Pedagogy
IN THE AGE OF
Media
CONTROL

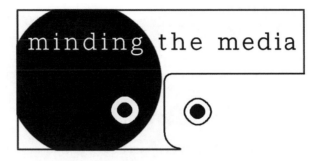

CRITICAL ISSUES FOR LEARNING AND TEACHING

Shirley R. Steinberg and Pepi Leistyna
General Editors

Vol. 3

The Minding the Media series is part of the Peter Lang Education list.
Every volume is peer reviewed and meets
the highest quality standards for content and production.

PETER LANG
New York • Washington, D.C./Baltimore • Bern
Frankfurt • Berlin • Brussels • Vienna • Oxford

Joao J. Rosa and Ricardo D. Rosa

Pedagogy
IN THE AGE OF
Media
CONTROL

Language Deception and Digital Democracy

PETER LANG
New York • Washington, D.C./Baltimore • Bern
Frankfurt • Berlin • Brussels • Vienna • Oxford

Library of Congress Cataloging-in-Publication Data

Rosa, Joao J.
Pedagogy in the age of media control: language deception
and digital democracy / Joao J. Rosa, Ricardo D. Rosa.
p. cm. — (Minding the media, critical issues for learning and teaching v. 3)
Includes bibliographical references and index.
1. Composition (Language arts) 2. Internet in education—United States.
3. Internet literacy—United States. 4. Media literacy—United States.
I. Rosa, Ricardo D. II. Title.
LB1575.8.R67   370.11'5—dc22   2010046185
ISBN 978-1-4331-0927-0 (hardcover)
ISBN 978-1-4331-0926-3 (paperback)
ISSN 2151-2949

Bibliographic information published by **Die Deutsche Nationalbibliothek**.
Die Deutsche Nationalbibliothek lists this publication in the "Deutsche
Nationalbibliografie"; detailed bibliographic data is available
on the Internet at http://dnb.d-nb.de/.

© 2011 Peter Lang Publishing, Inc., New York
29 Broadway, 18th floor, New York, NY 10006
www.peterlang.com

With love and gratitude we dedicate this book to the past and the future; to our beloved grandparents who paved the way for us to do what we do, and to our children and students who continue to inspire us as they navigate the road despite numerous obstacles along the way.

JOAO J. ROSA AND RICARDO D. ROSA

Contents

Foreword

Peter McLaren

It is no exaggeration to say that today we live in an era where control of the media is in the hands of the transnational corporations and the transnational capitalist elite. But, as the authors of this volume point out, it is not simply a question of who controls the media but how the media exerts control over us. That we are shaped and formed by electronic, print, and digital media is by now a commonplace. And much of the educational enterprise in today's schools involves the uncritical importation of what can be called "epistemologies of ignorance" (Malewski & Jaramillo, 2011)—ideological discourses embedded in the textual production of our lives, much of which comes to us by way of the media catechism that I refer to as "perpetual pedagogy." You might try, for instance, to leave the media alone, but it will not leave you alone. It will insistently teach you something about the world, regardless of whether or not you want to engage the message, or despite the reaction you might have when intentionally or unintentionally engaging it.

Few observers would disagree that our subjective formation as social agents is occurring at a very precarious time, a constituent moment during a world historical epidemic of overproduction, as living labor is being devoured in systematically new and more invidious ways and where the popular majorities have been consigned to the rag-and-bone shop of decaying fragments of the discarded self. Revealing a ubiquitous and pluriform power that forever seems undaunted, capitalism has grown a second set of jaws and is undergoing a ferocious re-feudalization by means of what David Harvey has described as "accumulation by dispossession" (Harvey, 2003): Neoliberal transformations in Western nations from the 1970s to the present that are being driven by privatization, financialization, management and manipulation of crises, and state redistributions.

Clearly at this time of intensified globalized financialization, we are suffering one of the worst moments in the crisis of capitalism. Accumulation by dispossession has marked the entire history of capitalism, and we are now seeing the results of a very long and systemic crisis that leads ineluctably to misery and suffering of momentous proportions. Conservatives continue to assert the U.S. domination of world markets, even if it means asserting military strength. The racist ideology that has survived abolition persists in new formations in the corporate media, in popular culture, in the social sciences, and in the very languages and theories of knowledge production that we take for granted, contributing to forms of epistemological genocide, or "epistemicide," where, as a manifestation of the coloniality of power, nondominant languages, dialects, cultural histories, and indigenous knowledges continue to be thrown into the dustbin of history.

There exists a rift between human agency and the historical realities in which agency must be lived, both individually and collectively. It is a commonplace assertion within progressive traditions and traditions of educational resistance that knowledge production is culturally embedded, and that when language mediates consciousness it often invokes the idioms of the social class that controls it. In addition, we have to account for the objective social conditions of exploitation. What has become clear is that our pedagogies of transformation must account for knowledge that is not only produced by bodies but also lived through real, sensuous, and feeling bodies.

Over the years, I have often been asked what I meant when I developed the term *enfleshment* with respect to the act of knowing. I meant by this term that the process of understanding cannot be reduced to the formal properties of language alone, but has to take into account its relationship to extra-linguistic forms of knowing, other forms of corporeal and praxiological meanings. Meaningful knowledge is, contra Habermas, not solely nor mainly the property of the formal properties of language. It cannot be abstracted "from all the concrete, particular, embodied, erotic, and expressive features of language in order to invest emancipatory possibilities from its formal properties" (McNally, 2001, p. 109).

Now if we begin to understand ourselves not only as the effects of language, but as extra-discursive bodies existing in geohistorical space, as corporeal social subject formations, and even more specifically, as racialized, gendered, and sexualized selves who have been placed grievously and differentially within objective social relations of production, that is, within the global division of labor, then we must look to our institutions of education as spaces of transformation where we can both fashion and refashion ourselves during this invidious war against working people waged by the capitalist class by means of media systems built at public expense and run by what Noam Chomsky calls "private tyrannies," mainly comprised of a half dozen international mega-corporations. Chomsky (1998) tells us that the war against working people is not a new war. It is simply a new phase of an ongoing war. Currently, this war has "a highly class-conscious business class" who "have long seen themselves as fighting a bitter class war, except they don't want anybody else to know about it" (p. 179). The goal of the business class is to "control the public mind" by means of corporate propaganda. Chomsky writes:

> There's no doubt that one of the major issues of twentieth century U.S. history is corporate propaganda. It's a huge industry. It extends over, obviously, the commercial media, but includes the whole range of systems that reach the public: the entertainment industry, television, a good bit of what appears in schools, a lot of what appears in the newspapers, and so on. A huge amount of that comes straight out of the public relations industry, which was established in this country early in this century, and developed mainly from the 1920s on. It's now spreading over the rest of the world, but it's primarily here. (1998, p. 180).

In Chomsky's discussion of the history of propaganda, he mentions how, during the 1930s, the dominant elites decided that, rather than punish strikers with clubs or guns, it was more effective to use what was called "the Mohawk Valley formula," or "scientific methods of strikebreaking," which Chomsky describes as the production of "Americanism." Chomsky writes:

> The basic idea is to present a picture of the world that looks kind of like this: There's "us," a big happy family in the community. The honest workman going off every morning with his lunch box, his loyal wife making the meals and taking care of the kids, the hardworking executive who's toiling day and night in the interests of his workers and the community, the friendly banker running around looking for people to lend money to. That's us. We're all in harmony. Harmony was a big word. We're all together. It's Americanism. (1998, p. x)

It should be scant cause for astonishment that now, in 2010, this description of our servile inurement to the strictures of the bourgeois state still largely fits. But the current global economic crisis is making the image of the benevolent corporate state harder to defend, especially when coupled with British Petroleum's recent oil spill in the Gulf of Mexico that has brought to public light dimensions of capitalism's despotic order. But even when BP's executive chairman Carl-Henric Svanberg continually repeated "We are about the small people" (reminding many Americans of Leona Helmsley's comment, "only little people pay taxes"), Republican senators still rushed to the defense of BP, claiming that corporations should not be targeted by the government. And while it is becoming harder to protect the public image of bankers, lobbyists, and developers, the propaganda machine is still largely successful at stemming a mass uprising by the people.

What Joao and Ricardo Rosa have accomplished in *Pedagogy in the Age of Media Control* is to provide for readers a conceptual seedbed in which to plant a new type of critical pedagogy that can deal with language deception in an era of digital democracy. They recognize that the interlocutor of critical pedagogy is the absent voice of history, the voice of the displaced, the marginalized, the most despised and exploited of humankind. We can remake history only if we first attempt to re-read history, by turning history "upside down from the bottom, not from the top" (Gutierrez, 1983, p. 21).

Tragically, what we are seeing today is that whatever historical memory was won by the civil rights movement is now being turned upside down from the top, as witnessed by the recent travesty surrounding the textbook standards approved in Texas (and adopted in other states). The elected state board of education overseeing the Texas social studies curriculum accomplished a watering-down of the rationale for the separation of church and state, and rejected language to modernize the classification of historic periods to B.C.E. and C.E. from B.C. and A.D. Thomas Jefferson—who is disliked by conservatives for advocating the separation of church and state—was cut from a list of figures whose writings inspired revolutions in the late 18th and 19th centuries, and replaced with St. Thomas Aquinas, John Calvin, and William Blackstone. The board required students to evaluate efforts by global organizations such as the United Nations to undermine U.S. sovereignty. In addition, the board solidified requirements on teaching the Judeo-Christian influences on the nation's Founding Fathers and required that the U.S. government be referred to as a "constitutional republic" rather than "democracy." Furthermore, students will be required to study the decline in the value of the U.S. dollar, including the abandonment of the gold standard. Attempts to include more Latino figures as role models were consistently defeated. The board also included a plank to ensure that students learn about Phyllis Schlafly, the Contract with America, the Heritage Foundation, the Moral Majority, and the National Rifle Association—all part of the conservative resurgence of the 1980s and 1990s. The head of the board, a dentist, pushed through a change to the teaching of the civil rights movement so that students will learn about the so-called violent philosophy of the Black Panthers in addition to the nonviolent approach of the Reverend Martin Luther King Jr. Students also will now study the "unintended consequences" of the Great Society legislation, affirmative action, and Title IX legislation. In order to counter the idea that the internment of Japanese during World War II was motivated by racism, the board passed an amendment that stressed that Germans and Italians as well as Japanese were interned in the United

States during this time. Rehabilitating the McCarthy period by claiming that the United States was infiltrated by communists after World War II (as supposedly confirmed by the later release of the Venona Papers) also won approval. Milton Friedman and Friedrich von Hayek, two champions of free-market economic theory, were added to the list of economists to be studied. The word "capitalism" was replaced by the term *free-enterprise system*. Board members who didn't accept sociological explanations for teenage suicide, dating violence, sexuality, drug use, and eating disorders because such explanations tend to "blame society for everything," countered sociological perspectives with "the importance of personal responsibility for life choices."

Not surprisingly, the board lamentably omitted the analysis of leftist historians such as Howard Zinn, which is perhaps the most egregious omission, but you wouldn't find leftist perspectives in textbooks even with a board dominated by Democrats. Over the luxuriant history of critical pedagogy, critical educators who have exercised their right to make revolutionary interventions into capitalism and its attendant social antagonisms, and the forms and modes of domination that keep it securely in place, have been often become the object of academic repression in the schools and the universities. We are clearly fighting an ideological civil war today, and whatever remains of critical analysis in our school systems is clearly being sabotaged. This should not be a cause for despair but an opportunity to ratchet up our struggle. That is the wager of *Pedagogy in the Age of Media Control*.

Critical pedagogy writes in a white heat, but it must connect with the oppressed, as in a multivoiced, polyphonic novel. Its characters must be recognizable to those who suffer most at the hands of the capitalist elite. The faith in our struggle can only be renewed by reclaiming a subversive history. Gutierrez warns that "what is criminal is not to be *sub*versive, struggling against the capitalist system, but to continue to be *super*versive, bolstering and supporting the prevailing domination" (1983, p. 21). We need to understand and negate the social relations of oppression imposed by the prevailing social order, all those mechanisms that prevent people from recognizing their objective location within the capitalist system and acting as the agents of their own lot in

history. Critical pedagogy is adorned with polemic and filled with struggle, but in recent years it has been shorn of its commitment to fighting
capitalism. It is imperative, then, that critical pedagogy becomes the
locus of the encounter of reformists and revolutionaries who attempt to
create a new social order outside of value production itself, an encounter
undertaken within the context of a concrete historical movement that
transcends dogmatism and is open to new ideas. We are all part of the
movement of history, what Anne Fairchild Pomeroy calls "the productive generation of novelty from the given then objectified as a new
accomplished given for appropriation" (2004, p. 59). We are not mech-
anistically determined in advance by modes and social relations of production, but rather exist as a processive creation within a world as
given, that is, in a world where our objective location limits the datum
which we can appropriate. There is no outside to the world of capitalist commodification so that critical pedagogy cannot be seen as a tran-
scendent force. It must work within the decaying and fallen world of
things, and those who have been reduced to things, the toilers and the
workers of the world.

The critical tradition of which the authors of this book are a part is
known by numerous terms such as *critical pedagogy*, *Freirean pedagogy*,
popular education, and *public pedagogy*, but one of the most common
terms is *social justice education*. It is no exaggeration to say that when
social justice education is advocated by teachers and educational scholars, the corridors of educational power listen with alarm. They are listening ever more intensely now. When the commissioner of the New
York State Department of Education, David M. Steiner, remarked to
Henry Giroux at the Nexus Conference in Amsterdam in 2007 that
"social justice promotes hatred. Hatred for the established order"
(Giroux, 2010), it was clear that the object of attack of many establishment leaders in education is critical thought itself. This is an example of
Steiner heaping ideological mystification upon distortion. But the real
pathos is neither the mystification nor the distortion of the truth, it is the
fact that critique itself is now seen as a major enemy of education. What
we are facing are not only retrograde positivists who champion instrumental rationality but also, as Giroux notes, conservative ideologues

who promote authoritarian forms of pedagogy that are in direct conflict with the concept of an open, participatory democracy. Tom Horne, the Arizona superintendent of public schools, has attacked ethnic studies programs on the basis that such programs are cynical and un-American.

These thinkers, who include Arne Duncan, the secretary of education under Obama, support what Giroux calls instrumental and practical classroom methodologies that, especially in the case of African Americans, function as part of a circuit of power that produces the school-to-prison pipeline. Their contrapuntal harangue echoes from throats filled with pebbles and hoarse from declaiming with relentless rage social justice as hostile to the survival of the state. Reactionary political values are smuggled under the guise of technical reasoning and remain immune to the criticism that education has succumbed to the idiom of the corporation, to the business ethic of self-interest, to knowledge as a prepackaged commodity, to the unlimited pursuit of the accumulation of capital, to the notion that progress is measured by the quantitative growth of consumption.

So, what is the role of the critical educator in the present epoch? I wish to say this unabashedly: to be an artist, an intellectual, a committed cultural worker and critical researcher. In these roles we can start to help students rehearse identities not yet permissible by the state. We can refuse the way that education is being refigured by the role now played by transnational capital. We can never create a pedagogy with faultless legitimacy, one that never contradicts the basic principles which directed them at the beginning—we don't possess a definitive and purifying pedagogy that will avoid detours from our original objectives. All of our pedagogies, including critical pedagogies, are dirty, and we must struggle to make them less dirty, less messy, and point them in the best direction that we can given the historical, cultural, and political contingencies that bear down upon us. This is not going to be an easy task at a time when critical pedagogy itself is in trammels, when it is subsumed by identity politics and leaves the question of class struggle largely unaddressed. How can educational transformation be accomplished without entering the world of the underemployed and the unemployed who supply the modern/colonial world-system with cheap labor? After all, the current system of world capitalism is unsustainable. This requires a new cultural compact and a new productive system that opposes the logic of capital and that creates a new social metabolism rooted in egalitarianism, community, and human development.

Such a compact stipulates that we must recover the memory of the "scourged Christs of America," as Bartolomé de las Casas referred to the indigenous peoples of our continent (Gutierrez, 1983, p. 21). We courteously acknowledge their presence but we engage in a structured refusal to listen to what they have to say. Clearly, we require another artisanship of pedagogical practices, what Walter Mignolo (2009, 2010) refers to as a "geopolitics of knowledge and knowing." This entails a political and epistemic delinking from Western Eurocentric practices and from a zero-point epistemology in which a knowing subject in the center of power maps the world for those who reside in the periphery. Developing another artisanship of pedagogical practices also means interrogating Eurocentered epistemologies as well as the production of decolonizing and decolonial knowledges through understanding our subjectivities as historical and biographical loci of enunciation. In other words, we need to engage in a geopolitics of knowing that will produce a geopolitics of knowledge that follows from a process of political and epistemic delinking from the grand Western episteme and cosmology. This follows from Santos's assertion that all ignorance is ignorance of a certain knowledge and all knowledge is the overcoming of a particular ignorance (2007, p. 229). The confrontation and conflict we witness among knowledges is actually the confrontation and dialogue among the different processes through which practices that are ignorant in different ways turn into practices that are knowledgeable in different ways (2007, p. 229).

Critical pedagogy guarantees neither political upheaval nor stable states of social brotherhood and sisterhood. Critical pedagogy provokes our educational imagination and gives us the space to wallow occasionally in the mystery of our humanity, and to cultivate the ability of individuals to take part in collective decision-making, to work to imagine postcapitalist social orders, to experiment in the creation of equality and social justice as well as social agency on a large scale—with a vision of creating a new internationalism. In our struggle for what Samir Amin

(2010) calls "a negotiated globalization without hegemonies," we must in the process realize that participatory democracy is both the telos of the movement towards socialism (which is the only alternative to chaos) and a set of principles and practices that will keep socialism from being hijacked by elite cadres who would come under the spell of the financial oligarchies or eventually lead to the path of autocracy or statocracy. Today, our immediate challenge as critical educators is to prevent the powers that be from restoring the same system that is currently under collapse, a system that has wreaked havoc on the globe. We must develop a philosophy of praxis that can be lived geopolitically, corporeally, and that is grounded in a commitment that is given birth each day in acts of protagonistic struggle.

The authors of *Pedagogy in the Age of Media Control* are part of this struggle for a decolonized and decolonizing critical pedagogy. In their discussion of the knowledge production of Disney, gaming and the marketing of games, African American stand-up comedy, dis/ability, race and Hollywood, and standard pedagogical models used in public school classrooms, they assiduously recognize that there is little that divides the social and the academic, that the wall that artificially separates them is the same ideological boundary that serves the interests of the transnational capitalist elite. They make it clear that popular culture can increasingly serve as powerful sources of knowledge, knowledge that can augment the active knowledge that students already possess in their struggle for survival. After all, students are already employing sophisticated analytical powers in their active, quotidian engagement with the social imaginary of the often harsh, concrete world spawned by neoliberal capital. As a result, the curriculum can be reimagined and re-envisioned such that the discontinuities between life inside and outside of schools can be integrated into a pedagogical project that transcends both domains, that provides the pedagogical contexts for a construction of active being, of inquisitive subjectivity, of moral courage and political praxis. We don't want people to adapt to the prevailing social order, filled as it is with so much strife, corruption, and exploitation. We want a critical pedagogy of maladaptation, a dialectical awakening to the importance of anticapitalist struggle. But we must not take a single line of march that focuses solely on the relationship of capitalist production, as important as this is; we need also to focus on the subjective incorporation of the working class into capitalist society and to find ways to resist this incorporation. Clearly we have learned from revolutions past and present that they either fail or turn into their opposite, absent of human development, absent of the embodied dreams and collective hopes of humanity and their mundane, quotidian practices and ways of life, absent of a critical pedagogy devoted to remembering the past and organizing our collective lives so as to actualize a new world outside of capital's value form.

Reading this wonderful book by Joao and Ricardo Rosa can help us participate in class struggle, in a systematic delinking from epistemologies of empire, and in a counter pedagogy linked to the struggles of new social movements. Following the lead of these authors, we need to commit ourselves to the fight to decolonize our pedagogies, our schools, our universities, beginning with the very vocabularies of liberation that we use to fight domination and exploitation. This book initiates such a challenge.

References

Amin, S. (2010, February 7). The battlefield chosen by contemporary imperialism: Conditions for an effective response from the South. *Monthly Review Zine*. Retrieved from http://mrzine.monthlyreview.org/2010/amin070210.html.

Chomsky, N. (1998). Propaganda and control of the public mind. In R. McChesney, E. M. Wood & J. B. Foster (Eds.), *Capitalism and the information age: The political economy of the global communications revolution* (pp. 179–189). New York: Monthly Review Press.

Giroux, H. (2010, June 24). Charting disaster: Why Duncan's corporate-based schools can't deliver an education that matters. *Truthout*. Retrieved from https://www.truthout.org/chartering-disaster-why-duncans-corporate-based-schools-cant-deliver-education-that-matters60553.

Gutierrez, G. (1983). *The power of the poor in history*. Maryknoll, NY: Orbis.

Harvey, D. (2003). *The new imperialism*. Oxford, UK: Oxford University Press.

Malewski, E., and Jaramillo, N. (In press). *Epistemologies of ignorance*. Charlotte, NC: Information Age.

McNally, D. (2001). *Bodies of meaning: Studies on language, labor, and liberation*. Albany, NY: State University of New York Press.

Mignolo, W. D. (2009). Epistemic disobedience, independent thought and decolonial freedom. *Theory, Culture and Society, 26*(7/8), 159–181.

Mignolo, W. D. (2010). The communal and the decolonial. *Pavilion, 14*, 146–155.

Pomeroy, A. F. (2004). *Marx and Whitehead: Process, dialectics, and the critique of capitalism*. Albany, NY: State University of New York Press.

Santos, B. S. (2007). From an epistemology of blindness to an epistemology of seeing. In *Cognitive justice in a global world: Prudent knowledges for a decent life* (pp. 407–437). Lanham, MD, and New York: Lexington Books.

Santos, B. S. (2009). A non-Occidentalist west? Learned ignorance and ecology of knowledge. *Theory, Culture and Society, 26*(7/8), 103–125.

Acknowledgments

This book could not have been possible without the encouragement and support of Donaldo Macedo and the courage of Shirley Steinberg. We owe a debt of gratitude to both for their vision and commitment to a more humane and just society. To Peter McLaren, who similarly, unselfishly shared his wealth of knowledge for the good of the project, we are eternally grateful. This project is anchored in the vigorous and critical discussions with mentors, colleagues, and students at the University of Wisconsin–Madison and the University of Massachusetts Dartmouth. These discussions have served as catalysts for our continued growth. We would like to express our profound gratitude particularly to Professors Michael Apple, Gloria Ladson-Billings, Carl Grant, Maggie Hawkins, James Gee, Mary Louise Gomez, Bernadette Baker, and Stacey Lee. Among the many colleagues at the University of Wisconsin–Madison, we would like to thank Keita Takayama, Chung-Pei Tsai, and Ming Fong.

As is the case with any project requiring a great deal of time, our families were particularly affected by the development of the book. With paramount understanding and patience they "put up" with our frustrations and late nights as we inched our way through it all. To them, who asked for so little and endured so much, we are forever thankful and appreciative. To our sister Leila Rosa, who has supported us in many endeavors and was a source of strength and encouragement, our many thanks.

Introduction

A perfunctory glance at the mosaic of this text will either be cause for jubilant vindication by those who dare to traverse the sometimes turbulent waters of change in search of new epistemological realities with which to engage students, or it will engender virulent reactions from those who, despite suffocating in the "placid tranquility" that is today's curricular canon, continue to revel in the safety of uncritical bodies of knowledge/pedagogies that incite resistance born out of the lucid cultural penetrations of youth. The development of this project was for us a way of delving into this world of possibilities, propelled primarily by the seldom thoughtfully answered question: Why do I have to learn this stuff?

Along the way, we have had to circuitously and candidly reflect on a call put forth by George Counts in *Dare the School Build a New Social Order?* (1932) when he alluded to the critical function of schools in observing that

> if the schools are to be really effective, they must become centers for the building, and not merely for the contemplation, of our civilization . . . our social institutions and practices, all of them, should be critically examined in light of such a vision. (p. 34)

In the realization that democratic societies cannot be sustained by a mechanistic, reverential contemplation of the past, but rather are formed and transformed through a living praxis that undermines the ideological hegemony that is sustained by the cultural commodification of capitalist societies, we are seeking not simple detours to the same destinations. The deconstruction of pedagogies of control must necessarily open up spaces for a radical reconceptualization of possibilities, of aims and of means, and in so doing necessitate the rewriting of the ideological scripts that serve a politics of entrenchment in the traditional for the sake of constrainment of movements.

We note that to some extent the battles that are currently being fought over education are somewhat illusory; this is not to say that the battles should not be fought, that they are somehow only discursive in nature, or that we should not engage in a visceral contestation of the malaise that anesthetizes students' lived capacity for critique. Critical media literacy is the present terrain of battle in that it leads to an unpacking of dormant sensibilities engineered and maintained primarily by a passive curriculum for the sake of unfettered consumption. As Rhonda Hammer (2009) lucidly points to the urgency of both the issue at hand and the possibilities, she notes

> the ubiquity of media in a multiplicity of forms and the prominent roles they play in our everyday experiences demand that media become a compulsory area of critical inquiry and investigation in all levels of educational curricula. This kind of critical thinking would liberate the majority of Americans to "think outside of the box" of the dominant ideology and corporate system and look for new political and social alternatives. (p. 170)

The prize in this struggle, in our opinion, reaches beyond "thinking outside the box" to an effective contestation of neoliberal politics of the magnitude of disaster capitalism (Klein, 2007) through the development of a collective praxis that upholds collective interests and public spaces.

Our purposeful engagement with the bodies of knowledge presented herein reflect above all a disdain for uncritical pedagogical interventions that segment the lived reality of youth from the world of academic work under an illusory (though systemically complicit) banner of "worthy knowledge." Our focus then is the exploration of the limitations of traditional conceptions of literacy while positing curricular alternatives that seek to bridge the false chasm between theory and educational practice. We argue that in market-driven, consumption oriented societies, our quest for critically analytical students requires that we engage in a multilayered approach that seeks (a) the reconceptualization of literacy itself from ideological extremes that often through a variety of discourses position students as passive recipients of knowledge; (b) a recentering and fusion of social spheres to academics with equal rigor; (c) a strategic targeting and honing of the critical instincts that students already possess as a matter of an instinct of survival; and (d) lastly, the integration of knowledge to ongoing local or national political projects.

Through the use of alternative curricular epistemologies, we utilize areas of popular culture to respond to a theoretical and practical void that often structures the debate of teachers/theorists who seek to rupture the false dichotomy between the social and the academic. Through the analysis of "Disney curriculum," African American stand-up comedy, dis/ability and race (as conceptualized in movies), and video games, we not only propose new ways of fusing the discontinuities between school and home but also, in the latter chapters, develop tangible nontraditional lesson plans that capture some of the nuances and possibilities of a re-envisioning of the curriculum that goes beyond the uncritical importation of media sources disconnected from a critical social engagement anchored in concrete social movements. We seek to decenter traditional lesson plans by demonstrating ways in which the lessons themselves can be constructed so as to center student voices and provide an entry point to the already analytical processes that students bring to bear on the world.

In chapter 1 we being by exploring the historicity of Disney as an enterprise and the systematicity with which the ideological discourses embedded in the textual productions of Disney can be represented as a "curriculum" in itself. We argue that the very systematicity of Disney is itself intertextual in nature, and that one of the ways in which Disney structures character subjectivity is through the use of language. With reference to popular Disney productions such as *Aladdin* and *Mulan*, we analyze the use of language (phonological characteristics) and the creation of character normativity.

Our argument is that, in multiple modes (ideology, context, representation, language), as an enterprise Disney capitalizes on that which is
projected as familiar, and in so doing relegates as "peripheral and
deviant" those practices and ways of being which are external to a purposefully constructed matrix of what it means to be "normal." In the case
of language, we demonstrate through an analysis of the scripts of these
various textual productions (and the reactions of individuals to these
scripts, as well as their phonological productions) that character subjectivity is fused to the use of language and that particular variants of
English are systematically representative of "abnormality/deviance";
hence the Disney curriculum is seen as a viable medium through which
teachers can engage issues of linguicism, classism, and racism within disciplines such as English Language Arts, Social Studies, or Health.

In chapter 2 we explore the phenomenon of gaming and the marketing of games by showing that culturally embedded knowledge production can take forms that are often viscerally masked through discourses
that normalize relations of domination (Giroux, 2000; Rosa, 2009). As a
medium of knowledge production, video game cultures are increasingly becoming critically important as entertainment outlets and multibil-
lion dollar industry but also in its capacity to shed light on forms of
information processing (Gee, 2003, 2007; Shaffer, 2008). According to the
NPD Group, a market research firm that tracks consumer trends for the
film, music, PC games, video games, and video industries, in 2007
national retail sales of video games, including portable and console
hardware, software and accessories, topped $9.5 billion, an increase of
28 percent over 2006.[1] The Entertainment Software Association, a U.S.
group representing computer and video game software publishers,
noted that during 2007, "On average, an astonishing 9 games were sold
every second of every day of the year"(ibid.). While these statistics are
indicative of the attraction that this new medium of diversion has cast
over an increasingly diverse demographic of players, our focus is on the
marketing packages of two games in particular, the original *America's
Army* and its successor, *America's Army: Special Forces*. We argue that the
evolution in the marketing of these games reflects a change in the way
individuals in a multiplicity of settings are able to socially position
themselves as to what is "authentic and real." We further argue that the

capacity to view these positionalities as "authentic and real" has become increasingly more plausible as a result to changes in U.S. foreign policy through global military intervention.

Chapter 3 explores the discourses represented and enacted through African American stand-up comedy and its relation to social, political, economic, and cultural formations. Here we argue that the medium of stand-up comedy has been a pervasive force historically in centering a penetrating analysis of the structured suffering of African Americans and in awakening a sense of possibility through its command of attention in "mainstream" markets without limiting its subversive agenda. Furthermore, we argue that the internal coherence of this medium is shaped by its delivery within the linguistic architecture of African American English Vernacular (AAEV). Therefore, the medium's most important impact has been and will continue to be the resistance to Standard English hegemony and the centralization of AAEV on terms that reflect the lived political experience of those who speak it.

What is examined here is the complex critical consumption and production of stand-up comedy as a political text and social movement that traffics in the unmasking of institutionalized structural inequalities (even as it at times sustains or realigns structural hierarchies of power in other forms), provides a space for engaged public criticism, and animates social action, especially when anchored to more concrete forms of political pedagogical work.

We then move on in chapter 4 to exploring an important omission in critical theories centering on representational politics. Here, we explore the representational intersections of "black bodies" and dis/ability as negative ontology, and by dialectical engagement, "whiteness" and able-bodiedness as not only affirmative field but "normative" space. Such analysis is critical because Hollywood codes are considerable players in spaces of identity (re)production and therefore, in part, help us further understand the formation of policy (a critical entry point in our field would be the racialization of special education and the concrete fact of overrepresentation of students of color in special needs programs). We read the representation of these "Othered" bodies, therefore, within the context of power relations. Furthermore, we argue that the transactions made between and against these two corporeal social subject formations function to seductively (re)erect regressive representations of each and sustain structures of institutional domination where both physical configurations are not only envisioned as deviant, but also positioned "as in need of control."

We also analyze the manner in which these symbolic forms gain their power through their anchoring within specific discourse communities, or what is more commonly referred to in the field of critical film analysis as "genre." In this case, we analyze Hollywood's discursive lean on the comic book and mystery genre.

Following critical media theorists, cultural studies scholars, and pedagogues who position mass media and mainstream film as mediums that often serve dominant interests and antidemocratic ends (Herman & Chomsky, 1988; hooks, 2006; Giroux, 2006), we contemplate these mechanisms in all of their various forms as major pedagogical machines whose power over public imagination needs to be reinvoked through a counter-pedagogy anchored to concrete social movements.

Chapter 5, our final chapter, opens a dialogue with teachers that goes beyond the customary discourses on "student interest." The authors discuss the difficulties encountered by teachers in bridging the increased demands of standardized models to the contextual realities of students. Each medium discussed in the earlier chapters is utilized in laying out lesson plans that model modes of engagement with disciplines as diverse as Mathematics, Health, Social Studies, History, English, and Technology while capitalizing on student knowledge.

In presenting this work, we hope to invite teachers to explore rival epistemological frameworks in developing meaningful educational roads that transform the lived experience of students into worthy areas of engagement and sources of knowledge. Our intent is to challenge teachers to consider new ways of looking at and understanding experience with the aim of fragmenting the artificial construction of boundaries between the academic and the lived.

Note

1. http;//www.theesa.com/newsroom/release_archives_detail.asp?releaseID=8

References

Counts, G. S. (1932). Dare the school build a new social order? New York: John Day.

ESA. (2010). Computer and Video Game Industry Reaches $18.85 Billion in 2007. Retrieved October 25, 2010 from: http://www.theesa.com/newsroom/release_archives_detail.asp?releaseID=8

Gee, J. P. (1996). Social linguistics and literacies: Ideology in discourses. London: Routledge/Falmer.

Gee, J. P. (2003). An introduction to discourse analysis: Theory and method. London: Routledge.

Gee, J. P. (2007). What video games have to teach us about learning and literacy. New York: Palgrave.

Giroux, H. (1997). Channel surfing: Race talk and the destruction of today's youth. New York: St. Martin's.

Giroux, H. (2000). Stealing innocence: Corporate culture's war on children. New York: Palgrave.

Giroux, H. (2006). Are Disney movies good for your kids? In K. Abowitz & R. Karaba (Eds.), Readings in sociocultural studies in education (6th ed., pp. 21–28). New York: McGraw-Hill.

Hammer, R., & Kellner, D. (2009). Media/cultural studies: Critical approaches. New York: Peter Lang.

Herman, E., & Chomsky, N. (1988). Manufacturing consent: The political economy of the mass media. New York: Pantheon Books.

hooks, b. (2006). Outlaw culture: Resisting representations. New York: Routledge.

Klein, N. (2007). The shock doctrine: The rise of disaster capitalism. New York: Picador.

Rosa, R. (2009). What type of revolution are we rehearsing for? Boal's theater of the oppressed. In M. Apple, W. Au, & L. Gandin (Eds.), The Routledge international handbook of critical education (pp. 240–253). New York: Routledge.

Shaffer, D. (2008). How computer games help children learn. New York: Palgrave.

Chapter One

Disney-fying Language

The Good, the Bad and the Foreign

Current conceptions of "curriculum" reflect historical tensions between various epistemological frameworks which historically have been fused with an underlying subtext revolving around race, class, gender, and ability (Ladson-Billings, 2000; Kliebard, 1995; Castenell & Pinar, 1993). Inasmuch as theorists have referenced each other and engaged in wider social conversations as to the nature of "worthy" knowledge and systems of dispensation and creation of such knowledge (Apple, 2000), the curriculum has been incrementally constructed through the formation of categories that ultimately legitimize some forms of knowledge and in so doing, systemically marginalize others (Cornbleth & Waugh, 1995; Leistyna, 2002; Davis, 2009). This process of curricular differentiation has over time created boundaries between the public pedagogic space and the school as distinct spaces, leading to curricular segmentation. Not wanting to romanticize the notion of the public pedagogic space, in the same manner in which this space must be engaged such that we may usefully benefit from it (Rosa, 2009), where it contributes to hegemonic forms of cultural reproduction that marginalize some while dialectically centering others, it also must be examined and, if necessary, challenged.

By public pedagogic space, we are referring to the myriad ways in which forms of popular knowledge and cultural production and reproduction serve to inculcate in the populace at large normative ways of being, feeling, thinking, and acting. To the extent that this space is freely accessed and its commodified products are consumed, knowledge production is proceeding outside the traditional parameters of the classroom. Media productions constitute one of these public pedagogic spaces that ultimately are just as, if not more, influential in the daily lives of students than the traditional school-based curriculum. It is not unusual, then, for students to be better able to engage in conversations about the intricacies of Hannah Montana and the Jonas Brothers than the importance of geography or history in affecting local or national issues. By focusing on the role of the public pedagogical space as an active rival creator of knowledge, our aim is to blur the distinction between the public and traditional education. This blurring of boundaries, while certainly redefining the pedagogic space, will most assuredly also have to take into account newer forms of thinking about curricular conceptualization and cohesion.

Disney's involvement in the production of curriculum traverses the terrain of normative entertainment into an ideological abyss that more and more fuses "fun" with pedagogy, and private with public. The Walt Disney World College Program, a prime example of this fusion of private and public, is a for-profit induction process that is widely available to students at public institutions across the United States. The ultimate goal of Disney's intern program is to provide college students the chance to learn the Disney business model in a "living laboratory" during a semester working at a Disney park. While the program accepts students from a wide array of academic areas, typical roles for "Cast Members" include Bell Services Dispatcher, Boutique Hostess, Concierge, Character Attendant, Custodial Worker, Food Services Hopper, Lifeguard, and Housekeeper. (After completing the Disney College Program, students may apply for other internships in the Disney organization that align more closely with their chosen areas of study.) The only requirement for participation is that students be at least second-semester freshmen in an accredited higher education institution. Once students go through a screening process by Disney representatives who travel to major colleges looking for potential inductees, they receive a let-ter informing them of their hiring status and requiring a commitment for attendance. What follows is a series of seminars (ten in all) over a four-day period during which the college students are introduced to appro-priate Disney practices at the Disney University in Orlando, Florida. While attending the program, the students' necessities are provided for, at a cost. Disney's pedagogical reach extends to both undergraduate and graduate students.

Similarly, at the Disney Institute, a professional development com-pany founded in 1986, the mission is the promotion of Disney philoso-phy and practice. The institute does not restrict its members to U.S. college students—it is a worldwide operation that includes 45 other countries besides the U.S. With the capacity to target programs specifi-cally to public or private organizations, at a cost of thousands of dollars per attendee, the institute purportedly targets Knowledge, Comprehension, and Application of the Disney business model. Potential attendees are informed that

> Disney Institute programs provide you with a business map that will help you chart a course for your organization, your division and yourself. Your return on this investment is across the board improvement. You'll realize this improve-ment in processes, your work environment and the delivery of customer ser-vice. You'll sense it in yourself and your employees who are inspired to strive for excellence. Above all, you'll see it in increased productivity and a renewed sense of purpose and potential.[1]

While the Walt Disney College Program clearly has an overt curriculum in that there is a specific skills set and knowledge base that Disney attempts to impart to students, this particular project seeks to engage in an analytical approach that goes beyond the mere description of con-sumer-oriented practices aimed at mystifying a youthful population with the euphemism of "internships" tailored to "Cast Members." As such, we recognize that the curricular boundaries of the Walt Disney College Program in offering a series of courses for program partici-pants, as well as the "opportunity to attend training classes, personal and professional-development activities and networking sessions with Disney leaders...[and the chance to] borrow a variety of books, DVDs,

CDs and other resources from Disney Learning Centers"[2] are but one limited dimension of the pedagogical impact of Disney. When considering its worldwide reach, that is its least demagogical in that the program specifics are freely available on the web. Disney's ventures into curriculum and pedagogy straddles the line between the explicit and implicit. As Giroux (2006) notes, the effort to push more explicit brand recognition allows Disney to "insert itself into a network of commodities that lends itself to the construction of the world of enchantment as a closed and total category." Giroux further notes that

> defining itself as a vehicle for education and civic responsibility, Disney sponsors "Teacher of the Year Awards," provides scholarships to students, and more recently, offers financial aid, internships, and educational programs to disadvantaged urban youth through its ice-skating program called Goals. (p. 22)

Educators visiting and registering themselves at Disney World are routinely sent "Educator Packages" complete with lesson plans with specific objectives to be used with classic Disney animated features such as Pinocchio in the development of character education. Such an engagement brings to the fore questions about which values Disney promotes, and for what purposes.

Our concern in this project is to focus on the dissonance between the projected image of Disney as the carrier of "wholesome values" and "innocent fun" with the historicity of its operations, and to critically engage with the discourse produced in Disney's capturing of "innocence" in Disney animation; both of these aims require that we critically situate the development of Disney in a sociohistoric context, but also that we instantiate a certain "presence of mind" that views the development of company discourse as continuously built in a dialectical engagement between the overt and that which is nefariously hidden.

All Things Disney

Begun by Walt and Roy Disney in 1922, Disney is a media and entertainment empire with a vast array of diversified commodity production strategically targeted at multiple audiences. Given its broad reach, it is virtually impossible today to escape the "magic of Disney." The influence of Disney is not limited to children; it is also instilled in and pro-moted by parents who grew up watching Disney films and documen-taries, reading Disney comics, and belonging to Disney clubs. This generational connection to the Disney enterprise exponentially increas-es the company's reach. According to the company's shareholder finan-cial statement, in 2008 revenues topped $37 billion, an increase of 7 percent over the previous year[3] The company's empire includes Studio Entertainment, Parks and Resorts, Consumer Products (everything from toys to home furnishings and clothing), Media Networks, and Interactive Media, and extends to 240 territories worldwide. Ownership of ABC affords the Disney company a significant share of the domestic televi-sion market: In the 2007–2008 season, "8 of the top 10 ABC-owned sta-tions ranked number 1 in their respective markets"(ibid.). The company is increasingly and strategically targeting emerging markets as sources of new revenue and spaces where the Disney brand can be marketed and expanded. The company's projection of "innocence" and make-believe that ensures that Disney guests are "transported from their everyday lives to worlds that could only be created by Disney" is contextualized by Disney's own report to its shareholders which uses a discourse more emblematic of a very real battle for market shares:

> We recognize that allocating capital profitably and managing our business to drive creative and financial success are the most important ways that we can serve our company. Our first priority in allocating capital is to fund strategi-cally attractive investments that can drive future growth and provide strong returns over time. These opportunities can include internal investment in exist-ing and new business acquisitions. We plan to continue expanding our creative pipeline of high-quality content and to strengthen our brands and reach on a global basis. These internal growth initiatives include investment in television, films, digital media and video game development. We will also continue to invest in developing local, Disney-branded content and expanding the reach of our Disney and ESPN-branded channels around the world. We recently released films made for China and India and currently have films in produc-tion for China, India and Russia. (p. 8)

Such language seems at odds with Disney's efforts to create individu-ally tailored "transformational experiences and products that connect with audiences on an emotional level" (p. 21). The disconnect between

Disney's practices aimed at securing ideal financial positioning and the projection of the Magic Kingdom's image of innocence is instrumental in clarifying a dissonance of being that allows for a critical engagement of the Disney Discourse. I utilize the term Discourse purposefully with a capital D to capture the theoretical concept referred to by Gee (1999) and to differentiate it from discourse in the conventional sense (i.e., language in action). As utilized by Gee, the term Discourse with a capital D refers to the

> different ways in which we humans integrate language with non-language "stuff," such as different ways of thinking, acting, interacting, valuing, feeling, believing and using symbols, tools and objects in the right places and at the right times so as to enact and recognize different identities and activities, give the material world certain meanings, distribute social goods in a certain way, make certain sorts of meaningful connections in our experience and privilege certain symbol systems and ways of knowing over others. (p. 13)

Here I use the term Discourse referring to the general conversations about Disney and the ideas represented by the company, and discourse to the specific use of language in some classic Disney productions.

Dorfman and Mattelart (1971) have articulately argued that Disney's system of cultural reproduction is in fact far from innocent in that in Latin America it was strategically used to undermine popular movements and the development of a popular consciousness that questioned U.S. social, cultural, and political ideology. They observed that

> Disney has been exalted as the inviolable common cultural heritage of contemporary man; his characters have been incorporated into every home, they hang on every wall, they decorate objects of every kind; they constitute little less than a social environment inviting us all to join the great universal Disney family, which extends beyond all frontiers and ideologies, transcends differences between peoples and nations and particularities of custom and language. (p. 28)

The act of trying to engage Disney then is somewhat risky in that the historic development of the company fundamentally represents a piece of Americana. As such, the questioning of Disney ideology is projected as an act of subversion that offends the sensibilities of what it means to be an American. Dorfman and Mattelart (1971) noted with insight that "We need not be surprised, then, that innuendo about the world of

Disney should be interpreted as an affront to morality and civilization at large" (p. 28).

Disney produces a very particular type of Discourse. It is specific in that there is a particular structure to the Disney vision that allows for some possibilities of outcome while simultaneously negating others. Some would argue that the Disney Discourse is in a sense heteroglossic (Smoodin, 1994), however, inasmuch as the Discourse is itself constructed against the background of the Anglo-heterosexual-male-able-bodied-capitalist norm, it is very much unitary. This heteroglossic vision of the Disney Discourse may itself be an illusion created by the relative explicitness or implicitness of the Discourse as temporally set in a "changing" sociohistoric frame, but even as the context inevitably mutates and the form adjusts, Disney cultural reproduction remains fixed within particular boundaries.

Although we are primarily concerned here with a linguistic analysis, in this case looking at aspects of phonology and grammar because these texts are intricately linked through content and form, the linguistic analysis cannot be divorced from the context of production. In this case, the production of discourse (language in action) is inextricably linked to Discourse. While arguing for the need to explore the symbiotic relationship between form and content in discourse analysis, Fairclough (1999) notes that "One cannot properly analyse content without simultaneously analysing form, because contents are always necessarily realized in forms, and different contents entail different forms and vice versa" (p. 184). Because content in this case refers to a series of visual representations, the analysis must not only include tools that allow for a linguistic analysis, but also provide a lens through which these representations can be analyzed at a semiotic level. The result is that the analysis ends up being and encompassing a hybridity of linguistics in a structural sense and a social approach capable of tackling issues of ideology.

It is of course impossible to delve into the dissection of Disney's ideological linguistic apparatus without considering the sociohistorical conditions under which it was created and is currently maintained. An understanding of the development of the company can provide a lens through which the intertextual nature of the discourse can be made more salient and linked synchronically.

Disney's financial history has had more vacillations than its adherence to a particular "message." Strategic partnerships with the U.S. government early on saved the company from financial ruin, while its more recent partnership with Pixar Animation Studios, for example, has produced a string of hits that have added to the company's value. The lucrative partnership with Pixar produced big hits such as *Toy Story 1, Toy Story 2* (total worldwide gross income of $485,015,179), *A Bug's Life, Monsters, Inc.* (total worldwide gross income of $529,061,238), and *Finding Nemo* (worldwide gross income of $864,625,978).[4] Even with spectacular revenues in hit years, the solvency of the Disney company has fluctuated as a result of not only bitter struggles between the Disney brothers, but also periodic creative slumps, particularly after the deaths of its founders (Smoodin, 1994). The arrival of Michael Eisner and Frank Wells in 1984 launched a period of hit movies that repositioned Disney as an entertainment power to be reckoned with by the beginning of 1990. An expansion into *R*-rated movies through the creation of Touchstone Pictures (distancing this genre from the Disney discourse) and the offer of Disney shares to upper-middle-class Americans (Taylor, 1987) brought in a new pool of investors capable of providing welcomed financial support to the company's filmmaking enterprise.

The opening of Disneyland in Japan and the expansion of its U.S. counterparts Disneyland in California and Walt Disney World in Florida, as well as the purchase of the ABC television network, allowed the company to continue to grow steadily, but reminiscent of earlier epochs of financial chaos, Disney is occasionally still plagued by diminishing profits and vicious battles among the executive staff (Taylor, 1987). The success story of the mid-1980s was in troubled waters in 2002 when *The Wall Street Journal* observed that

> Mr. Eisner spent much of the past summer sparring with two key Disney board members, Vice Chairman Roy E. Disney and Mr. Disney's investment adviser, Stanley Gold. Both have been critical lately of the entertainment company's faltering performance and lack of management depth. The tensions climaxed at a two-day board meeting in late September. The board endorsed Eisner's strategic plan, but fallout from that meeting has continued. (Orwall, 2002)

In December 2003 the same newspaper reported that Roy E. Disney Jr. had sent a letter to Michael Eisner demanding his resignation and started a national web-based campaign to remove Eisner as chairman of Disney. Crystallizing this bitter feud among the executive staff, on January 30, 2004, *The Wall Street Journal* reported:

> Pixar Animation Studios delivered a stunning blow to Walt Disney Co. by ending talks to extend their lucrative and long-running distribution deal for Pixar's computer-animated films. The move is a high-profile setback for Disney Chairman and Chief Executive Michael Eisner, whose company often has relied heavily on Pixar smashes like "Finding Nemo" to generate the profit Disney's own animated films couldn't produce in recent years. (Orwall & Wingfield, 2004)

In February 2004 *USA Today* reported that Comcast offered $54.1 billion for the entertainment powerhouse in a bid to create a global network and entertainment empire.

Whereas society at large becomes the ultimate regulator of the Disney Discourse by opting to spend or not spend money to sit in a movie theater to be retrained in the logic of being good consumer capitalists and to be socioideologically positioned so as to voyeuristically have dominant ideological narratives projected through the "innocence" of Disney animation, the company is more than willing to engage in all that is legally allowable and enforceable (and sometimes even that which is unallowable) to protect the Discourse itself.

Jon Lewis (1994) noted that in 1987, "Disney filed seventeen major lawsuits, naming some seven hundred defendants in the United States and another seventy-eight overseas. The following year, one suit alone named four hundred defendants, claiming copyright infringement ..." (p. 93). The images at issue represented a particular identity that Disney wanted to protect at all costs, or at least to directly profit from their representation. The values and modes of being that become imbued in the characters become synonymous with Disney. This is reflected in Paul Hollister's observation in 1940 that

> Article I of the Disney constitution stipulates that every possible element of a picture shall be not a mere pictorial representation of the character or an element of scenery, but an individual, with clearly defined characteristics. Disney lieutenants have grown gray in the service of repeating that Mickey is "not a mouse, but a person. (p. 26)

The production of these characters constitutes the creation of entities that embody and reflect particular values and ways of being that legitimize the familiar and delegitimize alternatives. In fact, it is more pervasive in that the construction of self dialectically and simultaneously both constructs and projects the image of the Other. While conducting research, Bell, Haas, and Sells (1995) encountered this spirit of rigorously policing the Disney Discourse and prosecuting those who transgress the boundaries of Disney engagement (from consumption to critique):

> When we corresponded with Disney personnel to gain access to the Disney archives in Buena Vista, California, we were informed that Disney does not allow third-party books to use the name Disney in their titles—this implies endorsement or sponsorship by the Disney organization. (p. 1)

In 2003 Disney filed numerous lawsuits to protect, police, and enforce its values as transmitted through animated images. If the image is created and brought to life and imbued with particular characteristics that become synonymous with the "American way," subversion cannot be tolerated, even if it comes from Disney's own employees. While this "policing" is more effective and efficient through a process of internalization, generated by rigorous enforcement of company policy, the process of material commodification and the structuring of discourse cannot be subjected to the possibility of ideological vacillations. It is in the context of establishing and policing boundaries to this discourse that David Kunzle (1971) observes:

> The system at Disney productions seems to be designed to prevent the artist from feeling any pride or gaining any recognition, other than corporate, for his work. Once the contract is signed, the artist's idea becomes Disney's idea. He is its owner therefore its creator, for all purposes. (p. 16)

The fictitious image of the happy Disney production camp portrayed by Hollister, even as it is complemented by the courteous smile and "welcome to Walt Disney World" greeting, must be contextualized. To be sure, the creation of the Disney image of innocence and the abstraction of the human condition from the projection of that immaculate, trouble-free world can be contrasted with a sometimes turbulent work history, exemplified by worker strikes and management feuds (Smoodin, 1994; Taylor, 1987).

Smith and Clark background this aspect of the Disney enterprise in their *Disney: The First 100 Years* (1999). Out of 211 pages of information on the Disney Company and its history of animation and entertainment, a single mitigated paragraph mentions conditions that deviate from the creation of a mythical happy camp. Referring to a strike that occurred *prior* to World War II, the authors note that

> at the same time that Walt and his artists were soaking up the culture in South America, a union problem that had been festering at the Disney Studio evolved into a bitter strike. The strike over wages and union representation would cause strained feelings among Disney staff members for years to come and would forever change the atmosphere on the Studio lot. (p. 52)

We have to assume that the workers who were striking for better conditions were not "Walt's workers," and that what caused the "strained feelings" was that fact, and not the conditions that prompted the strike. Some other authors occasionally have brought to light the disjunction between the "happy camp" and the lived reality of its members.

In 1999 the BBC reported that some 200 employees at the Disneyland theme park outside Paris had gone on strike in a dispute over pay. According to this report "Their action was not expected to be followed by the majority of the park's 10,000 employees, only about 10% of whom are union members."[5] The "happy camp" imagery must be taken in the context of these intermittent strikes over working conditions and compensation.

In 2000 the Hong Kong Industrial Committee (CIC) issued a report on twenty Disney contract factories in Guandong Province, China. Conditions were deplorable. The infractions ranged from work safety violations to excessive working hours to the application of fines for talking during work hours. International conditions with Disney subcontracted companies abstract the situation from a local level and project it to others, a dual victimization in the sense that, Disney is able to deflect attention away from these practices by claiming that it has little control of the companies it deals with yet it derives immense financial benefit from these dealings. As profits are reaped, in a business as usual atmosphere, it might be helpful to remember that Eisner came to Disney in 1984, at $750,000 a year and a performance bonus that could reach more than a $1 million (Taylor, 1987, p. 233).

By 2005, projecting a more global view of the labor practices of Disney associated enterprises, again the BBC reported that due to the pressure put on by the National Labor Committee, Disney would investigate the "stifling and dangerous" conditions at some of it's contractor companies in China, ranging from a chronically underpaid labor force, women being denied maternity rights, fainting from heat exhaustion as well as industrial accidents.[6] In the same report the BBC noted that "The Reuters news agency reported that one print factory producing books for Disney has been the scene of regular industrial accidents, in which workers had lost their fingers and palms."

Ten years after the 1999 Paris Disneyland strike, in a classic replay and with significantly more impact, workers again protested over wage demands forcing the cancellation of the "Disney Star 'n' Cars" parade at Walt Disney Studios and the Once Upon a Dream parade at Disneyland park in Paris.[7]

The Smith and Clark (1999) text was of course published through the Disney Company, hence the selective appropriation and dissemination of company history through foregrounding and backgrounding. The availability of data on the Disney Company is staggering, ranging from a narrow focus of analysis on particular movies, to company finances (Taylor, 1987), to the analysis of imperialist ideology as constructed in character subjectivity (Dorfman & Mattelart, 1971), to gender construction and the policing of Disney Discourse (Giroux, 1999; Smoodin, 1994; Wasko, Phillips, & Meehan, 2001; Bell, Haas, & Sells, 1995). One of the more interesting of these analyses on the level of ideology was written by Ariel Dorfman and Armand Mattelart in 1971. Their *How to Read Donald Duck* builds a convincing case for the functioning of ideology through Disney comics in Latin America. They assert that "Disney characters only function by virtue of a suppression of real and concrete factors; that is their personal history, their birth and death, and their whole development in between, as they grow and change" (p. 34).

In fact, the world of Disney can exist only to the extent that it is able to suppress all that entails struggle in the human condition. Bringing to mind the Disney theme parks' underground network of tunnels that prevent access to a daily reality of actual life and work abstracted from fantasy, the authors lay out a complex formulation by which Disney—

controlling for biological relationships, continuously extolling the image of the noble savage as foreign and subject to domination—intricately weaves a process of gender domination fused into colonialist practices. In contrasting this idea of the child as innocent with the theme of the foreigner's innocence, Dorfman and Mattelart (1971) observe that

> there are two types of children. While the city-folk are intelligent, calculating, crafty and superior, the third worldlings are candid, foolish, irrational, disorganized and gullible (like cowboys and Indians). The first are spirit, and move in the sphere of ideas; the second are body, inert matter, mass. The former represent the future, the latter the past. (p. 46)

The projection of the "foreign reality" onto the noble savage is of course commensurate with exploitative capitalist practices in which the crafty theft of the valuable is justified by the moral and intellectual superiority of the central western characters. In fact, it is not very different from the current opposite portrayal of the Middle Eastern as violent and unable to administer his own affairs, thereby legitimating the exploitation of the people of that region by companies such as Halliburton and Blackwater (now Xe) (Chomsky, 2004). In either case, the media ultimately plays a central role in legitimating the dominance of Western ideology and simultaneously ensuring the exploitation of the "foreigner." In a brilliant analysis, Dorfman and Mattelart observe that

> this world of projection and segregation is based upon the role and concept of entertainment as it has developed in capitalist society . . . all the conflicts of the real world, the nerve centers of bourgeois, are purified in the imagination in order to be absorbed and co-opted into the world of entertainment. (1971, p. 76)

This projection, under the guise of innocent fun, must be contextualized within a matrix of the legitimization of differential power relations. Giroux (1995) cautions that

> as an ideological construct that mobilizes particular cultural practices in diverse regimes of representations, whether they be theme parks, comics, or movies, Disney's appeal to pristine innocence and high adventure is profoundly pedagogical in its attempt to produce specific knowledge, values and desires. (p. 48)

As Wasko, Phillips, and Meehan (2001) have concluded, among the resisters (to Disney discourse) participating in the Global Disney

Audiences Project, the construction of gender subjectivity seemed to be just as problematic as Disney's focus on consumption and pricing. This is evidence of the changing nature of the contextual frame under which the Disney characters operate. While some may opt to see recent heroines (e.g., Esmeralda, Pocahontas, and Mulan) as independent and more aggressive compared to the older, more subdued images of, for example, Cinderella, these traits are in fact contained in the realization of the final typical romance that must reinstate the dominance of the male character. This dynamic becomes pervasive in that even as these heroines are psychosocially demonstrative of cultural shifts in acceptable norms for females, they remain bound to an idealized, sexualized aesthetic that itself becomes an entrapment. Clearly this dynamic reinforces the notion that even as the contextual frame explicitly changes, the underlying themes of female subservience remain implicit in the character's relation to the politics of the body and sexuality.

Nevertheless, cultural insights, even among those who resist "Disneyfication," are not without their share of contradictions. As in the Gramscian notion of hegemony, many of the participants in the Global Disney Audiences Project were able to mediate the psychological dissonance created by a nostalgic reminiscence of childhood by fracturing the Disney Discourse into the "classic" Disney (Walt's characters and values) and the "new" Disney (commercialism and hyper-consumption). Even though, as Wasko, Phillips, and Mehan observe, "the new Disney—with its emphasis on synergy across media and heavy merchandising—is seen as the merchandisation of culture, and is rejected"(2001, p. 335), this view did not necessarily lead to nonconsumption, but rather to a moderated consumption that reflects an embrace of "soft capitalism."

What the above-referenced studies indicate is that there is clearly a particular discourse that is instantiated in the production of Disney animated films, and that this discourse is not in any sense arbitrary. It follows a particular logic that is built into the company vision, and it does not stray from what is deemed appropriate to be presented as Disney material. Departing from the ideological position that indeed only some alternatives are possible in the construction of this overall narrative, we are still left with a pragmatic problem: It is one thing to say that such a discourse exists because of historic patterns and the impossibility of the existence of multiple alternatives, and another to say that this discourse in some ways correlates with language as it is built into character subjectivity. In fact, one can even question the overall significance of language as an indicator of individual subjectivity in any sense. It is to this aspect that we now turn.

The Role of Language

There is a vast array of literature (Baugh, 2002; Macedo, Dendrinos, & Gounari, 2003; Fanon, 1952; Labov, 1966; Pennycook, 2001; Rickford, 1999; Dillard, 1972) that positions language as a fundamental aspect of identity. To ignore this body of literature is to dismiss a plethora of research that situates language within a complex framework, whereby it is simultaneously constitutive of and constitutes differential power relations that are inevitably legitimized in hegemonic forms that legitimate particular realities and materialities. The role of language is so integral in the construction of identity (Anzaldúa, 1987; Macedo & Gounari, 2005; Labov, 2001; Norton, 2000; Garcia, 2008) that the very mentioning of it seems to defy our sense of the obvious. Not only do we rely on it in terms of the construction of our own identity, but we also impose all types of markers on those who we feel are somehow constructing new identities. In thinking of the various labels that we utilize within the sphere of education in categorizing students (e.g., English Language Learners, Limited English Proficient), it becomes obvious that such labels are ultimately problematic in that they reduce the identity of learners to our own conceptions of normativity with respect to language learning; nevertheless, they capture the extent to which we view language as a mediator of who we are in the world. Davis (2009) articulately captures this dynamic by reminding us that "Language that we, social scientists, researchers and policy makers create and use in our studies of society, its institutions, its populations, economic and social behavior, becomes codified and used to categorize, stigmatize, denigrate and separate citizens over time" (p. 123).

No one understands this better than those who are in the process of developing new linguistic identities within a context of power relationships (Norton, 2000). Only through this lens can we process newspaper stories of Asian students of English "opting" to have surgical procedures so that they would be able to clearly produce specific sounds of the English language.[8] On the norm, such "surgical procedures" are done mentally and routinely, for whenever an individual apologizes for his or her "accent," he or she is ultimately engaging in a surgical and tactical maneuvering of his or her identity within a matrix of what Gee (1999) refers to as the "socially situated identity." The apology then becomes an admission of one's incapacity to fully integrate into dominant culture to the extent that one is incapable of reproducing "native-like" phonological characteristics. As linguists John Baugh (2002), William Labov (1973), and Donaldo Macedo have demonstrated with their studies on language attitudes, beyond the centering of the identity of the speakers in such encounters, there is a heavy price to pay for those who find themselves on the side of the linguistically oppressed in any society.

Referring to the importance of language (linguistic capital) as a key component of one's identity, Bourdieu notes,

> discourse always owes its most important characteristics to the linguistic production relations within which it is produced. The sign has no existence (except abstractly in dictionaries) outside a concrete mode of linguistic production relation. All particular linguistic transactions depend on the structure of the linguistic field, which is itself a particular expression of the structure of power relations between the groups possessing the corresponding competences (e.g. "genteel" language and the vernacular, or, in a situation of multilingualism, the dominant language and the dominated language). (1977, p. 647)

The relationality of linguistic production was further highlighted by Bourdieu as he reminded us that

> the products of certain competences only yield a profit of distinctiveness inasmuch as, by virtue of the relationship between the system of linguistic differences and the system of economic and social differences, we are dealing not with a relativistic universe of differences that are capable of relativizing one another, but with a hierarchized universe of deviations from a form of discourse that is recognized as legitimate. (1977, p. 654)

An example of this can be seen if one compares speakers of high-status languages such as German and French with Spanish in the U.S. context. Whereas in the former languages phonological fossilization is experienced as a sign of intelligence and "high culture," in the latter the speaker would be interpreted (and often treated) as relatively inarticulate and "uneducated." In fact, the current virulent attacks against teachers in the state of Arizona for having "accents" are a clear example of this dynamic. The implication is that one's "accent" is somehow transferrable to students. This subject position is assigned as much through the historic background of colonization (and neocolonization) as it is by a conservative socially constructed xenophobic fear of hordes of Latin American immigrants who are supposedly at the immigration gates just waiting to barge down the door and take away working-class jobs (never mind the fact that they were here first). In either case, the fact remains that "accents" carry particular associations that determine, or at the very least impose, particular subject positions on the speakers through social conventions and biases. It is in this frame that Bourdieu observes:

> We know that properties such as voice setting (nasal, pharyngeal) and pronunciation ("accent") offer better indices than syntax for identifying a speaker's social class; we learn that the efficacy of a discourse, its power to convince, depends on the authority of the person who utters it, or, what amounts to the same thing, on his "accent," functioning as an index of authority. (1977, p. 653)

Disney, being fully aware of these subtle but general attitudes, fully exploits them in the construction of character subjectivity, and in doing so, not only contributes in the perpetuation of these attitudes but also indirectly structures the materiality associated with the attitudes. As Giroux (2006) observes with respect to language in Disney productions, "It is worth noting that racism in Disney's animated films does not simply appear in negative imagery or through historical misinterpretation; racist ideology also appears in racially coded language and accents" (p. 25). Of course Disney is not the only contributor to this process, nor by any means the principal one, but Disney's wide reach in terms of audience gives it a particularly strong role in maintaining these linguistic attitudes, which are embodied in material effects. In this sense, critical theorist Henry Giroux's notions of public pedagogy becomes central in illustrating the pedagogical force of spaces that exist outside the social sphere of schooling as transmitters of cultural knowledge.

In 2003 while working at a major Midwestern university, we devised a study to research language attitudes based on phonological character-istics in particular Disney productions. We only had two requirements for the texts to be analyzed: that the texts contained characters that would have to be clearly represented as "good" or "bad" as articulated in the ultimate victory or destruction of a character in the finality of the text; and that the text centered on a living culture that was outside of the social context of the United States. The second requirement ensured that the syntactic and phonological variations and cultural assumptions encountered would have to be projected onto the characters, hence the possibility of examining existing cultural models as native to the United States or as text-driven. These two parameters were met by the movies *Aladdin* (1992) and *Mulan* (1998), in which characters are very clearly delineated and the settings are outside of the "life-worlds" of the aver-age American consumer.

As we analyzed both textual productions we noted particular pat-terns in language usage and, just as important, systemic patterns in the reactions to the phonological productions therein. In *Aladdin*, the char-acter requirement is ultimately satisfied with the banishment of the character Jaffar through the astute context manipulation of Aladdin himself. The ultimate demise of Jaffar leaves no doubts as to the con-struction of morality in the text. There is a coveted prize (the lamp and, subtly, the affection of Jasmine) and two antagonistic forces in the per-sonae of Aladdin and Jaffar. The development of the plot ultimately leads to the triumph of one and the decimation of the other, hence the resolution of the plot and the attainment of the prizes, the lamp and Jasmine. The setting in India fulfills the second requirement, that the plot development be located in an ostensibly different environment. The mythical city of Aggrabah necessitates the historical imposition of par-ticular cultural norms because the interpreter of the text hypothetically has no schema to draw from in the interpretation of form and context.

Mulan repeats this sequence, though in a more intricate manner. In *Mulan*, the objective is the saving of a town, an objective that positions the heroine Mulan against the villain Shan-Yu. The plot development is ultimately resolved with the saving of the town, the banishment of the villain, and the ultimate reduction of the lead character into a bride (the natural sequence for the Disney heroine). Regardless of the ideological apparatus that allows for gender dynamics to be constructed as such (that is to say, for her to save the town and the population only to be diminished and held captive to the status of "bride"), the banishment of Shan-Yu clearly satisfies the first condition. In satisfying the second requirement, the setting is ancient China. As in *Aladdin*, the setting forces the text creator to impose particular historical constructions in a geographical space that is outside the norm of white middle-class America. This imposition not only positions the interpreter in an imaginary locale, outside her or his immediate norm of reference, but even where an interpreter might have an understanding (albeit already tainted) of historical conditions relative to the geographic space, this understanding is played upon in the construction of character and national identities.

A methodological consideration in this endeavor is the unit of analysis. Why choose a particular set of stanzas for analysis as opposed to another? After all, although character construction must be fluid in the sense that the overall structure of the character must remain whole, throughout the textual construction, different character facets must be must be foregrounded and backgrounded so as to portray the character as somewhat "life-like." The methodological dilemma associated with this fluidity is resolved through an a priori establishment of analytic parameters.

In this case, the use of language in the construction of character subjectivity is analyzed through particular "tools" of discourse analysis, namely, identity construction, relationship forming, and the distribution of social goods (Gee, 1990). Identity construction as a constant in character creation is particularly relevant: "Cues or clues to assemble situated meanings about what identities and relationships are relevant to the interaction, with their concomitant attitudes, values, ways of feeling, ways of knowing and believing, as well as ways of acting and interacting" (Gee, 1999, p. 86).

As a category of analysis, "stanzas" relating to the distribution of social goods implicitly embed dominant values in character construction. In this particular case, rather than breaking down the dialogue into stanzas in an effort to understand the visual representation of the linguistic interaction, I have opted to complement the linguistic component with a physical description of the represented frames. It would be problematic if values embedded in the characters directly contradicted master narratives of how characters should or should not behave. Likewise, the foundation of relationships is observed in stanzas that embody both of these former categories. Several conversational sequences reflecting these three modes were selected for analysis. Although this analytical format attempts to fragment these categories for the sake of analysis, often in everyday speech these categories overlap into a symbiotic relationship that allows for multiple functions to be carried on simultaneously; as such, the separation of these categories is an artificial construction, a tool to assist in analysis, as it were. Figure 1 visually represents the format of analysis.

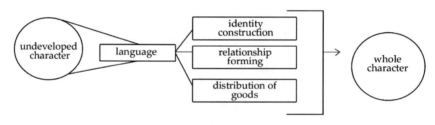

Figure 1.

It is through language, or specific forms of language, that identities are created, adjusted, and re-created. At this point in the analysis, it is important to point out that we do not see an inherent systematicity of language that would "naturally" lead one character to speak in one way as opposed to another (hence the segmented connection between character and language). This being the case, the syntactic and phonological choices made in the process of character construction become meaningful in that they are one among a range of possible alternatives. In the first section of the analysis we focus specifically on the link between language and identity construction.

The first unit of linguistic analysis embodies two of these building tasks while alluding to the third; both identity and social relationships are central to chapter 13 of Disney's Mulan. Through this initial interaction between Mulan and her guardian dragon Mushu, subjectification becomes crucial in that the characters are in a sense embodying, through linguistic interaction, their primary role positions. Mushu establishes himself primarily as a guardian of family honor and protector of Mulan. Mulan has the responsibility of taking her father's place in the army, thereby playing the role of a dutiful daughter (even though the "substitution" traditionally would be fulfilled by a son). This subject position must be understood within a wider ideological frame where family honor becomes the distributed social good; that is to say, in one way or another, it is not just a cathartic agent, but also remains perpetually that which is coveted. It symbolizes Mushu's return to an honored position with the ancestors, as well as Mulan's redemption with the family for transgressing her filial obligations as well as the established regulatory patterns of a gendered reality. Conversational sequence A1 exemplifies the contradictions between gender relations and filial duty to family honor and wider social responsibility, with the subordination of the former.

Conversational Sequence A1

Chi Fu: By order of the Emperor, one man from every family must serve in the Imperial Army. The Xiao family [a family member steps up, bows to the guard and takes the conscription notice from the guard]. The Yi family.

Yi's Son [holding his old father back]: I will serve the Emperor in my father's place.

Chi Fu: The Fa Family.

Mulan: No.

[Fa Zhou gives his cane to Fa Li and walks toward Chi Fu. Fa Zhou bows before the horsemen]

Fa Zhou [standing proud]: I am ready to serve the Emperor. [Fa Zhou reaches for the conscription notice]

Mulan [running outside to keep her father from taking the conscription notice]: Father, you can't go.

Fa Zhou [turning to see his daughter]: Mulan!

Mulan: Please sir, my father has already fought bravely—

Chi Fu: Silence! You would do well to teach your daughter to hold her tongue in a man's presence.

Fa Zhou [looking away from Mulan]: Mulan, you dishonor me.

[Grandma Fa guides Mulan back away]

In terms of linguistic production, chapter 13 (conversation sequence A and B) is particularly fascinating with respect to stylistic registers (Halliday, 1985) or social languages (Gee, 1999), syntactic distributions, and the use or non-use of the post-vocalic R. Stylistic registers or social languages refer to the types of languages we use in a given situation. These registers serve to create socially situated identities in everyday interactions. Lexical choice and syntactic construction are some distinct ways of identifying social languages or variations in registers. As Gee (1999) notes,

> each social language has its own distinctive grammar. However two different sorts of grammars are important to social languages, only one of which we ever think to study formally in school. One grammar is the traditional set of units like nouns, verbs, inflections, phrases and clauses. . . . [T]he other—less studied, but more important—grammar is the "rules" by which grammatical units like nouns and verbs, phrases and clauses, are used to create patterns which signal or "index" characteristic whos-doing-whats-within-Discourses. (p. 29)

Conversational Sequence A

Conversational sequence A demonstrates the use of language in the representation of a collective.

[Mushu appears as a giant shadow being cast on a rock with flames on either side. Mushu's real appearance remains out of sight]

Mushu [in a Southern Baptist Preacher's voice]: Did I hear someone ask for a miracle!? Let me hear you say aye!

Mulan [Running and hiding behind a rock]: Ahhhhhh.

Mushu: That's close enough.

Mulan [from behind a rock]: Ghost.

Mushu: Get ready Mulan your serpentine salvation is at hand. For I have been sent by your ancestors—[notices Cri-Kee making a hand shadow of a dragon on the rock and stamps him down with his foot] to guide you through your masquerade. [bending down to Cri-Kee] C'mon, you're gonna stay you're gonna work. [returning to Mulan] Heed my word, 'cause if the army finds out that you are a girl, the penalty is death. [big flames shoot up from the rocks]

Mulan: Who are you?

Mushu: Who am I? Who am I? I am the guardian of lost souls. [Mulan smiles big in anticipation of seeing her guardian] I am the powerful, the pleasurable, the indestructible [coming out from the rocks to show his real size] Mushu! Oh hah, hah, pretty hot, huh? [Khan stomps on Mushu. Mulan pushes Khan back]

Mulan: Ah, my ancestors sent a little lizard to help me?

Mushu: Hey, dragon, dragon, not lizard. I don't do that tongue thing [flips out his tongue to show Mulan what he means].

Mulan: You're uh...

Mushu: Intimidatin[g]? Awe-inspirin[g]?

Mulan [making a hand gesture to denote his smallness of size]: Tiny.

Mushu [with a look of disappointment]: Of course. I'm travel-size for your convenience. If I was my real size, your cow here [patting Khan on the nose] would die of fright. [Khan tries to bite Mushu] [pointing to the ground speaking to Khan] Down Bessy. My powers are beyond your mortal imagination. For instance, [leaning in and looking at Mulan's chest] my eyes can see straight through your armor. [Mulan covers her bust with her left arm and slaps Mushu with the right] Ow. [angrily] All right, that's it! Dishonor! Dishonor on your whole family. [aside to Cri-Kee] Make a note of this [Cri-Kee grabs a leaf and a pen and starts writing]. [Loudly with gusto] Dishonor on you. Dishonor on your cow. Dis—Mulan [pleadingly while covering Mushu's mouth]: Stop! I'm sorry, I'm sorry [kneeling down in front of Mushu]. I'm just nervous. I've never done this before.

Mushu: Then you're gonna have to trust me. And don't you slap me no mo[r]e, we clear on that? [Mulan nods emphatically]. All right. Okey dokey, let's get this show on the road. Cri-Kee, get the bags [Mushu starts walking to the camp]. [to Khan] Let's move it heifer.

In this case, the register or social language used by Mushu in meeting Mulan and establishing his own identity is an intertextual nod to an inflamed Southern preacher who warns of the dangers of the situation while characterizing his own position as the salvation to possible doom. In effect, Mushu's register or social language, as evidenced by phonological and syntactic output, is more or less static throughout the textual construction, becoming cemented to characteristics like copula deletions and uses of the post-vocalic *R* characteristic of African American Vernacular English (AAVE). By phonology I refer to the production of sound units or phonemes. The critical reader may immediately question the notion of an "essentialized" AAVE, yet as many linguists have observed, AAVE is characterized by distinct linguistic productions. Wolfram (1991) observes:

> Phonological patterns can be diagnostic of regional and social differences, and a person who has a good ear for dialects can often pinpoint a person's general regional and social affiliation with considerable accuracy based solely on phonology. Certainly, the use of a few critical pronunciation cues can narrow down a person's place of origin to at least general regions of the United States, if not the precise county of origin. (p. 51)

In the last "stanza" of this scene, for example, Mushu's phonological output makes use of a common AAVE speech pattern when the character says "And don't you slap me no mo[r]e, we clear on that?" The dropping of the *R* in "more" is characteristic of AAVE. While the dropping of this phoneme appears to be a minute phonological difference, it certainly is sufficient to establish contrast with the subsequent vowel, thereby producing a distinct speech pattern.

In a similar instance of dropping a phoneme, when Mushu responds, "Intimidatin[g]? Awe-inspirin[g]?" we note the phenomenon of consonant neutralization common to AAVE. Wolfram (1991) notes that the nasal segment represented as [ng], when occurring at the end of a word in an unstressed syllable, is often represented in AAVE as the production of the sound [n]. This process is in fact characteristic of AAVE speech patterns. Reflecting on this particular exchange we also note another common AAVE speech pattern, in a relationship of syntactic agreement. In this case, the negative in the sentence guides the use of indefinite form. In this exchange, the character could have perfectly well stated, "And don't slap me any more."

Wolfram (1991) further observes that

> in standard dialects, *any* is used in the postverbal indefinite (that is, the form comes after the verb in the sentence, such as He didn't have any money) whereas *no* may be used in most vernacular dialects (e.g., He didn't have no money). . . . Many of the distinctive dialect differences of syntax involve agreement patterns between words or morphemes, and *they are the most prominent social markers within American English* [italics added]. (p. 59)

Similarly, Rickford (1999) has pointed out that among the features of AAVE are the realization of the final *ng* as *n* in gerunds, deletion or vocalization of *R* after a vowel, and more varied intonations with "higher pitch range and more rising and level final contours than other English varieties" (p. 5). Certainly these linguistic features are abundantly exemplified in these textual productions. Why are these features particularly important in this context? Such an inquiry is anchored in an ideological frame where lexical choice (content and form) is ultimately meaningful. If the reader will recall, one of the requirements for the unit of analysis was that the setting and context would have to be imposed; that is to say, the phonological qualities of the voices would have to be "constructed." This being the case, the register used by the character Mushu becomes even more problematic. The textual production in fact contains other comedic characters, yet these characters, while relieving structural tension through humor, are not ultimately portrayed as "bungling fools" phonologically and syntacticly linked to a particular racial collective. The linking of character subjectification and a racialized group becomes more striking in the absence of similar constructions with the supporting characters.

The Disney textual presentation in effect supports and perpetuates this link with long-term effects on our perceptions of subjectification and linguistic production. Theorizing this link cannot be abstracted from the structured materiality of the linguistically oppressed. In fact, Disney accomplishes this task selectively with Mushu's character. If the characterizations were done to resemble common speech patterns generally, we would have to wonder why the supporting comedic characters did not for instance represent the common *R–W* substitutions so commonly found in Chinese English speakers. The social languages used by the characters are structured so as to either conform or deviate from dominant linguistic conventions. Whereas Mushu's speech contains morphological irregularities such as syntactic contractions of "going to" to "gonna" and "want to" to "wanna," as well as "ain't" for "am not," other characters use more "standard" Anglo middle-class discourse. Consider, for example, a sequence of dialogue where General Li (the hero's father) and Chi Fu are debating the general's choice in promoting Shang to the rank of captain. This sequence disrupts the hierarchical relationship of Shang to Chi Fu while solidifying the relations between father and son.

Conversational Sequence B

[Chi Fu watches and then walks into the tent. General Li and Li Shang are in the tent.]

General Li [motioning with his pointer to a map of the region]: The Huns have struck here, here and here. I will take the main troops up to the Tung Shao Pass and stop Shan-Yu before he destroys this village.

Chi Fu: Excellent strategy, sir. I do love surprises, Ha ha, ha, ha.

General Li: You will stay here and train the new recruits. When Chi Fu believes you're ready, you will join us... Captain. [General Li hands a sword to Shang]

Shang: Captain?

Chi Fu: Oh, this is an enormous responsibility, General. Uh, perhaps a soldier with more experience—

General Li: Number one in his class, extensive knowledge of training techniques, [leaning back smugly stroking his chin] an impressive military lineage. I believe Li Shang will do an excellent job.

Shang [excitedly]: Oh, I will. I won't let you down. This is, I mean, I...[somberly] yes, sir.

Several factors are apparent in this sequence. First and most obvious in this sequence is the choice of lexicon used to establish these relationships. The dialogue does not use syntactic contractions such "gonna" in the place of "will." The general could have just as easily said "You're gonna stay here and train the new recruits," but this construction would not have been consistent with the image that Disney is attempting to project of standard versus nonstandard speech patterns. Even more commonly accepted contractions such as "you'll" for "you will" are reduced to the point where they appear nonexistent. In fact, the very lexical choices "Impressive military lineage, extensive knowledge, enormous responsibility" reflect a more Anglo, middle-class discourse.

The coherence of dialogue is momentarily broken by Shang in the last line of the dialogue when he expresses surprise at the unexpected promotion. This deviation from the norm not only heightens the awareness of the formal speech patterns of the general through contrast, but also attests to a particular fluidity in the use of social languages that is absent from other characters. The linguistic dis-fluencies have a mediating role in the dialogue, attesting to Shang's "normality" in being able to socially position himself and adjust to the ongoing dialogue. This adaptation is nonexistent with the character Mushu, and it is also nonexistent with the central evil character, Shan Yu. The effect of these non-adaptations in speech is that Mushu is portrayed as a familiar yet unserious character who is constantly joking and shirking responsibilities, while Shan Yu becomes so stilted and stiff through lexical hypercorrection as to appear "abnormal." The "stiffness" of Shan Yu's speech can be seen clearly in a conversational sequence where his relationship to his soldiers is being constructed. In this scene, Shan Yu presents some materials to his men and in a pedagogic manner creates a socially situated identity of group leader.

[Cut to Shan Yu sitting on top of a tree. He cuts off the very top with his sword. His falcon swoops by and drops a doll. Shan-Yu takes the doll, sniffs it, looks surprised, and drops down to the ground]

Shan-Yu [tossing the doll to Hun Strong Man]: What do you see?

Hun Strong Man [feeling the doll]: Black pine, from the high mountains. [Long Hair Hun Man takes the doll from Hun Strong Man. Bald Hun Man #1 takes a hair as it passes by him]

Bald Hun Man #1: White horse hair. Imperial stallions.

Long Hair Hun Man [sniffing the doll]: Sulfur, from cannons.

Shan-Yu: This doll came from a village in the Tung Shao Pass, where the Imperial Army's waiting for us.

Hun Archer: We can avoid them easily.

Shan-Yu [shaking his head]: No, the quickest way to the Emperor is through that pass. Besides, the little girl will be missing her doll. We should return it to her.

[End Interlude]

Anyone engaged with this text will certainly understand that these are the "bad" characters in the production, not from the visual representations themselves but rather from the phonological and syntactic constructions; the voices are lower and syntactic construction is again stilted by the hyper-adherence to conventional morphological rules.

These constructions create a triad in terms of possibility of being. Mushu's position is highly racialized, and even where somewhat familiar, he is projected as a mischievous trickster who is not ideal. The main "good characters" are projected as being able to flexibly adjust their social languages in creating varied socially situated identities, and the "evil" characters are projected as in a hyper-corrective mode that becomes "abnormal" in its linguistic inflexibility. One can visualize this dynamic on a continuum of linguistic production, ranging from highly systematized (racialized character) to flexible (good character) and ultimately to a structured production (bad character).

In the second textual production, Aladdin, the same methodological pattern was followed. Again we see developing in the analysis of the sequences patterns that relate to the construction of character subjectivity. In this production the distributed social good is power; this is situational because power symbolizes something different for each of the main characters. For Jafar power is literally the power of the sorcerer to command the kingdom, for Aladdin power is the possibility of transforming himself to obtain the object of his desire (Jasmine), and for Jasmine power is the ability to control who she will marry, in possible violation of the law. Conversational sequence C is important in this production to the extent that it captures the flouting of Aladdin's newly found "power" as a transformed prince, hence the creation of a new socially situated identity for this character. Interestingly, the scene also embodies a triad of relationships in Jafar's challenging of the legitimacy of the new prince, as well as Jasmine's assertion of individuality and refusal to be represented as a "prize."

Conversational Sequence C
(Identity/Relationship Building)

(More and more fanfare build up until Aladdin flies off Abu's back on Magic Carpet and flies down to the Sultan. Jafar slams the door shut.)

Sultan: (Clapping) Splendid, absolutely marvelous.

Aladdin: (Takes on a deeper voice.) Ahem. Your Majesty, I have journeyed from afar to seek your daughter's hand.

Sultan: Prince Ali Ababwa! Of course. I'm delighted to meet you. (He rushes over and shakes Ali's hand.) This is my royal vizier, Jafar. He's delighted too.

Jafar: (Extremely drily) Ecstatic. I'm afraid, Prince Abooboo—

Aladdin:—Ababwa!

Jafar: Whatever. You cannot just parade in here uninvited and expect to—

Sultan:...by Allah, this is quite a remarkable device. (He tugs at the tassels, and they tug his moustache.) I don't suppose I might...

Aladdin: Why certainly, Your Majesty. Allow me. (He helps the sultan up onto the Carpet, and he plops down. Jafar pins the Carpet down on the floor with the staff.)

Jafar: Sire, I must advise against this—

Sultan:—Oh, button up, Jafar. Learn to have a little fun. (He kicks away the staff and Carpet and Sultan fly away. Iago, who was standing on the head of the staff, falls down, repeatedly bopping the staff with his beak as he descends. Sultan and Carpet fly high into the ceiling, then begin a dive-bomb attack, flying under Abu, scaring him. The flight continues in the background, while Jafar and Ali talk in the foreground.)

Jafar: Just where did you say you were from?

Aladdin: Oh, much farther than you've traveled, I'm sure. (He smiles. Jafar does not.)

Jafar: Try me. (Iago lands on the staff.)

Sultan: Look out, Polly! (They all duck in time as the Carpet whizzes centimeters over their heads. Carpet returns and the sultan chases Iago around the room.)

Iago: Hey, watch it. Watch it with the dumb rug! (The carpet zooms underneath Iago, who sighs, wipes his brow, and crashes into a pillar. He crashes to the floor, and his head is circled by miniature sultans on carpets, saying "Have a cracker, have a cracker." The real sultan begins his final approach.)

Sultan: Out of the way, I'm coming in to land. Jafar, watch this! (He lands.)

Jafar: Spectacular, Your Highness.

Sultan: Ooh, lovely. Yes, I do seem to have a knack for it. (Carpet walks over to Abu dizzily, then collapses. Abu catches it.) This is a very impressive youth. And a prince as well. (Whispers to Jafar) If we're lucky, you won't have to marry Jasmine after all.

Jafar: I don't trust him, sire.

Sultan: Nonsense. One thing I pride myself on Jafar, I'm an excellent judge of character.

Iago: Oh, excellent judge, yeah, sure...not!!!

(Jasmine walks in quietly.)

Sultan: Jasmine will like this one!

Aladdin: And I'm pretty sure I'll like Princess Jasmine!

Jafar: Your Highness, no. I must intercede on Jasmine's behalf. (Jasmine hears this and gets mad.) This boy is no different than the others. What makes him think he is worthy of the princess?

Aladdin: Your Majesty, I am Prince Ali Ababwa! (He pricks Jafar's goatee, which springs out in all directions.) Just let her meet me. I will win your daughter!

Jasmine: How dare you! (They all look at her surprised.) All of you, standing around deciding my future? I am not a prize to be won! (She storms out.)

Sultan: Oh, dear. Don't worry, Prince Ali. Just give Jasmine time to cool down. (They exit.)

Jafar: I think it's time to say good bye to Prince Abooboo.

As we can see in this scene, multiple effects are achieved through linguistic production. When Aladdin says, "Ahem. Your Majesty, I have journeyed from afar to seek your daughter's hand," linguistic dis-fluencies are used to displace the former identity of a common street boy to the embodiment of a prince. In fact, while this appears to be a relatively minute change in dialogue, it signals that the producers of the text are aware that there needs to be variation in the social language used to make the character "fit" the scene, or at the very least make it appear convincingly that the character is projecting this change. This is done not only in terms of the syntactic construction with the dis-fluency, but also by controlling the phonological output (pitch) to indicate status differential in speech. Lexical choice also indicates an adjustment in social language: "Journeyed," "afar" and "seek" are certainly part of a lexicon that a common "street boy" would not be routinely use.

This sequence demonstrates some of the same characteristics found in the previous analysis, in that the central "good" characters are represented as having the capacity to moderate the social language to flexibly adjust to new scenes and interactions, while the "bad" characters are projected as relatively inflexible in linguistic output to the point of seeming "abnormal." Jafar exemplifies this alternate modality when he greets Aladdin by saying, "Whatever. You cannot just parade in here uninvited and expect to—."

The character certainly could have said "You can't just come in here" or "you can't just walk in here," but the substitution of "cannot" and "parade" for these other more quotidian linguistic productions would have diminished the capacity of language to shape the subjectivity of the character in accordance with the parameters set forth for "bad" characters. Lexical choice, then, indicates a difference of being. In fact, whereas Jafar's character produces highly stilted speech such as "Sire, I must advise against this," and "Your highness, no. I must intercede on Jasmine's behalf," the king, who is portrayed as a "good" character, responds to Jafar's admonition by stating, "Oh, button up, Jafar," a clearly flexible use of language that is reflected in the productions of all of the "good" characters, yet virtually nonexistent in Jafar's language. Iago, the meddling parrot, a mediating character who by the end of the movie is incorporated into the camp of the "good" guys, is also able to play with syntax, and in so doing is able to achieve a type of generational bonding with the audience, particularly the younger viewers. When Iago dislocates the negative in an interaction with Jaffar by saying, "Oh, excellent judge, yeah, sure . . . not!!!," the pattern resembles a common linguistic output in adolescents' slang that emphasizes the improbability of the statement. These fluctuations in language production are selectively evident in the characters, and as such create the "normal" and "abnormal" ("standard" and "nonstandard") identities that Disney projects as "good" or "bad."

In another conversational sequence there are some similar links between character development and language use. In this case, the scene reflects interactions relating to the distribution of a social good, namely the power sought by Jafar and contested by Aladdin.

Conversational Sequence D

(They both look up and see a gigantic genie lift the palace into the clouds. Aladdin whistles and Carpet flies up to greet him. They fly up near the genie's head.)

Aladdin: Genie! No!

Genie: Sorry, kid—I got a new master now. (He places the palace on top of a mountain.)

Sultan: Jafar, I order you to stop!

Jafar: There's a new order now—my order! Finally, you will bow to me! (The sultan bows, but Jasmine does not.)

Jasmine: We'll never bow to you!

Iago: Why am I not surprised?

Jafar: If you will not bow before a sultan, then you will cower before a sorcerer! (To Genie) Genie, my second wish—I wish to be the most powerful sorcerer in the world! (Genie extends his finger. Aladdin tries to stop him, but he cannot, and another Genie (tm) brand lightning bolt strikes Jafar, returning him to his normal look.)

Iago: Ladies and gentlemen, a warm Agrabah welcome for Sorcerer Jafar!

Jafar: Now where were we? Ah, yes—abject humiliation! (He zaps Jasmine and the sultan with his staff, and they both bow to him. Rajah comes running at him. He zaps Rajah, and the tiger turns into a kitty-cat.) Down, boy! Oh, princess— (lifts her chin with his staff)—there's someone I'm dying to introduce you to.

In this sequence, Jafar is engaging in the construction of a new socially situated identity as the new authority figure. This conversational sequence reflects some of the linguistic structures that we have seen in some of the other sequences. As we can clearly see, Jafar's lack of use of contractions help to create the linguistic "stiffness" or inflexibility that becomes attached to his character. At several points during this sequence he could have opted to contract his speech as in an everyday conversational style by substituting, for example, "you'll" for "you will." Yet the character's inability to manipulate syntactic construction creates a distance and formality that positions this character as outside the norm of familiar linguistic interactions. This positioning is also reflected again in the lexicon that the character draws from in the dialogue. "You will cower before a sorcerer" and "abject humiliation" are lexical choices that we don't readily find in the other characters. Contrast this with the Genie's response to Aladdin's plea to stop assisting Jafar: "Sorry, kid— I got a new master now." The use of "sorry kid" in this sequence organizes Genie's actions as not entirely menacing in the sense that the very word "kid" connotes a friendly and informal relationship with Aladdin. The Genie is transgressing out of duty or obligation, but not necessarily malice. In a certain sense, it is as if the language that Genie uses allows the viewer to empathize with the socially situated identity enacted by Genie, even as it is doing damage to the kingdom. This is yet another case where lexical choice indicates the ability of the character to moderate social language so as to appear "normal." Whereas in *Mulan*, Mushu becomes a highly racialized character, the Genie in *Aladdin* breaks this mold to the extent that it is part of the construction of the character that he is able to mutate and morph into different personae, thereby allowing the character to escape the process of racialization.

Although Disney is operating within an "English domain," the selective variation in the linguistic construction of character subjectivity suggests that these wider social attitudes structured in a binary of "Standard

English" as familiar and "nonstandard" variations as foreign or alien have been absorbed by the company. In fact, they have become part of the apparatus of the construction of normalcy (Disney discourse), hence, they display Disney's complicity in the perpetuation of xenophobic attitudes toward all that is constructed as being outside the parameters of "standard" white middle-class linguistic variations. The Disney textual presentation supports and perpetuates this link with long-term effects on our perceptions of subjectification and linguistic production.

Disney-fying Language: Assessing Linguistic Differentiation

To test the systematicity between character development and language use, a study was designed to investigate not only the reactions that undergraduate students in a Midwestern university had to different linguistic variations, but also the attitudes that prompted these reactions. The study was primarily survey research. The students were exposed to three sets of voices from the Disney films *Mulan* and *Aladdin* and then were asked to qualify their attitudes about the voices. The first set consisted of three voices of animated characters from *Aladdin*, the second set of three voices from *Mulan*, and the last set of a combination of voices from both movies. After the presentation of each voice set, students were asked a series of questions to determine which voices the students attributed to "bad" and "good" characters, as well as their reasons for these choices. The results were later coded and statistically analyzed to determine the propensity of choice relative to linguistic variation.

For the first set of voices the students were asked to identify the voice belonging to the "good" character. In this series, the first voice was an excerpt with phonological stress on particular syllables deviating from "standard Anglo middle-class" linguistic output; as a result, this particular character appeared to have an "accent." The second voice was that of the main character (hero) of the movie, and the last was that of the villain. As much as possible, the investigator minimized the context by limiting the exposure so that the context or frame could not be derived from listening to the voices. Sequentially, the voices presented were those of the street seller, Aladdin, and Jafar.

In the second set of voices, the objective was to single out the "bad" character. In this sequence, the "bad" character was in the first position, and the following voices belonged to the heroine and a mediating supporting character. Sequentially, the voices were those of Shan-Yu, Mushu, and finally Mulan. In the last sequence, the investigator included all "good" voices, that is to say, no villains were included in the samples. The subjects were asked to identify the good character. The voices presented were those of Aladdin, Mulan, and Mushu.

All of the students were able to identify the villainous characters by listening to a sentence or part of a sentence . More problematic was the identification of the "good" character once the voices in the sample included only "good" characters. When this scenario was presented, some students had such difficulty choosing that they opted to label all three samples as belonging to "good" characters.

Just as interesting as were the descriptors that students used in referring to the characters. Some of the more common descriptors for the "good" characters were: Friendly, smooth, soft tones, clear, higher tones, compassionate, innocent, moderately pitched, perhaps white, white American, no apparent discernable accent, comforting, Midwest or West Coast accent. In contrast, terms utilized to describe the "bad" characters based solely on listening to their phonological characteristics were: Deep, dark, low pitch, threatening, no clear discernable accent, sinister, vicious, deceitful, low, coarse, mean, vicious.

This limited yet telling study shows that particular phonological productions are attributed positive characteristics while others are perceived as negative. Furthermore, these attributions are systematic, and as such indicate a particular complicity on the part of Disney. How else can we explain the systematic correspondence between character production and linguistic output?

Clearly, language is playing a mediating role in the way that reality is constructed so as to align with dominant "mainstream" narratives, hence "white American," "comforting," and "compassionate" are diametrically opposed to "threatening," "sinister," and "deceitful." Linguoracism is grounded in material realities and inextricably linked to dimensions of power that ultimately reproduce hegemonic forms of control through forms of cultural reproduction.

The filtering of these pervasive ideological discourses in the repro-duction of cultural forms necessarily creates an exigency for the produc-tion of counter-discourses that strategically undermine econo-viability of sustaining these Discourses while simultaneously positing alternate possibilities grounded in more humane representational forms. This is not to say that there are specific people in the Disney Company that are systematically conspiring to create these images through the use of lan-guage, but rather that Disney, to the extent that it appropriates a wider discourse on what is the norm in terms of language attitudes, fully exploits these attitudes, and in so doing perpetuates stereotypes which in the long run structure the very materiality of those who find them-selves subordinated linguistically.

The linking of the ideological positions espoused here with curric-ular practice sets forth a synergy between the public sphere and curricu-lum development and implementation. As Giroux notes among the various lessons that must be learned from these forms of cultural repro-duction,

> it is crucial that the realm of popular culture that Disney increasingly uses to teach values and sell goods be taken seriously as a site of learning, especially for children. This means, at the very least, that it must be incorporated into schools as a serious object of social knowledge and critical analysis . . . parents, community groups, educators and other concerned individuals must be atten-tive to the messages in these films in order to both criticize them when necessary and, more importantly, to reclaim them for more productive ends. (2006, p. 26)

This link allows for a reconceptualization of curriculum that would necessarily venture beyond the educational sphere as currently concep-tualized to disrupt the linearity of curriculum and create a pedagogical space where the boundaries between the public and the educational spheres become fragmented. This disruption would require not only an alternate way of conceptualizing curricular cohesion, hence appeasing those who favor the primacy of regulation and governmentality as struc-tured into the current mode (Hirsch, 1988), but simultaneously a post-progressive pedagogy that uses rival epistemological frameworks and also is open to new methods of conceiving and evaluating what gets counted as knowledge.

Once we break down the barriers between the public and the educational, possibilities become limitless in that reality can better be engaged from multiple dimensions without limiting the inherently pedagogical space of the public through the fragmentation of knowledge. Given the adjustments and mutations of market economies that ordinarily seek to increase commodification and consumption, it only seems fitting that the educational establishment capitalize on the availability of these culturally embedded texts for an active engagement with a vast array of social justice themes, such as the permanence of racism through linguistic production. The analysis of language production in the public pedagogic space can lead to a creative tension that ultimately opens spaces of dialogue, a necessary step toward transformative change in a progressive pedagogy that envisions the establishment of boundaries of social responsibility, particularly for culture/commodity producers such as Disney as a matter of public health.

Notes

1. http://www.disneyinstitute.com/About_Us/Our_Story.aspx
2. https://www.wdwcollegeprogram.com/sap/its/mimes/zh_wdwcp/students/education/edu_additionalopportunities.html
3. The Walt Disney Company 2008 Annual Report
4. Retrieved from http://hubpages.com/hub/The-top-Animated-Movies-of-all-Times on October 28, 2010.
5. http://news.bbc.co.uk/2/hi/business/574387.stm
6. http://news.bbc.co.uk/2/hi/business/4165654.stm
7. http://www.themeparktourist.com/news/20091224/801/strike-hits-disneyland-paris-causes-parade-cancellations
8. Demick, B. (2002, April, 7). English 101: Get a longer tongue. The Seattle Times.

References

Anzaldúa, G. (1987). *Borderlands/la frontera: The new mestiza*. San Francisco: Aunt Lute Books.

Apple, M. W. (2000). *Official knowledge: Democratic education in a conservative age*. London and New York: Routledge.

Bakhtin, M. (2000). Unitary language. In L. Burke, T. Crowley, & A. Girvin (Eds.), *The Routledge language and cultural theory reader* (pp. 269–279). London and New York: Routledge. (Original work published 1934).

Baugh, J. (2002). *Beyond Ebonics: Linguistic pride and racial prejudice*. New York: Oxford University Press.

BBC News. (1999). Strike at Disneyland Paris. Retrieved November 1, 2010 from:http://news.bbc.co.uk/2/hi/business/574387.stm on November 1, 2010

BBC News. (2005). Disney probes China labour claims. Retrieved October 28, 2010, from: http://news.bbc.co.uk/2/hi/business/4165654.stm

Bell, E., Haas, L., & Sells, L. (1995). *From mouse to mermaid: The politics of film, gender, and culture*. Bloomington, IN: Indiana University Press.

Bourdieu, P. (1977). Economics of linguistic exchanges. *Social Science Information, 16*(6), 645–668.

Brown, H. D. (2000). *Principles of language learning and teaching*. Englewood Cliffs, NJ: Prentice Hall Regents.

Castenell, L. Jr., & Pinar, W. F. (1993). *Understanding curriculum as a racial text: Representations of identity and difference in education*. Albany, NY: State University of New York Press.

Chomsky, N. (2004). *Hegemony or survival: America's quest for global dominance*. New York: Henry Holt.

Cornbleth, C., & Waugh, D. (1995). *The great speckled bird: Multicultural politics and education policymaking*. Mahwah, NJ: Lawrence Erlbaum Associates.

Davis, R. D. (2009). Minorities vs. minority groups: How language defines, defiles and denigrates for life. In S. Steinberg (Ed.), *Diversity and multiculturalism: A reader* (pp. 123–130). New York: Peter Lang.

Demick, B. (2002, April 7). English 101: Get a longer tongue. *The Seattle Times*. Retrieved from: http://www.thefreelibrary.com/English+101%3 A+Get+a+longer+tongue+Some+Koreans+believe+surgery+will . . . -a084666449

Dillard, J. L. (1972). *Black English: Its history and usage in the United States*. New York: Vintage.

Dorfman, A., & Mattelart, A. (1971). *How to read Donald Duck: Imperialist ideology in the Disney comic*. Valparaiso, Chile: Ediciones universitarias.

Fairclough, N. (1999). *Language and power*. London and New York: Longman.

Fanon, F. (1952). *Black skin white masks*. New York: Grove Weidenfeld.

Garcia, O. (2008). *Bilingual education in the 21st century: A global perspective*. Chichester, UK: Wiley-Blackwell.

Gee, J. P. (1990). *Social linguistics and literacies: Ideology in discourses*. New York: Routledge.

Gee, J. P. (1999). *An introduction to discourse analysis: Theory and method*. London and New York: Routledge.

Giroux, H. (1995). Memory and pedagogy in the "Wonderful World of Disney." As cited in Bell, E., Haas, L. & Sells, L. (1995). *From mouse to mermaid: The politics of film, gender and culture* (pp. 43–61). Bloomington, IN: Indiana University Press.

Giroux, H. (1999). *The mouse that roared: Disney and the end of innocence.* Lanham, MD: Rowman & Littlefield.

Giroux, H. (2006). Are Disney movies good for your kids? In K. Abowitz & R. Karaba (Eds.), *Readings in sociocultural studies in education* (6th ed., pp. 21–27). New York: McGraw-Hill.

Gomery, D. (1994). Disney's business history: A reinterpretation. In E. Smoodin (Ed.), *Disney discourse: Producing the Magic Kingdom* (pp. 71–86). New York: Routledge.Halliday, M. A. K. (1985). *An introduction to functional grammar.* Baltimore: Edward Arnold.

Hirsch, E. D. Jr. (1988). *Cultural literacy: What every American needs to know.* New York: Vintage.

Hollister, P. (1940).Genius at work: Wwalt Disney. As cited in E. Smodin, (Ed.). (1994). *Disney discourse: Producing the Magic Kingdom* (pp. 23–41). New York: Routledge Press.

HubPages. (2010). The top ten animated movies of all times. Retrieved October 27, 2010, from: http://hubpages.com/hub/The-top-Animated-Movies-of-all-Times

Kliebard, H. (1995). *The struggle for the American curriculum.* New York: Routledge.

Kunzle, D. (1971). Introduction. In A. Dorfman & A. Mattelart (Eds.), *How to read Donald Duck: Imperialist ideology in the Disney comic* (pp. 11–24). Valparaiso, Chile: Ediciones universitarias.

Labov, W. (1966). *The social stratification of English in New York City.* Washington, DC: Center for Applied Linguistics.

Labov, W. (1973). *Language in the inner city: Studies in black English vernacular.* Philadelphia: University of Pennsylvania Press.

Labov, W. (2001). *Principles of linguistic change, social factors.* Malden, MA: Blackwell.

Ladson-Billings, G. (2000). Racialized discourse and ethnic epistemologies. In N. Denzin & Y. Lincoln (Eds.), *Handbook of qualitative research* (pp. 257–277). London: Sage.

Leistyna, P. (2002). *Defining and designing multiculturalism: One school system's effort.* Albany, NY: State University of New York Press.

Lewis, J. (1994). Disney after Disney: Family business and the business of family. In E. Smoodin (Ed.), *Disney discourse: Producing the Magic Kingdom* (pp. 87–104). New York: Routledge.

Macedo, D. (1985). *The Capeverdean Language Project: Final report.* Washington, D. C. : Department of Education.

Macedo, D., Dendrinos, B., & Gounari, P. (2003). *The hegemony of English.* Boulder, CO: Paradigm.

Macedo, D., & Gounari, P. (2005). *The globalization of racism.* Boulder, CO: Paradigm.

Norton, B. (2000). *Identity and language learning.* Harlow, UK: Pearson Education.

Orwall, B. (2002, November 21). Tensions persist between Eisner and Roy Disney. *The Wall Street Journal*, p. B1.

Orwall, B., & Wingfield, N. (2004, January 30). The end: Pixar breaks up with distribution partner Disney. *The Wall Street Journal*, p. B1.

Pennycook, A. (2001). *Critical applied linguistics: A critical introduction*. Mahwah, NJ: Lawrence Erlbaum.

Rickford, J. (1999). *African American vernacular English: Features, evolution, educational implications*. Malden, MA: Blackwell.

Rosa, R. (2009). What type of revolution are we rehearsing for? Boal's theater of the oppressed. In M. Apple, W. Au, & L. Gandin (Eds.), *The Routledge international handbook of critical education* (pp. 240–253). New York: Routledge.

Smith, D., & Clark, S. (1999). *Disney: The first 100 years*. New York: Disney.

Smoodin, E. (1994). *Disney discourse: Producing the Magic Kingdom*. New York: Routledge.

Taylor, J. (1987). *Storming the Magic Kingdom*. New York: Knopf.

Theme Park Tourist. (2009). Strike hits Disneyland Paris, causes parade cancellations. Retrieved October 28, 2010, from: http://www.themeparktourist.com/news/20091224/801/strike-hits-disneyland-paris-causes-parade-cancellations

The Walt Disney Company. (2008). The Walt Disney Company 2008 Annual Report. Retrieved October 27, 2010, from: http://corporate.disney.go.com/investors/annual_reports/2008/index.html

The Walt Disney Company. (2010). Disney Institute. Retrieved November 1, 2010, from: http://www.disneyinstitute.com/About_Us/Our_Story.aspx on

The Walt Disney Company. (2010). Disney College Program. Retrieved October 26, 2010, from: https://www.wdwcollegeprogram.com/sap/its/mimes/zh_wdwcp/students/education/edu_additionalopportunities.html

Wallace, L. (1972). *Language, psychology and culture: Language, science and national development*. Stanford, CA: Stanford University Press.

Wasko, J., Phillips, M., & Meehan, E. (2001). *Dazzled by Disney?: The global Disney audiences* project. London and New York: Leicester University Press.

Wolfram, W. (1991). *Dialects and American English*. Englewood Cliffs, NJ: Prentice Hall.

Chapter Two

Struggles in the Semiotic Landscapes

Reading between the Images

I remember when America...when I was little America used to be a different kinda country...we didn't fuck with nobody...Now we be fucking with people in El Salvador and shit...(Audience laughter)...How we gonna lose? 35 people in El Salvador...(audience laughter)...right...we be sending advisors and shit...(takes out pretend gun and shoots) That's how it goes pal...(Audience laughter) Take my advice and do it that way (audience laughter)!

—Richard Pryor, Here and Now

High school students hate history. When they list their favorite subjects, history invariably comes in last. Students consider history "the most irrelevant" of twenty-one subjects commonly taught in high school. Bor-r-ring is the adjective they apply to it. (Lowen, 1995, p. 12)

So begins one of the most provocative inquiries into historical understanding that we have ever read, James Lowen's *Lies My Teacher Told Me* (1995). Two of Lowen's central points in the text are particularly well supported by our experiences in teaching this discipline for many years in U.S. public schools. The first of these is that historical understanding, starting from our early introduction to the field, often is so embedded in lies that it is only when students attend college (if they are fortunate enough to engage with critical professors) that they begin to demystify what by then is taken as a commonsense version of history. The second is that this process often occurs in part through a process that Lowen terms "heroification," or a cult of personality that disarticulates collective struggles through the aggrandizement of particular historical figures: The civil rights struggle becomes about Dr. King's "I Have a Dream" speech, the genocide of Native Americans becomes about Sitting Bull or Crazy Horse, and the class struggles during the revolutionary war is about George Washington's unfailing character. This process of disarticulation of history from collective struggles serves to sustain an ideological hegemony that effectively irons out current social contradictions by relegating past historical knowledge to abstract events with few connections to the present, thereby leading to what Giroux (1981, p. 40) has referred to as a "crisis of historical consciousness," or a type of "social amnesia." Giroux points to the importance of a historical consciousness to both radicals and conservatives when he notes,

> while it is true that both radicals and conservatives have often drawn upon history to sustain their respective points of view, this should not obscure the potentially subversive nature of history. Nor should it obscure the changing historical forces that sometimes rely upon "history" to legitimate existing power structures. Historical consciousness is acceptable to the prevailing dominant interest when it can be used to buttress existing social order. It becomes dangerous when its truth content highlights contradictions in the given society. (1981, p. 40)

Giroux's claim is that the wider social culture of positivism sustaining a type of technocratic legitimation during the twentieth century undermined the preceding concern with social progress in favor of technological development more conducive to "technical growth." As he observed,

> whereas progress in the United States in the eighteenth and nineteenth centuries was linked to the development of moral self-improvement and self-discipline in the interest of building a better society, progress in the twentieth century was stripped of its concern with ameliorating the human condition and

became applicable only to the realm of material and technical growth...inherent
in this notion of progress and its underlying technocratic rationality is the source
of logic that denies the importance of historical consciousness. (1981, p. 41)

A fundamental premise that we advance in this chapter is that the fundamental tensions between tendencies toward progressive social movements and the more anesthetizing discourses that mystify reality through decontextualizing the teaching of subjects such as history and social studies rest in the manipulation and rearticulation of language (through various formats) in ways that allow contradictory readings of the world to become socially digestible. Yet, at the same time, it is in the critical analysis of this very rearticulation of language (in its various formats) that psychological and social tensions can be produced to allow for more critical readings of the word and the world, thereby disrupting meta-narratives that institutionalize relations of domination as "commonsense" reality. From a pedagogical standpoint, this analysis, while necessary in all fields of inquiry, cannot be grounded in fragmented realities artificially created in the classroom by teachers concerned more with raising standardized test scores than a critically meaningful education. Such analysis must be entrenched in the daily experiences of students, however much that might conflict with the educator's own background and experiences. In the bridging of these experiences, education takes on an ethical dimension that provides spaces of liberation for both participants in the endeavor. In this chapter we look at the marketing and sustaining of one of these spaces of youth engagement that contributes to cultural hegemony as a means of interrogating dominant narratives and pointing to the possibility of counter-discourses.

Knowledge production can take forms that often are viscerally masked through discourses that normalize relations of domination (Giroux, 2001; Rosa, 2009, 2010; Macedo & Steinberg, 2007; Leistyna, 2004).

As a medium of knowledge production, video game cultures are increasingly becoming critically important not only for their own sake as entertainment outlets and multibillion-dollar industries, but also for their capacity to shed light on forms of information processing (Stephenson, 2009; Gee, 2003, 2007; Shaffer, 2008), and to capture the dialectical process whereby cultural artifacts both inform and reflect the very manner in which we process these relations of domination. Boggs and Pollard (2009) point to this critical understanding when they assert that

> the steady growth of a militarized society in the United States cannot be understood apart from the expanded role of media culture in its different forms: TV, radio, internet, publishing, video games, and film. An unsurpassed source of information, opinion, and entertainment, the corporate media have become the main linchpin of ideological hegemony in the United States, a repository of values, attitudes and myths that shapes public opinion on a daily basis. (p. 455)

The evolution of the game industry, from the initial static models introduced through the Atari systems to the current lifelike simulation models that thrive on realism and the integration of the player into the game world, has accompanied sociohistoric shifts that allow a normativity of particular discourses in the relation between the player and the mode of knowledge production. It is important at the outset to state that the aim of this chapter is not to declare that video games are inherently good or bad as entertainment modes. Such pronouncements ultimately give rise to dichotomous positions that are reductionist in nature, shedding little light on opportunities for pedagogical intervention. As Giroux (2006) has noted with respect to Disney animation,

> the roles assigned to women and people of color, along with ideas concerning a rigid view of family values, history, and national identity, need to be challenged and transformed. That is, such images and their claim to public memory need to be rewritten as part of a script of empowerment rather than simply dismissed because they serve to undermine human agency and democratic possibilities. (p. 26)

Instead, we go beyond this dichotomous position, because as Gee (2007) has pointed out, such pronouncements could not be made outside the cultural models which one opts to use as frames of analysis. Indeed, while Stephenson (2009) noted that

> despite their importance in youth culture and newfound cachet as an educational tool, video games continue to be demonized for destroying childhood— or, at least destroying the nostalgic version of childhood in which a child can safely and comfortably hang out outside playing ball all day. (p. 588)

She went on to observe that

> games provide an important space for representation—a space in which representations are presented and preserved, protested and changed. Despite being marketed as "child's play," games are, in fact, terrain on which battles related to the politics of representation are regularly fought. (p. 588)

The aim of this chapter is to examine the packaging and processing of two games in particular (*America's Army* and *America's Army: Special Forces*) in light of these sociohistoric shifts through the use of the tool of discourse analysis (Gee, 2003) as well as Kress and van Leeuwen's (2006) theory of visual design. The manufacturing of e-commodities associated with the production of video cultures is without doubt a phenomenon that transcends geographic borders. Even though such cultures are always framed in accordance with local specificities, this particular realm of cultural production has, at least in the United States, engendered pro and con movements, congressional hearings, and industry-wide debates, not to mention a plethora of current academic research on the benefits of exposure to video literacy (Gee, 2003, 2007; Shaffer, 2008; Sethi, 2008).

According to the NPD, a market research firm that tracks consumer trends for the film, music, PC games, video games, and video industries, in 2007 national retail sales of video games, including portable and console hardware, software, and accessories, topped $9.5 billion, an increase of 28 percent over 2006.[1] The Entertainment Software Association (ESA), a U.S. group representing computer and video game software publishers, acknowledged that during 2007, "On average, an astonishing 9 games were sold every second of every day of the year."[2] Relative to other media formats, the same association reported that "Halo 3, the best-selling title of 2007, took in more revenue in its first day of sales than the biggest opening weekend for a movie (Spider-Man 3, $151 million, and Harry Potter and the Deathly Hallows, $166 million)."[3] Astounding though they are, these figures do not adequately convey the extensive infrastructure required to sustain the public demand (natural or manufactured) for these entertainment modes. Although video games often are depicted as a realm of escape for youth through the apparatus of marketing, the *2007 Report of Sales, Demographic and Usage Data* published by ESA suggests that the social imaginary that links the consumption of video games solely to children is misguided. According to ESA, 67 percent of U.S. heads of households play computer or video games and the average game player is 33 years old (p. 2). In addition, in 2007, 24 percent of gamers were over the age of 50 (p. 2). Lest one think that gaming is gender specific, consider that the same source reported that overall, females represent 38 percent of total gamers and males 62 percent, yet women 18 and older represent a greater proportion of the game-playing population (31%) than boys 17 and younger (20%) (p. 3).

While these numbers are staggering, they fail to capture the extent to which producers of gaming software zealously compete for market share as well as the multimodality of games (Stephenson, 2009). With such massive figures and a clear and rising percentage of the population becoming more active in gaming, it becomes ever more important to examine the discourse through which games are packaged and marketed, because these discourses must also reflect particular cultural models that allow us to be drawn to or repelled by games themselves. As Kress and van Leeuwen (2006) note, "Pictorial structures do not simply reproduce 'reality.' On the contrary, they reproduce images of reality which are bound up with the interests of the social institutions within which the pictures are produced, circulated and read. They are ideological" (p. 45).

It is precisely due to their ideological nature that we believe critical pedagogical interrogations of such cultural productions can help to create spaces of creative tension that would allow students to rupture dominant narratives positioned as "value-free" commodities in an increasingly consumption-oriented society. Citing Dill et al. (2005), Stephenson (2009) notes,

> ...a protectionist attitude toward children and gaming does little to unpack the issues of racial representations, power and violence reproduced in games. The general invisibility of characters of color is one issue to address in a medium in which more than two thirds of main characters are white. In addition, the widespread use of ethnic stereotypes and overrepresentation of non-white characters as villains for the hero to destroy are important, but largely overlooked in videogame culture. (p. 593)

In fusing "traditional" curriculum to and through the experiential base of students, critical educators, rather than alienating students with quotidinal pedagogies of "confiscation and control," are able to strategically utilize this living experience of gaming in the development of a presence of mind (Leistyna, 1999) that lends itself to the repositioning of self in society. In other words, the development of *conscientização* (Freire, 1974) is grounded principally in the living realities of students (whatever these may be) rather than in arbitrarily and externally created and imposed curricula that often segment the "academic" from the "real" in an effort to sever theory from practice, and, vice versa, in the search of "objective truth" based on positivism, rigidly policed through test-centric policies. Giroux (1981) captures this mode of understanding historical processes when he notes that

> the severance of knowledge and research from value claims may appear to be admirable to some, but it hides more than it uncovers. Of course, this is not to suggest that challenging the value-neutrality claims of the culture of positivism is tantamount to supporting the use of bias, prejudice and superstition in scientific inquiry. Instead, what is espoused is that the very notion of objectivity is based on the use of normative criteria established by communities of scholars and intellectual workers in any given field. (p. 44)

Such a process further leads to a historical configuration in which knowledge becomes "not only countable and measurable, it also becomes impersonal," leading to a set of dynamics in which

> rather than comprehending the world holistically as a network of interconnections, the American people are taught to approach problems as if they existed in isolation, detached from the social and political forces that give them meaning. The central failing of this mode of thinking is that it creates a form of tunnel vision in which only a small segment of social reality is open to examination. More important, it leaves unquestioned those economic, political and social structures that shape our daily lives. Divorced from history, these structures appear to have acquired their present character naturally, rather than having been constructed by historically specific interests. (Giroux, 1981, p. 46)

James Lowen (1995) alludes to this inability of normative pedagogical practice to make links to a more critical orientation that utilizes the present in illuminating our construction of the past by noting that in the field of history and in the utilitarian construction of a sanitized and measurable past,

> none of the facts are remembered because they are presented as one damn thing after another. While textbook authors tend to include most of the trees and all too many twigs, they neglect to give readers even a glimpse of what they might find memorable: the forests. Textbooks stifle meaning by suppressing causation. Students exit history textbooks without having developed the ability to think coherently about social life. (p. 15)

Our efforts to engage gaming and the marketing of games as rival epistemological frameworks rests on a fundamental embrace of the "reality of youth" and the realization that pedagogical interventions are much more effective when they embrace rather than exclude knowledge that is grounded in one's living reality.

Methodological Framing

In our analysis we follow a particular line of inquiry that puts forth a set of propositions that structures our own framing of the content. First, we stress that language usage is always a carefully constructed political endeavor. Second, we propose that given the present fusion of imagery and text in the production of meaning in our society, analysis of semiotic landscapes must accompany more traditional "written text" analytical formats. Finally, we stress that the creative tension associated with such analytical approaches can assist teachers in deconstructing dominant social narratives and in the process developing more critically aware students.

The object of analysis in this particular case are the games *America's Army* and *America's Army: Special Forces*. We begin with some basic assumptions about the nature of language and language usage. As in the previous chapter, we assume that our use of language is always political; that is to say, in any particular interaction requiring verbal or written communication, we choose words carefully to reflect the nature of power dynamics at play (Gee, 2007). Consider, for example, that the discourse one uses in an academic committee meeting is not the same as one would use in a local singles bar on a Friday night. Clearly in these two very different environments, the social language that one uses is carefully chosen as to reflect "authenticity" in the immediate space. Language then is the primary instrument used in creating what Gee (2007) refers to as a "socially situated identity," a marker that proclaims to those around me that "Yes I do belong here (wherever that here may be)." Gee (1996) argues that making sense in the construction of socially situated identities through the creation of texts is "always social and political. Making sense is always an attempt to recruit "appropriate" hearers and readers; and hearers and readers, within their own social and political contexts, recruit speakers' and writers' meanings in diverse and value-laden ways" (p. 121).

Gee proposes a set of tools which, when taken in conjunction, can serve as a means of analyzing the construction of these socially situated identities. As he notes, in any one particular communicative exchange the construction of these identities need not necessarily make use of all of the tools; in other words, one need only instantiate sufficient characteristics in any one particular communicative act to substantiate or claim a particular identity. Beyond these tools of analysis appropriated here from linguist James Gee, we also make a distinction between what we refer to here as FTFs (Fixed Text Formats) and VTFs (Virtual Text Formats). FTFs are texts that are created so as to position us as passive consumers (even if we are expected to identify with particular points of view); with VTFs the consumer is asked to interact with and within the text in an active model that creates an exigency for choice of action. A movie, for example, may constitute an FTF because one's interaction with it remains at the level of watching it and at most, identification with the general themes presented. On the other hand, VTFs require continuous adjustments and shifts in action that ultimately affect the outcome of the social engagement. Consider for example fantasy football and its effects on the NFL and the profit margins of teams. In this case, the choices that individual consumers make based on their positionalities determine the overall viability of players, not just in the domain of "fantasy," but also on the actual field, as team profits become central to the overall scheme of things.

In addition to these tools of analysis, given that in the case of video games we are naturally dealing with a textual production that relies on a blend of images and written text, we will also be considering some aspects of Kress and van Leeuwen's (2006) *Reading Images: The Grammar of Visual Design*. For Kress and van Leeuwen, images similarly structure language in ways that position individuals in particular identities: "We take the view that language and visual communication both realize the same more fundamental and far-reaching systems of meaning that constitutes our cultures, but that each does so by means of its own specific forms, and independently" (2006, p. 17). Even as they note the capacity of images in emphasizing particular aspects of communication, they also observe two factors that underscore the importance of the deconstruction of the visual. First they note that

> the different modes of representation are not held discretely, separately, as autonomous domains in the brain, or as autonomous communication resources in culture, nor are they deployed discretely, either in representation or in communication, rather they intermesh and interact at all times. (p. 39)

Second, and ultimately worrisome from a pedagogical standpoint, they observe that

> newspapers, magazines, public relations materials, advertisements and many kinds of books today involve a complex interplay of written text, images and other graphic elements, and what is more, these elements combine together into visual designs by means, by means of layout. The skill of producing texts of this kind, however important their role in contemporary society, is not taught in schools. In terms of this new visual literacy, education produces illiterates. (p. 15)

The interpersonal function of images which often are intermeshed with text (and in other contexts, audio) create a relation between the viewer and the actor, the image as well as the intended representation of said object. What is interesting is that often this "intermesh" is layered (Kress & Van Leeuwen, 2006). Filmmakers often utilize this principle in positioning movie watchers so as to identify with particular causes through imagery. In doing so, the identity of the viewer becomes molded to the intent of the producer/director. This process is not unidirectional (Boggs & Pollard, 2009), nor is it a single text format (relying on more than just images); often there may be a contradiction between the producer's intent in creating a particular socially situated identity in the viewer through the imagery presented, and the viewer's own background knowledge of a specific theme, and therefore his or her processing of the text. In such instances, a viewer may utilize his or her knowledge to interrogate the textual production, or he or she may simply dismiss the production as banal or without merit of consideration. In either case, even in the dismissal, the viewer is positioned so as to assume the identity of critic, and so rely on his/her socially situated identity of "expert" in that particular domain. Stephenson (2009) points to this multi-meaning possibility when she reflects on the mediated capacity of the audience's interpretation:

> Negotiated and oppositional readings are possible with any text. However, within games, the element of interactivity opens up additional spaces for these alternative readings . . . because other media, such as books, films or television programs give much more limited opportunities (if any) for such types of interactivity, research has posited that the immersion (or "presence") felt by players as well as identification with characters (or avatars) is a unique characteristic of new media like games and virtual worlds. (p. 594)

Images then, like words or sound, can be specifically molded in particular ways so as to create contexts and actors within those contexts; again, the advertising industry understands this principle extremely well.

Examples of this principle of molding or overlaying images and sound can be found in old western movies. In most old westerns, the Native American is ordinarily characterized as "savage" and treacherous; rather than rely on just the dialogue and imagery to convey this message, movie makers often used music to create a feeling of danger in scenes portraying Native Americans. This principle fits particularly well in contexts where English is not the native language, because viewers are more likely to use contextual information to infer meaning. Along the same lines, consider the recent television commercials for performance-enhancing drugs. The manufacturers of drugs such as Viagra® and Cialis® routinely use imagery traditionally associated with masculinity (motorcycles, camping, fishing, NASCAR) to promote the sales of their products. While it may seem almost banal to point out such overlays of image and sound, the commercials themselves can only work to the extent that they can effectively capture within their frames or sound bites the concept of masculinity.

Given that the packaging of the army games contains both written and visual text that interplay in creating a coherent whole, the question then becomes, how does the layout contribute to the development of the narrative such that the subjectivity of the reader is positioned to maximally identify with the textual metafunction? As Kress and van Leeuwen (2006) observe, "Any semiotic system has to have the capacity to form texts, complexes of signs which cohere both internally and with the context in and for which they are produced" (p. 41).

In looking at the packaging of the two versions of the army game, one finds a textual production that not only structures the socially situated identity of potential players, but also simultaneously allows for a permeation of social discourses that are ideologically laden with the increasingly multifaceted role of the military as an instrument of foreign policy. In many ways, of course, to refer to the military's role as "increasingly multifaceted" is a misrepresentation of history in that it suggests that somehow the military as an institution was in the past historically less invasive. Lest one forget instances of military suppression and repression and selectively embrace the events of Normandy, Iwo Jima, and the liberation of Italy (in the process dismissing the highest virtue of democracy: the ability to question), a critical interrogation of the utilitarianism of the military as an instrument of policy must also examine secret guerilla wars going back at least as far as the Russian revolution, the invasion of Mexico, the bombing of Laos, My Lai, Haiti, Nicaragua, Abu Ghraib, Grenada, the invasion of Panama, Guantánamo, links to internal (e.g., Blackwater, Xe) and external paramilitary organizations, the development of weapons systems designed for crowd control (internally and externally), the use of the U.S. Coast Guard for border control, and numerous other "interventions" (Zinn, 2005; Chomsky, 1989, 2005; Boggs & Pollard, 2009).

The visceral reactions to any attempts to entertain some of these histories, ironically even in normative capitalist consumption, point to the

ideological nature of such commodity production, as well as the perceived danger in having a population at large capable of interrogating
social policies aimed at repression and control. The creation of the game
Rendition Guantánamo, for example, a game in which a wrongfully
convicted terrorist attempts to flee the prison, was met with such resistance that it was ultimately pulled off the shelves.

In reality, however, the reference to the military's increasingly "multifaceted" role in foreign policy suggests more a shift in the parameters
of discourse than changes in the integral operations of the military. In
other words, it isn't that somehow the military is actually engaging in
"newer" activities, but rather that we, as a matter of discourse, engage
these activities differently. Only such a shift in discourse, or our accep-
tance of such discourse, could move respected theologian Pat Robertson
to publicly claim that we should "take out" Venezuelan president Hugo
Chavez because we perceive him as a political threat ("taking out"
implies the use of specific branches of the military to assassinate a world
leader). Such a shift in discourse is not the purview of communicative
acts by individuals who upon pronouncing their hatred face such a
backlash that they are forced to reconcile their public position with
more carefully constructed language; instead, it is a national phenomenon that allows us to detach ourselves from destructive acts through the
use of language and its capacity to shield or cloak what otherwise would
be unthinkable. Take as an example the use of terms such as *collateral
damage, insurgency, smart bombs, targeting, theater of operations,* and *sectarian violence.*

As a military term, collateral damage was first used in the national
media in 1968 during the height of the Vietnam War. As Zinn (2005) has
noted, the eventual end of the Vietnam War was structured more by the
impending possibility of social revolution by a youth population slowly awakened to the horrors of war, rather than by an enlightened political establishment conscious of the social destruction caused by one of
the greatest military assaults in the history of mankind. Only such language could reconcile the sustained physical destruction of a land and
the deaths of some 4 to 5 million people (depending on the source used).
In 2000, BBC News observed that as many as 38,000 people had been

killed and 64,000 injured in Vietnam since the end of the war in 1975 thorough accidental detonation of unexploded ordinances. The BBC went on to report that in total, there were still an estimated 300,000 tons of similar ordinances still left to be cleared.[4] In present-day Angola, similar conditions exist in part due to the expansion of our military-industrial complex in earlier decades. While statistics themselves erase the magnitude and devastation of war by shielding readers and viewers from the real carnage of war through an engagement with numbers (as opposed to faces), we have to assume that as the numbers climb, the continuing deaths will be categorized as "collateral damage" rather than described as the mutilation of children as a result of misguided foreign policy. The use of the term in social discourse in more recent wars continues the trend of semiotic violence through this use of language as a sliding signifier in ways that mask the very real nature of war. No doubt Madeleine K. Albright's assertion in 1996 that the deaths of the 500,000 children in the first Iraq war as "worth it" must be taken in this frame where we systemically disconnect the brutality of war from the language that we use to describe the event itself.

Reading Visual Landscapes

The packaging of the prototype army game (*America's Army*) is inferior with respect to the complexity of narrative that it develops in comparison to the latter version of the same game (*America's Army: Special Forces*). In the original, the image is nontransactive. It makes an offer but certainly no demand. The omission of a central actor on the front cover signals that the attempt to create specific socially situated identities is virtually nonexistent other than that of generic "player." Both the image and the text associated with this version of the game are restrictive in appealing to multiple identities. While the viewer/reader is offered a symbolic identification with the U.S. Army through the text, the cultural model of the role of the military is abstracted from the image, thereby leaving the viewer/reader to construct an accompanying narrative based on an individualized reception and framing of an idealized model.

The lead image on the cover is symbolically and primarily depicted in red, white, and blue. In this version of the game, the generic soldier is subordinated to the overall narrative constructed by the cover. "America's Army" is prominently displayed at three different sight levels; the upper portion of the cover institutes the authority/authenticity with the claim "The Official U.S. Army Game." A symbolic patch with the standard AA logo bisected by a white star on a red and blue background seems to project out of the page. A carefully crafted white border around the patch creates a vector between the upper claim of authenticity and the bottom visual. In reality, this "intermesh" between text and visual reinforces the two. The visual of generic soldiers on the bottom are secondary in the sense that the manufacturers of the game don't seek to create a specific affinity between the viewer/reader and the image, because the soldiers are "generic" and the image is set as a long shot. Under the image of the soldiers, the standard narrative (traditionally infused with foreign policy exploits) proclaims "Empower Yourself Defend Freedom." To the right of this graphic the U.S Army star is supported by text reading "U.S. Army." This visual, while constructing an overall narrative, does not in itself create appeals to specific socially situated identities, even though it does lend itself to a particular generic cultural model of the U.S. armed forces.

In the later version of the game, *America's Army: Special Forces*, the image on the game jacket is centered and transactive. The reader is invited to a close look at the elite Special Forces unit member. The image is captured as a close-up. In any other context the distancing of the image and its very transactive nature would require the viewer to be able to see the actor's eyes, as they would ensure the establishment of affinity with the viewer. Kress and van Leeuwen (2006) note the importance of actors in the spatial integration when they observe

> in pictures they are often also the most salient participants (Actors), through size, place in the composition, contrast against the background, colour saturation or conspicuousness, sharpness of focus, and through psychological salience which certain participants (e.g. human figure, and even more so, the human face) have for viewers. (p. 61)

In this case, however, the image goal is not the establishment of affinity, but rather the structuring of a sense of awe at the power of the operative. The use of a dual-scope on the center image has the effect of not only distancing the possibility of the personable but also creating the image of a high-tech soldier with a very specialized skill set. In this particular semiotic landscape, the overall narrative foregrounds some information and in the process dialectically backgrounds secondary actors. The centered image or lead actor is given both rank and purpose linguistically through the designation of "Special Forces" and the caption "Empower Yourself Defend Freedom." The placement of the Special Forces patch creates a natural vector between the realization of the top idealized image and the lower half's highlighting of purpose. The purpose in this case is the insertion of the reader in a sociopolitical discourse that has been commonplace in U.S. politics since the very foundation of the country and shows no signs of abating in the 21st century: Empowering the self through the defense of freedom. The term *empowering* in this case is particularly interesting because in terms of a demand it obviously only works for those who feel less than empowered. As a 2007 NPR report[5] on the state of recruitment observed,

> The Army has been offering recruits bonuses of up to $20,000. It also brought in more recruits without high school diplomas, who scored low on aptitude tests, and who had to get waivers for criminal offenses. Many defense analysts say this policy is lowering the military's standards, but the Army rejects that claim.

Beyond these givens of rank and purpose, there are other aspects that are projected through this section of the game's cover. First, in smaller print the image reminds the viewer/reader that the experience of playing the game will be "complete," yet the completion of the game is also linked to a major function of the entire project, which is to project authenticity. To the right of the inscription ("Includes the complete game *America's Army: Special Forces*") the viewer is faced with a graphic of the symbolic army star highlighted by "U.S. Army." The authenticity aspect in creating the socially situated identity of the viewer is reinforced and is such a central aspect of the image that it is also captured in the top half of the image as if to highlight it. The idealized image of the operative is slightly cut by a vector that proclaims "The Official Army Game" followed by "America's Army." Again, it is the authenticity that is projected which gives the image credibility.

The secondary actors still serve the process of creating the overall narration, yet they are subordinated by the center as well as the linguistic output. Behind the idealized image of the special operative several images are strategically placed in the background. The location of the images both fill the open landscape created by the centrality of the lead actor, but also create a counter-narrative that enhances the connection with the viewer in creating other identities that can complement the overall narrative. In the top left quadrant (to the left of the central image) we see a faded search and rescue operation with a soldier jumping out of a helicopter into a raging sea to succor an individual. To the right of the image we see a plane fading into the background with paratroopers already in the air. In the bottom left quadrant of the image we see yet another version of rescue: what appear to be two medics standing in front of a landed helicopter with the Red Cross emblem prominently displayed.

The totality of these images on the front cover suggests the centrality of the lead actor, the operative of the Special Forces, yet it also captures the multiplicity of identities and likes that can be processed as "belonging" in the game. While one image (the central) suggests the killing of those who would threaten freedom, the secondary images focus either on a more pacific narrative of providing aid to the injured or an infiltration of sorts of enemy territory. In either case, the viewer's socially situated identity can be channeled to identify with whatever image is commensurate with one's idealized vision of the role of the military.

The images and language on the inside cover again serve to consolidate the central message to the viewer/player: authenticity and player immersion. Because the inside cover doubles the layout size once opened, the spatial integration of the central image is proportionately greater. "De Oppresso Liber" narrates the image and is dominantly placed over the actors. Again, the image restates the original demand of the defense of freedom. Linguistic intertextuality is fused into the ideological narrative because one viewer/reader is asked to mold this particular image to the common historical and sociopolitical discourse of the liberation of the oppressed. Further authentication (though hardly need-ed at this point) is consolidated with the offer "Designed, Created and Developed by the U.S. Army." This offer is strategically placed at eye level because the viewer is positioned to watch the four operatives from a low angle. The central actor is lying down in front of a helicopter with a machine gun pointing to the viewer's left. There is in this case an attempt to create an affinity with this actor, because the viewer can clearly see his eyes and subsequently his intentionality. The three other operatives in the image are clearly already in the "action," with one crouching behind the helicopter firing to the viewer's left. The smoke ris-ing from the background validates the immediacy and realism of the image.

In front of the helicopter an image of a crouching soldier (with a beard) is positioned pointing a rocket launcher in the same direction. The level of affinity attempted with the viewer here is different, because the image is taken as a long shot and no effort is made at capturing the sol-dier's gaze. While this actor is embedded in the "action," the disso-nance between the bearded soldier and the U.S. military is resolved with the caption on the lower right "Fight Alongside Indigeneous Forces." To the viewer's immediate right (still in the central image) is a different operative who is standing and firing to the viewer's right side. Again, the image is structured so as to place the viewer's reader in the middle of the action, both with the image angle and the various battle positions.

Because the image is positioned as a horizontal layout, the system requirements statement is positioned to the right of the central image. In other words, in terms of relaying the narrative itself, the written text becomes secondary. Nevertheless, even this message is superimposed on the image of a flying helicopter attempting to lower a rescue operative who helps in establishing the lower right quadrant in being placed between the narrating texts. On the lower right quadrant two images are positioned side by side with clearly dissecting lines forming vectors between the two. Kress and van Leeuwen (2006) note that "Vectors can demonstrate transactional relations what in language is realized by words of the category 'action verbs' is in pictures realized by elements that can be formally defined as 'vectors'" (p. 44). Above these images and positioned on either side of the lowering rescue operative the viewer is again given options. To the left of the soldier the text reads "Combat Medics Train to Save Lives and to Assess Casualties" and to the right, "New Combat Systems More Weapons and the Hardware to Modify Them." The lower left image is positioned as a long shot of an ongoing battle, and because the soldiers are crouching down and the image is at eye-level, the viewer/reader is positioned to do the same. Under this particular image the text reads "Enhanced Realism Fight Alongside Indigeneous Forces." To the right of this image, a close-up shot of a soldier waiting in an ambush position is displayed. The clarity of his facial features invites identification and suggests realism. Under this image the text reads "Greater Game Immersion Real-Time Soldier Shadows and Higher Resolution Graphics." In this layout, authenticity and versatility in the creation of socially situated identities are key. The dialogue and invitation to the viewer is continuous, even as the final text reads "Complete various missions and qualify for special training."

The back page is just as complex, yet it again reinforces the central themes of the previous two pages. Clearly delineating vectors proclaim in the uppermost section of the page "The Official U.S. Army Game," followed by a lower reading of "America's Army." This text is followed by the image of two Special Forces operatives with communication gear. The images are in close-up and complemented by the narration of text reading "Experience Authentic Training and Operate as a Member of the World's Most Elite Fighting Force, the U.S. Army Special Forces. *America's Army* Immerses You in the Exciting World of the Famous Green Berets." Under the text and similar to the front page, the image is followed by the Special Forces patch which becomes a demarcating structure from the lower three graphics.

The three lower images coalesce around the theme of realism and specialized action. In the lower left, four operatives are pictured looking in different directions (except directly at the viewer), pointing their weapons as if preparing for or in the process of firing. The image is labeled "Multiplayer Missions." As in most video games, the label captures the sense of community orientation in the development of collective sensibilities. The actor closest to the viewer/reader is wearing a beard and dressed in a leather jacket, certainly not conventional U.S. Army attire. While a central aspect of the game is to convey authenticity of the U.S. military (the Army in particular), the viewer/reader is being invited to participate in a military action that may indeed involve people from other regions of the world who share a similar goal as the central actors of the game, the U.S. Army. The roles of counter-insurgents/Indigenous forces and targeting specialists/advisors are particularly interesting in that as a society we seem to be more and more willing to engage in discourses that allow the possibility of such actions as a means of accomplishing political objectives.

Countering Dominant Narratives

The maintenance of institutions such as the School of the Americas at Fort Benning, Georgia, from 1946 to its closing in 2001 indicates that as a matter of policy, the reliance on U.S.-trained operatives in destabilizing political regimes across the world has always been a strategic maneuver aimed at ensuring the promulgation of U.S. economic, political, and military interests. One need only point to the destabilization of the Allende government in the 1970s, the many attempted assassinations of Fidel Castro, the destabilization of Nicaragua's electoral processes, and the interventions in Guatemala, El Salvador, Honduras, and so on (Zepezauer, 2002; Chomsky, 1989; Falla, 1994). It was U.S. support of brutal regimes such as those of General Lucas Garcia (1978–1982) and General Efrain Rios Montt (1982–1983) through military training or financial support in Guatemala that led the anthropologist Ricardo Falla to observe that "in 1982 and 1983, blood flowed like water"(1994, p. 8). In the years prior to the early 1980s, particularly following the 1979 Sandinista revolution in Nicaragua, the Guatemalan army began a policy of repression in the country that escalated to the scorched earth policy of 1982. Falla observes

> the period ended with terrible massacres that were like open wounds in the living map of Guatemala, particularly in the indigenous areas of the country.

There were 440 villages destroyed, according to the army, and the dead (primarily civilians) numbered between 10,000 and 20,000 by conservative estimate;
more reliable statistics are between 50,000 and 75,000. (1994, p. 8)

To many Central American historians, the atrocities of the 1980s can be
traced to the CIA backing and financing of the military coup of the government of Jacobo Árbenz Guzmán (a freely elected leftist leader) for the
protection of the economic interests of the U.S., particularly the United
Fruit Company. George Vickers of the Washington Office on Latin
America captured the relationship of the U.S. and Guatemala in a PBS
interview with Charles Krause when he said that "During the 1950s, the
1960s, and the 1970s, the United States was an important supporter of
the Guatemalan army. It trained it. It provided political support, logis-
tical support, material support, and politically supported its fight against
the Communist guerrillas."[6]

The financial backing, military training, and use of U.S. military
personnel in "advising" these regimes cannot be abstracted from the violent repression of peoples across the world, nor can it be reconciled
with our claims to support freedom and democracy. The successor to the
School of the Americas, the Western Hemisphere Institute for Security
Cooperation (WHINSEC), also in Fort Benning, continues the tradition
of the training of military personnel from a myriad of countries in the
western hemisphere.

On a wider scale, the training of the mujahadeen in Afghanistan to
counter Soviet influence, the installation of Hamid Karzai as president
of Afghanistan in 2002, the support of Saddam Hussein during the Iran-
Iraq war in the 1980s, and many other similar questionable uses of the
knowledge and expertise of the U.S. government (Blum, 2000; Grey,
2006) indicate that the discourse of the defense of freedom is not always
in line with the actions of the U.S. government and its military. The
first official visit by a foreign dignitary to the George H.W. Bush White
House was Mobutu Sese Seko, a notorious human rights violator considered by many to be one of the most repressive political leaders in
recent African history. Although President Bush called Mobutu "one of
our most valued allies," the *American Historical Review* reported in 2001
that at the time of his death in 1997, Mobutu had amassed as much as

$5 billion in Swiss bank accounts, and "also spent millions on mansions on the French Riviera, threw lavish receptions for heads of state and foreign dignitaries, and purchased countless other luxuries, including 14,000 bottles of 1930 vintage wine (the year of his birth)."[7] "Involvements" with such leaders and regimes often require the use of military or government "advisors" who inevitably must form alliances with "factions/indigenous forces" that are more amenable to U.S. interests, even if in the process, the human rights of native populations are systematically violated.

Returning to our analysis of the image on the *America's Army: Special Forces* packaging, to the immediate right of the graphic of this indigenous ally, another image of a solitary soldier pointing an automatic weapon is labeled "State of the Art Graphics." The weapon in this case forms a natural vector with the Special Forces patch. The instrumentality of it is in redirecting the vision of the viewer/reader back to the nature of the elite squadron one would be joining. Finally, to the lower right, two operatives utilize a specialized vehicle for cover while another is seen in the distance firing at an enemy position. This particular image is labeled "Authentic Weapons and Vehicles."

A key feature that permeates both the inside jacket and the back flap of the packaging is the architectural background. The dirt ground and the building have a clear "Middle Eastern aesthetic." The viewer certainly could not mistake this scenery as South American or European. In fact, the very military uniform which the Special Forces operative utilizes is designated by the U.S. Army as desert terrain gear.

The prototype Army game as a textual production is both technologically and graphically inferior to the later version. As one examines both covers, several similarities and differences become clear. The games' jacket covers are dimensionally equal and standard in size. Both covers are targeted to specific populations, and both suggest authenticity, albeit in different ways. The authenticity claimed by both games, while very "real," serves to work out a dissonance of sorts in the potential players that ultimately becomes the lynchpin to its effectiveness; that is to say, while the objective is to make the games as real as possible, the same authenticity functions to disarticulate true killing in war from the socially constructed video killing which, though graphic in some cases, always allows the player the freedom to press the reset button and begin anew. As Gee notes, the success of the video industry in developing these pedagogical tools rests in part on the capacity to allow the players to assume a certain degree of risk while they master play without "permanent damage."

Authenticity as captured in this packaging is ultimately central to the construction of the socially situated identity and becomes progressively more pronounced in the later version of the game. While the packaging of the first game is targeted to a more generic consumer in that the intended player's role is more limited, in the later version a wide array of possibilities present themselves, and the targeting of the player becomes more concentrated with respect to roles yet more broad in terms of reach. While in the first game only a narrow range of identities may be assumed by the player, the latter version allows the player the versatility of opting to be a specialist in clandestine operations (targeting/assassinations), a demolitions expert, a communications officer, a counter-insurgency expert, or a lifeline medical expert (noncombatant) as well as team member. This versatility of roles allows the game to target players with different sensibilities with respect to the military, hence becoming what Kress and van Leeuwen (2006) refer to as a "transactive image." It invites an interaction of affinity between it and the viewer. Even if one somehow wanted to argue against using the game as a diversion by arguing against killing per se, one could still be a medical officer and save the lives of "unit members."

The social and pedagogical implications of disarticulating these commodity productions from the social context in which we live downplays the extent to which there is an fusion between one's claiming of identities in the games and the sociohistoric trajectories that structure particular discourses as normative. In the case of the *America's Army* games, the commodity itself is produced by a military institution, and while it may seem contradictory that a military institution would be producing games, there is clearly a link between the production of the game and the furthering of the goals of the institution. No sensible human being on the planet would believe that the U.S. Army is now in the business of producing children's games for the sake of producing the games. In fact, the games have become a means of recruitment like any other.[8]

The realism of games provides a voyeuristic space in which uninterrogated consumption can serve to articulate or disarticulate contextual realities that are inevitably structured in the social relations of both players and the represented. It is this realism that forced the market withdrawal of the game *Six Days in Fallujah*, developed by Atomic Games of Raleigh, North Carolina, for Japanese publisher Konami with the consultation of army personnel. While being interviewed for ABC News, Jeremy Zoss, the communications manager for Atomic Games' sister company, noted that

> the game's premise is a historically accurate re-creation of the battle to re-take Fallujah in the current Iraq war...there are few other mediums than video games that you could get the kind of experience that you could get in this game. ...Games can do things that movies can't. They can put you there as part of it. There are many ways to put you in the role of a soldier...you do it in the wrong way and it can give the wrong message.[9]

"The message" is central to our concern here because it is the lynchpin that not only paves the way for a captive audience but also disarticulates the relational dynamics between the viewer/reader, the actors, and the represented. We are conscious of the dangers of naturally linking video games to violent acts. We make no such claim here, but we propose that these games (and their packaging and marketing) can serve as pedagogical tools that can help critical teachers to interrogate the social relations that allow for particular discourses to become so normative as to be captured in an "entertainment" mode, and in the process to develop more critically aware and socially active students capable of interrogating relations of domination in the very formation of normativity.

Visual landscapes are increasingly being fused to the world of written text and multiple realities, and the ultimate maintenance of democratic structures requires that students be able to deconstruct and reshape their own positionalities in relation to those around them. As we laugh at the late master Richard Pryor's critical interrogation of the use of "advisors" in the Latin American context, we must come to grips with the reality that such contestations must today be multimodal and make use of spaces that are created to sustain hegemonic practices, thereby curtailing democratic sensibilities. As Stephenson (2009) points out,

> acknowledging that videogame representations are complex, ideological, and frequently problematic is a necessary first step in using video games as a site for teaching and practicing critical media literacy....Teachers trained not only in the operation of the game, but also the language of media literacy can facilitate analysis and discussion of representatiton and scaffold students' understanding and readings of game representations. (p. 599)

Democracy requires both the active participation of students in their own education and the fortitude to challenge the dominant discourses that permeate every social stratum through an anaesthetizing of the senses to human suffering. The slumber of the population is not innocent by any means, nor is it rootless; it is the calculated molding of students to become passive bystanders/consumers in a world that is constantly being repositioned to serve the interests of the dominant class. Only critically aware students capable of engaging the multitude of currently available semiotic landscapes can reconcile the call for the "defense of freedom" with the buying of elections, the hiring of drug lords, the invasions of peaceful countries, the assassinations of heads of states, the maintenance of secret prisons, the courting of ruthless dictators, and the presentation of yellow ribbons as modes of displacement to mystify and conceal the strategic class interests that perpetuate and embolden the highly militarized society in which we now live, under the banner of patriotism. As Arundhati Roy (2003) eloquently notes, "flags are bits of colored cloth that governments use first to shrink-wrap people's minds and then as ceremonial shrouds to bury the dead"(p. 47), and until we can deconstruct the various modalities (linguistic and otherwise) under which this process occurs, we will remain susceptible to a politics of mystification and fragmentation that continues to wreak havoc with our democratic sensibilities and collective interests.

Notes

1. http://www.theesa.com/newsroom/release_archives_detail.asp?releaseID=8
2. Ibid.

3. http://www.theesea.com/newsroom/esa_newsletter/february2008/index.html
4. http://cdnedge.bbc.co.uk/1/hi/world/asia-pacific/1024627.stm
5. http://www.npr.org/templates/story/story.php?storyId=17551758
6. http://www.pbs.org/newshour/bb/latin_america/december96/guatemala_12
30.html
7. http://www.historycooperative.org/cgi-bin/justtop.cgi?act=justtop&url=http://
www.historycooperative.org/journals/ahr/106.3/mr_3.html
8. http://www.npr.org/templates/story/story.php?storyId=124216122
9. http://abcnews.go.com/Technology/GameOn/story?id=7750809&page=1

References

Bennett- Jones, O. (2000). BBC News. (2000). Vietnam war's new victims. Retrieved
October 25, 2010 from: http://cdnedge.bbc.co.uk/1/hi/world/asia-pacif-
ic/1024627.stm

Blum, W. (2000). *Rogue state: A guide to the world's only superpower*. Monroe, ME: Common
Courage Press.

Boggs, C., & Pollard, T. (2009). American militarism, Hollywood and media culture. In
R. Hammer & D. Kellner (Eds.), *Media/cultural studies: Critical approaches* (pp.
457–481). New York: Peter Lang.

Chomsky, N. (1989). *Necessary illusions: Thought control in democratic societies*. Boston:
South End Press.

Chomsky, N. (2005). *Imperial ambitions: Conversations on the post-9/11 world*. New York:
Metropolitan Books.

Dill, K. E., Gentile, D. A., Richter, W. A., and Dill, J. C. (2005). Violence, sex, race and age
in popular video games: A content analysis. In E. Cole & J. Henderson Daniel
(Eds.), Featuring females: Feminist analyses of the media. Washington, DC:
American Psychological Associationr

ESA. (2010). Computer and video game industry reaches $18.85 billion in 2007.
Retrieved October 25, 2010 from: http://www.theesa.com/newsroom/release
_archives_detail.asp?releaseID=8

ESA. (2010). ESA announces video game industry's record sales-$18.85 billion in 2007.
Retrieved October 25, 2010 from: http://www.theesa.com/newsroom/esanewslet-
ter/february2008/index.html

Falla, R. (1994). *Massacres in the jungle: Ixcan, Guatemala, 1975–1982*. Boulder, CO:
Westview.

Freire, P., & Macedo, D. (2000). Pedagogy of the oppressed. New York: Continuum.

Gee, J. P. (1996). *Social linguistics and literacies: Ideology in discourses*. London:
Routledge/Falmer.

Gee, J. P. (2003). *An introduction to discourse analysis: Theory and method*. London: Routledge.

Gee, J. P. (2007). *What video games have to teach us about learning and literacy*. New York: Palgrave.

Giroux, H. (1981). *Ideology, culture and the process of schooling*. Philadelphia: Temple University Press.

Giroux, H. (2006). Are Disney movies good for your kids? In K. Abowitz & R. Karaba (Eds.), *Readings in sociocultural studies in education* (pp. 21–27). New York: McGraw-Hill.

Grey, S. (2006). *Ghost plane: The true story of the CIA torture program*. New York: St. Martin's.

Gump, J. O. (2001). Mobutu: King of Zaire. The American Historical Review, Vol. 106, No. 3. 1108 Retrieved October 28, 2010 from: http://www.historycooperative.org/cgi-bin/justtop.cgi?act=justtop&url=http://www.historycooperative.org/journals/ahr/106.3/mr_3.html

Hammer, R., & Kellner, D. (2009). *Media/cultural Studies: Critical approaches*. New York: Peter Lang.

Heussner, K. M. (2009, June 4). 9 Video games that went too far. Retrieved October 28, 2010 from: http://abcnews.go.com/Technology/GameOn/story?id=7750809&page=1

Kress, G., & van Leeuwen, T. (2006). *Reading images: The grammar of visual design* (2nd ed). London: Routledge.

Leistyna, P. (1999). *Presence of mind: Education and the politics of deception*. Boulder, CO: Westview.

Loewen, J. (1995). *Lies my teacher told me*. New York: Touchstone.

Macedo, D., & Steinberg, S. (2007). *Media literacy: A reader*. New York: Peter Lang.

NPR. (2007, March 2). 'America's Army' Blurs Virtual War, 'Militainment.' Retrieved October 28, 2010 from:

http://www.npr.org/templates/story/story.php?storyId=124216122

PBS. (1996). Guatemala's future. Retrieved October 26, 2010 from: http://www.pbs.org/newshour/bb/latin_america/december96/guatemala_12–30.html

Rosa, R. (2009). What type of revolution are we rehearsing for? Boal's theater of the oppressed. In M. Apple, W. Au, & L. Gandin (Eds.), *The Routledge international handbook of critical education* (pp. 240–253). New York: Routledge.

Rosa, J. (2010). Discursos linguisticos e realidades nas salas de aulas: Vencendo a luta pelo controle. Praia, Cape Verde: University of Cape Verde Press.

Roy, A. (2003). *War talk*. Boston: South End Press.

Schaffer, D. (2006). How computer games help children learn. New York: Palgrave.

Seabrook, A., & Bowman, T. (2007). Army faces tougher recruitment in 2008. Retrieved October 25, 2010 from: http://www.npr.org/templates/story/story.php?storyId=17551758

Sethi, M. (2008). *Game programming for teens* (3rd ed.). Boston: Course Technology.

Stephenson, R. (2009). "Doing something that matters": Children's culture video games, and the politics of representation. In R. Hammer & D. Kellner (Eds.), *Media/cultural studies: Critical approaches* (pp. 587–600). New York: Peter Lang.

Zepezauer, M. (2002). *The CIA's greatest hits: The real story series.* Boston: Odonian.

Zinn, H. (2005). *A people's history of the United States: 1492 to present.* New York: HarperCollins.

Chapter Three

"I Ain't Scared of You Motherfuckas"

Stand-up Comedy as a Space of Linguistic and Political Resistance

If I've done anything to upset you, maybe it's what I'm here for...I kept pushing my material further, more topical, more racial, more digging into a system I was beginning to understand better and attack more intelligently. (in Kercher, 2006)

DICK GREGORY

See [when] racism sets in, I love it [cause] I fight against that. Cause, humor breaks through all that shit. [laughter]. Doesn't it. (Pryor, 2000)

RICHARD PRYOR

Growing up, I was drawn to humorists and comedians. If we are going to raise people's awareness of issues like our rights as women or people of color or workers in a culture that is often hostile to the protection of those rights, we must reach people in a space in which they are open to ideas that may not seem to be in their interests at first. And that's gonna take everything we can throw at them: vice presidential documentaries, rock stars in favor of debt cancellation, and jokes. Lots and lots of jokes. I find wherever there's an open, laughing mouth, the open heart can't be too far behind. (Olson, 2007)

SARAH JONES

"Mainstream" media and mass communication commodifies and trivializes all aspects of human relationships. In this age, it becomes difficult to point to elements of transgression and rather simple to dispense with the entire media mechanism and claim it as a commitment to disarticulate human agency and an effort to (re)engineer sleepwalkers. When television programming captures our vulnerabilities of pain, fear, suffering, and struggles to survive and recontextualizes them into zones of entertainment in the form of "survival" programming, it easily moves us into passive indifference toward those who bear the most social cost and simultaneously revictimizes victims by seeing their oppression as failure to compete. Such programming would certainly look different if instead of playing with survival on the edge of some remote Pacific island, the contestants/actors were placed in East St. Louis, New Orleans, Gary, Indiana, the favelas of Rio, or the slums of Port-Au-Prince, bearing the weight of long-term discrimination and neglect. Despite the media's debasement of humanity and distraction from more pressing matters, we know that power operates in more complex ways and reception can be critical. Polyvalent practices of contestation exist even in the most regressive of spaces. It's insufficient to merely recognize them; we must chronicle their full complexity and their amorphous and temporal qualities, because domination knows no last acts or last word. We must also theorize ways in which resistance(s) may be expanded and subversive agendas may flow through efforts at co-option and still maintain a critical internal coherence and contribute to progressive political struggle.

In this chapter, we take up stand-up comedy generally and African American stand-up comedy (AASC) specifically. Why African American stand-up comedy? We consider this cultural genre because of its significance in shaping American comedy and humor in general. It remains a powerful political and aesthetic medium produced and articulated by a subordinated group that has proved capable in reaching wide audiences and also shaping the counter-comedy of other groups. Its subversive agenda is marked not only by the contours of content, but more importantly by the centralization of the politics of language—an underanalyzed aspect of its transgression. It remains both a penetrating subterranean medium that is able to capture private feelings and articulate them into public consciousness, and a seductive terrain consumed by groups outside of African American culture. Furthermore, it is linked to the dominance of the worldwide circulation of American popular culture, which gives it an added importance for analytical engagement. We also invoke the call made by Sarah Jones above and Martin Luther King Jr. in his provocative speech against the Vietnam War: "we must seek every creative method of protest possible" (King, 1967) We examine the social values transmitted and the possibilities embedded for the fracturing of dominant ideologies and ways in which it may instantiate deeper democratic structures and critical sensibilities.

The use of humor and satire as sites that make more transparent the structured suffering and the contradictions of power are well established across geographic and historical contexts as well as artistic forms of expression: Political cartoons, literature, plays, commentary, poetry, and song lyrics are obvious examples. From ancient Egypt's *Satire of the Trades* and the *Papyrus Anastasi I*, Aristophanes' comedic poetry (influential in shaping public opinion in Athenian democracy), medieval Europe's *Canterbury Tales,* and George Orwell's *Animal Farm*, to the political commentaries of Michael Moore and Stephen Colbert, the counter-marketing of Adbusters, the parodies of "traditional news" in *The Onion*, and contemporary routines of African American comics, the weapon of wit has been utilized to challenge authority. Like any other form of cultural resistance, it has its limitations and must constantly be pushed to make it do what we'd like it to. Malcolm X once sharply criticized the dominant media for seeking comments on social injustice from African American comics, yet, within his own oratory, he often utilized humor to make significant connections. In deconstructing the nationalist narrative and myth of "land of immigrants" by pointing out the fact that African Americans were "kidnapped," for example, he went on to say, "although some of you think you came here on the Mayflower [laughter/applause]" (X, Malcolm, 1963). Tracing these actuations in culture is important because it often forecasts the social indignation that allows for organized social and political action.

The roots of stand-up comedy in the U.S. date back to 19th-century popular entertainment such as vaudeville. Certainly, the practice may be further historicized. For the purposes of this chapter, however, we are referring to stand-up as a bounded practice that involves a self-identi-fied comic performing for a live audience, the recitation of humorous narratives and bits in the form of a monologue, and the delivery of per-formance in various settings (usually comedy clubs and theaters). We refer to critical stand-up comedy as comedy that utilizes satire and other techniques in the effort to expose social, political, and economic contra-dictions.

Stephen Kercher (2006), historicizing satire in the U.S., deeply traces the brilliant uses of critical satire through various mediums in the two decades following World War II. This period is highlighted because the perception is that it was a relatively calm time in U.S. history (Kercher, 2006). He notes that few historians considered humor in their historical theorizations, and points to a handful of critical historians such as Todd Gitlin and Jackson Lears who take it up. It was Lears (1994), notes Kercher, who stated in Fables of Abundance that "in the end, the most effective response to the [fifties] relentless crusade for comfort was scabrous humor, which exposed the foolish pretensions of established authority and buried its representatives beneath the weight of their own technology" (p. 7). This historical context was marked by extensive satirical interrogation of the cold war, anticommunism, McCarthyism, and race relations. Despite its often critical edge, Kercher (2006) notes that "liberal post-war satire was directed to a small and influential cohort of educated, middle-and upper middle class liberals" (p. 8) who sought change mainly through the ballot box. The role of stand-up com-edy within the anatomy of satire has been critical, given its propensity to reach diverse audiences.

Two comics are credited with setting the stage, in the early 1950s, for the voices of political dissent that would come later. Mort Sahl frequent-ly appeared on stage with newspaper in hand and satirized current events and the cultural conformity of the time. He was eventually black-listed for the production of satire that questioned normalized narra-tives of the assassination of John F. Kennedy (a friend for whom he sometimes wrote jokes for his speeches). Lenny Bruce was banned from several U.S. cities and convicted of obscenity in New York in 1964, a conviction for which he later received a posthumous pardon from New York governor George Pataki, who cited the commitment to uphold First Amendment rights. Bruce's comedy revolved around social criticism and his graphic encounters with police officers. These comics ruptured the parameters of acceptable political discourse through comedy, and were credited by a number of African American comics as having influenced their own material and ability to cross over into multiple cultural terrains. African American comics in the 1960s were largely in the margins, playing exclusively for black audiences. The exceptions were Timmie Rogers, Nipsey Russell, and Slappy White (Watkins, 1994), who had to learn to navigate the sensibilities of white audiences while keeping much of the racial references. They were, of course, subjected to censoring and other forms discriminatory disciplining. In the case of Russell, who abandoned African American English Vernacular and experimented with Standard English, it meant self-censoring the political comedic edge. These comedians, however, never reached national recognition. The contribution that the vehicle of stand-up has made to political resistance may also be registered by the efforts at repressing it, as the various examples above amply demonstrate.

The 1950s produced abundant critical satire and some stand-up. It foreshadowed what was to come on the shoulders of the countercultural movements of the 1960s. It was these movements, with their various strains, that ushered in particular discourses that made/make AASC unique and brought African American comedians (male, mostly) to public visibility. During this epoch politically profound African American stand-up comedy was born, or, to be more precise, made public. Its critical edge was limited by the opportunities that existed for transgression given the cultural and social context and the internal constraints of its own diverse voice (given the marginalization of women).

It was first "nurtured on the street and in burlesque theatres, coffeehouses, ethnic nightclubs, and an assortment of unsavory, obscure dives until they gradually surfaced and began to dominate mainstream humor in the sixties. As in the struggle for equal rights, however, there was formidable opposition to the rise of this irreverent, underground humor" (Watkins, 1994, p. 481). By the 1970s this edifice was further solidified by the rise of comedy clubs and the wider circulation of stand-up on television. In the 1980s several late-night talk shows and variety shows frequently televised stand-up, and more importantly, shows devoted to this medium surfaced: A&E's *An Evening at the Improv* and HBO's *Comedy Hour* and *Young Comedians Showcase* were just some examples. By the 1990s many African American comics had accessed dominant media mechanisms, and audience demand intensified. Although we make no claims about major disruptions in the institution's agenda-setting power, it must be stated that entry of these comedians further opened political activity.

The most profound contemporary moment in the development of African American stand-up was the production of Russell Simmons' *Def Comedy Jam,* which originally ran from 1992 to 1997, then returned to HBO's lineup in 2006. This production launched the careers of many African American stand-up comics and the critical strains of humor that shape so much of that comedy. Also significant were the launchings of *Uptown Comedy Club, Comic Justice,* and *Comic View.* The current scene is marked by the presence of these comics in diverse media as well as the circulation of their comedy on digital venues and network-sharing internet sites that are capable of further opening up wider political spaces of resistance.

The function of humor and comedy in the articulation of the African American lived experience of historical oppression runs deep. Richard Pryor once quipped that African American humor began on the slave ship. The slave master observed a slave laughing and asked, "What are you laughing about?"; the African responded, "Yesterday I was a king" (Pryor, 1976). Comedy provided a space for the formulation of theories that intervened, not only in creating a healing place (hooks, 1994), but also in contributing to a formulation of anti-oppressive epistemologies that helped to rupture the hegemony of normalized structures and cultures of domination throughout U.S. history. As Ralph Ellison insightfully observed, comedy "[allowed] us to laugh at that which is normally unlaughable . . . comedy provides an otherwise unavailable clarification of vision that calms the clammy trembling which ensues whenever we pierce the veil of conventions that guard us from the basic absurdity of the human condition" (Kercher, 2006, p. 281). Yet, our analytical focus here is not on the private politics of humor, but rather the public manifestation of stand-up. African American stand-up is most pronounced in the late 1950s and the 1960s and remains the most profound expression of an anti-oppressive cultural current.

Comedy routinely crosses discursive parameters and touches on social issues and relations of power, which is often ascribed to zones of the taboo. It moves through complex social relations in an engaged language, since the very response of laughter signals an interaction between the utterance and the background knowledge of audiences. All of this is mediated, of course, through language. Media critic David Marc observes that

> without the protection of the formal mask of narrative drama, without a song, a dance, or any other intermediary composition that creates distance between performer and performance . . .the stand-up comedian addresses an audience as a naked self. . .the exposure of the stand-up comic to public judgment is extraordinarily raw and personal. (quoted in Watkins, 1994, p. 481)

The disinclination of most African American comics to engage in these prosthetic mechanisms signals the development of a critical aesthetics built through elements of the lived experience of the audience. African American stand-up comedy does what critical theater of the Brechtinian variety seeks to do: It serves as a testimony whose effect and power can be gauged by its ability to establish resonance and/or dissonance. It enters spaces that conventional academic theory making does not enter because it is often laced in elitist, specialized language. In countering the critique of profane routines, Richard Pryor instructively stated, "there is no such thing as profanity in what I do. I talk to people in their own words" (quoted in Watkins, 1994, p. 538). The very routine of the stand-up comic signals a space where the dialectical relationship between theory and action can be seen to merge in the very body of the comedian.

Many scholars have written eloquently about how African Americans have erected cultural signposts that speak to the group's survival and sense of hope in the midst of the most vicious of white supremacies. This literature also bears witness to the deep and extensive cultural contributions African Americans have made to the widening of democracy. Concurrently, the most profound of the analyses hold in tension these aesthetic and politically responsible contributions on the one hand, and on the other, regressive elements that often are attributed to exaltation by the dominant social, political, and economic context. Surveying the cultural terrain, we find extensive literature on oral traditions, the creativity borne out of the Harlem Renaissance (a historical inscription encoded in the Eurocentric imagination, for Europe remains the focal point of intellectual emulation), the mobilization of culture in protest politics, literature, dance, music, art, and aesthetics. One location that is underanalyzed, particularly for its power in centralizing a certain sociological imagination and counter-discourse, is the distinctive nature of the African American stand-up comedy narrative, particularly as it is expressed and constituted through African American Vernacular English.

Certainly, we are not suggesting a unitary essentialist narrative. Such a position would reinscribe a politics of romanticization, essentialism, and ethnic authenticity that shuts down critical engagement. Nor are we suggesting that the medium is so diverse that it collapses in the face of human agency. This genre has contributed to a powerful, and often unacknowledged, form of resistance to domination. The central question and tension that has arisen in most analyses of this genre has been this: Does African American stand-up serve to integrate audiences into particular dominant ways of being in the world, or is it a cultural vehicle for resistance and symbolic ruptures? These analyses have been limited on two fronts: They have lacked the complexity of analysis engendered in cultural elements such as hip-hop (the complex tensions I alluded to above) and they have been centered primarily on the content of performance. We must continually differentiate between those comics and productions that are politically responsible and those that reproduce current relations of power either by reproducing stereotypes of African Americans or by omitting references to operations of power and thereby contributing to a discourse of "arrival of the African American." Yet, without romanticizing those comics that evade the analysis of power, we also admit that even as they avoid it, they contribute to progressive politics indirectly. What Mel Watkins calls, "the central strain of African-American humor" (1994, p. 512), meaning its political nature through content, travels beyond the composition of jokes. This genre is already a significant and positive political force if it is theorized not only on the structure of content but also as a communicative medium. We argue that the dominant structure of its narrative points awakens a sense of political possibility, while not abstracting the ways in which it simultaneously perpetuates subordinate social relations. To avoid the latter, we outline a critical cartography of African American stand-up comedy connected to a broader public pedagogy, dialogue, and political project that may very well position it as a deeper transformative and democratic force that moves it beyond "entertainment, spectacle, consumption, and tourism" (Giroux, 1999, p. 65).

Stuart Hall, one of the most profound cultural theorists of our time, interprets the medium as one anchored to the frame of a positively charged and "normative" whiteness, or what he calls a "white chorus line" (2002, p. 277). He concludes that "black stand-up comics still ape their ambiguous incorporation into British entertainment by being the first to tell a racist joke" (2002, p. 277). His analytical focus is not only on the medium, but rather the medium in relation to the wider structure of British media. In terms of the social and political context,

> telling racist jokes across the racial line, in conditions where relations of racial inferiority and superiority prevail, reinforces the difference and reproduces the unequal relations because, in those situations, the point of the joke depends on the existence of racism. Thus they reproduce the categories and relations of racism, even while normalizing them through laughter. The stated good intentions of the joke-makers do not resolve the problem here, because they are not in control of the circumstances—conditions of continuing racism—in which their joke discourse will be read and heard. The time may come when blacks and whites can tell jokes about each other in ways which do not reproduce the racial categories of the world in which they are told. The time, in Britain, is certainly not arrived yet. (2002, p. 279)

Hall seems to have an ambivalent position on comedy uncharacteristic of the complex frameworks he's introduced in cultural studies. One wonders what makes jokes (which are, of course, only one aspect of stand-up comedy, particularly African American stand-up comedy) different from any other cultural and intellectual production. In other words, if those social evils exist, particularly in societies whose very national narratives are anchored to them, virtually any attempt to *do* culture may be theorized as an effort to reproduce the categories, and therefore easy to co-opt. Hall is clear in stating that the context of the analysis is Britain. This, of course, leads us to think through possibilities that stand-up comedy may encode in different contexts. We argue that in the U.S. context, the historical racial tensions have produced more politicized responses on the terrain of culture, not excluding African American stand-up comedy and, later, Chicano stand-up, Queer stand-up, and so on.

We may gain a glimpse of this in the 2006 Fringe International Festival in New York City, which featured black British comedians performing for a racially diverse American audience. The cultural critic Astride Charles (2007) pointed out that two themes dominated the narrative of the black British comedians. First, "voice, the sound of it, was a recurring topic throughout the show" (p. 1). Second, there was the predictable contrast between black British and black American culture. But she also inferenced a third theme—the politicization of the routines—and this led her to the final question of the piece: "It would be interesting to see how these black British comedians developed their art and, specifically, how they, if they, politicized their material because they are performing in an intensely race-conscious American landscape" (p. 1). This was a very perceptive critique echoing Hall's own reading of the British context and signaling our point that one of the dominant characteristics of African American stand-up comedy is its critical engagement with issues of difference and domination even "in conditions where relations of racial inferiority and superiority prevail" (Hall, 2002, p. 279). Even while a counter-cultural comedy exists, we must also reiterate that the orbit of African American stand-up comedy is complex and multivocal. Hall may be correct in his reading of black British stand-up, yet he may be read as suspicious of all stand-up. He is also a bit deterministic, however, even though he powerfully rejected the determinism behind Frankfurt School readings on mass communication in his elaboration of the concepts of "encoding" and "decoding" and possibilities of audience agency through "negotiated" and "oppositional codes" (Hall, 1980). As a text (particularly those narratives that treat processes of racialization, gendered realities, class, and other markers of difference), stand-up comedy is never closed off. Different histories, positionalities, and ideological frames are brought to bear in the process of viewing (Fiske, 1989), and its very creation indexes diverse ideological anchors. There are certain ideological exposures in Chris Rock and Eddie Griffin that are markedly different from those in Bill Cosby, Eddie Murphy, and the late Bernie Mack. Furthermore, Hall reads stand-up as a bounded and fixed practice incapable of conscientious political change. We argue that the genre already encodes creative and positive political tensions in the U.S. context, but may very well be moved along more critical lines because it is a medium in actuation, like all cultural/artistic mediums. The line of inquiry that must be opened, therefore, is how are we to inspire more critical interventions along this terrain? We turn to this question toward the end of the chapter.

African American stand-up comedy is already, by its very structure, an act of transgression, given its historicity. Where its narratives encode signs of political activity or regressive tendencies remains a matter to be debated, yet to leave the argumentation solely on this level leaves us with no language to assess its very architecture as a medium. As noted above, historically it was born within and contributed to the shaping of a concrete social and political movement—the 1950s and 1960s civil rights movements. As Amilcar Cabral has so eloquently put it, "culture plunges its roots into the physical reality of the environmental humus in which it develops" (Cabral, 1970, p. 1). Granted, culture is never static, but the historical roots of any cultural medium matter. Culture engages the fundamental symbolic activity which led to its production: the naming of the social conditions that cause misery from a people historically dehumanized. We cannot leave the analysis hovering solely over the comic and the production of her or his craft. This would in effect reinscribe dominant forms of western ethnocentric analysis where the individual takes center stage. The analysis of this medium needs to be blurred so that we are dialectically theorizing production/reception, performer/audience, the act, and the social, political and economic context. It is only here that we begin to more fully appreciate the art and build responsible and effective transgressive politics. These spaces are critical for the reconstitution of any truly democratic arrangement. Henry Giroux (1992) insightfully observes that "voices forged in opposition and struggle provide the crucial conditions by which subordinate individuals and groups can reclaim their own memories, stories, and histories, as part of an ongoing collective struggle to challenge those power structures that attempt to silence them" (p. 206). We need to recognize the comic voice as communal, because the space of entry is already predetermined by contextual disposition. There exists a familiar narrative pattern. In other words, it's not that all African American stand-up comedians explicitly challenge relations of power, but instead that the medium proclaims (as all mediums make certain claims) that there are certain types of activities, identities, and discourses that one must engage in order to be recognized as a comic within this discursive and cultural space.

The space of comedy speaks to the dialectical processes of meaning-making on the part of both the comic and the audience. Just as the comic "works" the audience, he or she is simultaneously shaped by the sphere of reception. The particular discourse chosen to convey the humor is already informed by a reading of the audience and the particulars of the historical, social, and political context. The construction of the comic narrative is never a totally private matter; the comic is always engaged in a social act. To whom do we speak? is the first question the comic encounters in the production of comedy. The fact that critical stand-up has its audience(s) is a powerful pronouncement of the failure of the ordinary political establishment's ability (or rather, desire) to engender active public participation. Given the gap between public policy and public sentiment, the public is certainly not anaesthetized. Engagement is sought through alternative channels, and stand-up is just one of those channels. Even as public space is shut down through neoliberal policy making, this medium (despite the current commodification) is opening up spaces for theorization centering on demands for a more democratic public life.

Comics cross ideological boundaries at times as they exhibit through their routines the same contradictions that we all move through. However, given the historical weight of processes of racialization (and its connection to class) in the U.S., it is no coincidence that the subject of race and class are constantly surfacing. Increasingly, women are also producing comedy that analyzes and exposes the intersections of these markers and patriarchy. In fact, one of the brightest points in the contemporary African American stand-up comedy scene is the deconstruction of socially constructed black masculinity, often centered in the routines of black male comics. Adele Givens is one comedienne who is effective in challenging these constructions as she dialectically tears down the cultural parameters of what it means to be a "lady."

It is important to note once again, however, that the comics aren't always necessarily intentionally seeking political, social, or economic redress. It is less about the "activist" tendencies of the comic and more about the contextual grounding and lived experiences of those to whom the comedy is directed. That is not to say that there aren't comics explicitly committed to addressing social evils. Dick Gregory and Richard Pryor were exemplary in this regard. Pryor was astutely aware of efforts to co-opt his politics and consistently resisted network censors. One channel of co-option continues to be the integration of comics into sitcoms where humor is made to appeal to a more general audience. On the eve of the cancellation of his 1977 series he said

> [television] could be such an informative medium. One week of truth on TV could just straighten out everything. One hundred twenty-seven million people watch television every night; that's why they use it to sell stuff. . . . They're not going to write shows about how to revolutionize America. The top-rated shows are for retarded people. (Pryor, 2000, p. 58)

Even Pryor eventually succumbed to the temptation. After signing a five-year contract with Columbia Pictures in 1983, his work was increasingly less controversial as he softened his comedic identity for onscreen productions.

The majority of comics, however, are living out and through a social script that already charts a cartography of relevant subjects and topics. To deviate from the script means distance from respective audiences, given the dialectical relationship between cultural grounding and voice. Of course, we are not suggesting a rigid script, but rather the continued perpetuation of asymmetrical relations of power (even as it shifts historically) and the counter-discourses and cultures that these relations produce and re-produce. The counter-discourses are, of course, more pronounced at specific historical junctures when social movements are more pronounced.

The best-known comics in the 1960s gained their notoriety primarily for their social consciousness. Jackie Mabley (later known as "Moms"), one of the most successful entertainers in the vaudeville Chitlin' Circuit, was known for her biting indictments of racism. Redd Foxx, Slappy White, and Nipsey Russell all utilized social commentary against racism (Kercher, 2006). They were not as outspoken as comedians who followed them because the boundaries of discursive transgression were tightly controlled, and as they attempted to cross boundaries into venues where white audiences were the norm, their routines were increasingly co-opted. This was particularly true for Russell, who attempted to stylistically shift his routines from African American Vernacular English to Standard English (Watkins, 1994). Tracing their individual biographies for moments of political subversion and/or co-option is not as significant as the context through which they lived. The context becomes important in the structuring of any theory of resistance because that becomes an important location for opportunities of transgressions. They crossed the boundaries they could cross in their particular context. Of course, the political nature of their work cannot be overly romanticized, because their movement in stand-up comedy (and beyond) was also signaled by their own economic interests. As the civil rights movement of the 1960s intensified, so too did the political commentaries and satire.

Aside from its historical genesis, the medium itself is political resistance in yet another way. The narrativization of African American stand-up comedy is most often articulated within African American English Vernacular (AAVE) in order to maintain its distinctive cultural transmissions and legitimacy in relation to the intended audience (both African Americans and Others who consume working-class African American cultural capital). This, again, was made abundantly clear in the manner in which voice and language became the central marker that the British comedians performing in the U.S. had to negotiate. In fact, to signal insider status, many comedians accentuate the nuances and linguistic creativity of AAVE. The depth of reliance on certain phonological, grammatical, semantic, and syntactical features of the language are less pronounced after the comedian exits the stage. We noted this reality in various interviews with stand-up comics, and it may be readily noted in linguistic differences in a comic's speech during an interview and while performing on stage.

Through this medium, there exists a powerful politics of linguistic recognition and a chronicling of the capacity of the language to perform on the same level as the socially legitimated "standard" variant and beyond. The need for this activity is monumental given the rampant assault on AAVE. (The most recent media and public display of this assault was the 1996 Oakland "Ebonics" controversy.) African American stand-up comedy is a public display countering linguistic devaluation (which is always about writing its speakers outside of humanity), particularly as we take note that it communicates one of the most complex psychological and social function known to humans—humor (and all those techniques that make it work: word play, double-edged irony, pitch and tone of voice, and so on). The effectiveness and efficiency of the language may be traced to its very capacity to capture the inherent spirit of wit—brevity (Freud, 1960) and precision. Yet, it captures much more of the stylistic, rhythmical, and African American cultural capital. Richard Pryor was acutely aware of the function and significance of language. In recounting the events on a trip to Africa, Pryor stated, "an African man asked us, 'what language do you speak at home?' We looked at each other and said, 'what? English?' [he responded] 'Everybody speaks English, but what language do you speak when you're at home.' One of the brothers looked at him and said, 'huh, Jive? [laughter]" (Pryor, 1982). In another routine, he recounts a dialogue with a white person who asked about the boxer Leon Spinks, "don't you think he's dumb?" Pryor reflects on what that piece of language communicated politically and personally: "I thought about how this motherfucka would see me if I agreed with him. Leon may not articulate the language, but shit it ain't his to begin with. I'd like to see how you do in here [meaning in the AAVE discursive community]. [laughter and applause]" (Pryor, 1978). This a potent illustration of W.E.B. Du Bois's notion of a double consciousness as it relates to linguistic capital. That is, "this sense of always looking at one's self through the eyes of others, of measuring one's soul by the tape of a world that looks on in amused contempt and pity" (1903, p. 2), and of a two-ness, of being "an American, a Negro; [...] two warring ideals in one dark body, whose dogged strength alone keeps it from being torn asunder" (1903, p. 5). Pryor's work and a great deal of the strains of African American humor that followed have been significant in the analysis of this process through the content of performance and through the brilliant points of reference communicated through the act of code switching.

Nevertheless, the continued articulation of AAVE in settings that are white, middle-class, and/or mixed opens up the possibility of a more informed and nuanced understanding of linguistic equality and respect. The perception of AAVE as an inferior variant or slang permeates the imagination of most Americans. Yet, there are more than matters of technical linguistics and the centralization of linguistic conflict to consider. There is also the matter of awakening a sense of possibility through cultural conflict, for language is both the codification and the vehicle through which culture is articulated. Several theorists of African American culture have written powerfully of their encounters with Standard English and the manner through which it was wielded in institutions for the purposes of inflicting harm, shame, and a sense of inferiority (Delpit, 2002; hooks, 1994). Stand-up comedy routinely enters Standard English for the purposes of analyzing the absurd behaviors of those who utilize it. In so doing, it counters the inferiority so often felt in the context of institutionalized and "normative" ways of being. It enunciates a counter-discourse through the representation of its speaker (usually the comic or a character created by the comic) as a rational thinker, collected and cool. It also counters the notion that speakers of AAVE can't enter the standard code due to some deficiency on the part of the speaker. Comics code switch routinely.

The comedienne Sommore enacts multiple activities when she compares and contrasts cross-racial and cross-class anxieties over current economic conditions. "They need to watch the way black people survive through the economy," she advises (Sommore, 2007). She relates how a white woman was shocked and distraught at the crimes of Enron. She code-switches, "I can't believe they misrepresented their financial earnings!" then responds by reverting to AAVE; "Bitch, that's called 'ballin'"

(Sommore, 2007). She places a great deal of significance on the language's ability to name the social condition more efficiently and accurately. There is also a linguistic anchoring to the historical condition, as the utterance marks and infers that "this is not new to us." The reference to history is a primary tool used by comics to make knowledge claims. When these claims move through AAVE they further make transparent the absurdity of "normative" and hegemonic knowledge constructions. The narrative structures of African American stand-up comedy follows Paul Ricoeur's (1981) theoretical work on how the novel blurs the boundaries of time. Stand-up also often merges language, history, and comedy in the creation of "new forms of human time, and therefore new forms of human community" (quoted in Burke, Crowley, & Girvin, 2000, p. 342). He goes on to say that this creativity is "also a social and cultural act; it is not confined to the individual" (p. 342). The power of these critiques is that they move both outward and inward as they simultaneously challenge forms of consent from below. Indeed, African American humor is often double-edged. There exists the self-deprecation and internal critiques (particularly critiques of religion) alongside serious critiques of domination. Relentless self-criticism through comedy undermines the myth that subordinated groups are subordinated because they don't work on themselves. Rather, the self-criticism coupled with the ongoing satire of relations of power illuminates the reality that those who are oppressed can work on themselves endlessly and remain dominated unless the very material conditions that sustains negative relations of power is changed.

There are clear connections between the articulation of AAVE, comedy, and the narration of the social, political, and economic conditions that African Americans have been subjected to and have resisted throughout the history of the U.S. The relationship between language, knowledge, and power is consistently centralized in stand-up. It (re)constitutes verbal repertoires of resistance through its broad dissemination and politics of self-definition and oppositional consciousness. Ngugi Wa'Thiongo (1986) has eloquently captured this dynamic: "The choice of language and the use to which it is put is central to a people's definition of themselves in relation to their natural and social environment, indeed in relation to the entire universe" (p. 4). Claudia Mitchell-Kernan observes that "nowhere is the symbolic importance of language in promoting in-group identity and unity more evident than in the domains of specialization which reflect social distance within the black community and between the black community and other speech communities" (1980, p. xviii). So, it is a cultural construct whose architecture is positioned to keep outsiders out through cultural nuances intelligible to insiders. It is also about the instantiation of a form of cultural politics.

The range of topics treated within the medium of comedy and the specificities of the language speaks to the countering of the politics of historical erasure and political invisibility. It simultaneously elicits laughter and insight. Frantz Fanon, the critical psychiatrist who illuminated the psychopathology of colonization, powerfully remarked that

> to speak means to be in a position to use a certain syntax, to grasp the morphology of this or that language, but it means above all to assume a culture, to support the weight of a civilization...A [person] who has language consequently possesses the world expressed and implied by that language. (Fanon, 1952, p. 419)

African American stand-up comedy is an aesthetic vehicle that centralizes the concerns and anxieties of African American working-class life, and lives on the economic lifeline and translates it into a form of social engagement where those anxieties are made public rather than private. Its reading of history and society is in many instances oppositional because it's transmitted through a linguistic capital constitutive of historical struggle, which demands the inclusion of suppressed memories. Richard Pryor's *Bicentennial Nigger*, released in 1976, utilized various terms of reference in the effort to illuminate the causation of present oppressive realities and their historical roots. The thematic catchphrase of the album was articulated by a preacher delivering the bicentennial prayer: "We're celebrating two hundred years of white folks kickin' ass [applause]...we offer this prayer. And the prayer is, how long will this bullshit go on? [laughter and applause]. [response from the audience: "how long, amen."] HOW LONG! How looong will this bullshit go on?" (Pryor, 1976). In relating the lack of positive African American representation in film, he goes on in the following track: "That's why we gotta make movies. [applause]. But we gotta make some hip movies, because we done made enough movies about pimps, 'cause white folks already know about pimpin.' We the biggest hos they got. [laughter and applause]" (Pryor, 1976).

The comedic narrative is laced with references to whiteness. In perpetuating these scripts, comics are functioning to make processes of racialization and social constructions of whiteness more transparent. At times, these imaginations of whiteness are stereotypical, yet their emergence is a counter to white stereotypes of African Americans (hooks, 1998). The counter-stereotype makes the humor work and further points out the irrationality of the entire social situation. It also functions as a public curriculum that counters racism through the very exposition that African Americans can and do see the operation of whiteness. As bell hooks (1998) observed, "racist thinking perpetuated the fantasy that the Other who is subjugated, who is subhuman, lacks the ability to comprehend, to understand, to see the working of the powerful" (p. 41). Just as it communicates its message outward, it also serves as a mechanism for healing (hooks, 1989) because it disarms the terror of whiteness through the production of counter-memories and "political self-recovery" (hooks, 1998).

Bakhtin (1981) also attempted to partly illuminate the relationship between language and a historical presence of mind through the concept of heteroglossia. He wrote,

> at any given moment of its historical existence, language is heteroglot from top to bottom: [I]t represents the co-existence of socio-ideological contradictions between the present and the past, between different epochs of the past, between different socio-ideological groups in the present...all given a bodily form. (p. 291)

In so doing, a space is provided for "the development of ideas and practices"(Duncombe, 2002), although never fully disconnected from the reality of capitalism as producer of culture (especially as the medium is connected to mainstream media and efforts at market manipulation and expansion). If hip-hop and rap remain the CNN of black America (according to Chuck D), African American stand-up comedy is its more penetrating *Meet the Press*. To feel the cultural pulse of any community, we must look at what it laughs at. We must enter this space, not as voyeurs but with an ethnographic sensibility and a disposition commanded by respect.

When the late Bernie Mack entered the *Def Comedy Jam* stage for the first time—possibly the most viewed performance of the series—he initiated his routine by saying, "I ain't scared of you motherfuckas!" and was met by thunderous applause and laughter. He continued by ending every punch line in the routine with the same catchphrase. In the process, he increased the laughs per minute in each progressive catchphrase utterance. What's of importance in this example, is that the catchphrase made no relation to the string of jokes preceding or following it. In essence, it served as a nonconnecting connector with a deep connotative meaning. This leads us to the question one viewer posted following the routine on a YouTube clip: "Might sound stupid, but why was is it so funny when he said, "Kick it" and "I ain't scared of you motherfuckers"? Another post answers: "Because it is!" These two responses are, in themselves, very nuanced. I will refrain from engaging them because the identity markers of the respondents are unknown, but I would venture to guess that the first poster was outside of working-class African American reality and the other one within. Yet, why was Mack able to gather what seemed an immediate response of laughter and applause at the catchphrase?

What Mack and the audience are engaged in here is a contextually situated meaning-making process functioning on the basis of a shared relationship. The utterance is more relevant and scripted into the context and culture given its resonance, and yet the significance cannot be readily explained by participants within the context of its production. We argue that the resonance is established primarily through the mobilization of two distinct cultural cues. First, there is a deeper reciprocal action in contexts where an audience is predominantly African American and working class. Entertainers and comedians working the Chitlin' Circuit at the height of racial segregation routinely point out that the demands placed on the quality of performance was intense given audience interaction. The best example on the circuit was, of course, Harlem's Apollo Theater. Richard Pryor claimed "[when I first played Harlem's Apollo Theater] I was scared to death. Them niggers will eat you up if your shit ain't right" (Robbins & Ragan, 1982, p. 35). Smitherman and others have labeled this dynamic "call and response," a form of "spontaneous verbal and non-verbal interaction between speaker and listener in which all of the statements ('calls') are punctuated by expressions ('responses') from the listener" (Smitherman, 1977, p. 23). Mack signaled his knowledge of this dynamic. Mel Watkins (1994) recounts a similar interaction between Moms Mabley and the Apollo Theater audience. "[She] scanned the audience with a tired, exasperated look, and said, 'yeah, I know how y'all feel'" (p. 132). More significantly, Bernie Mack invokes the historical dimension of the shared relationship and the various ways in which the very bodies of those present have been historically encoded first as objects and then as subjects to be feared. These dominant discourses have been amply documented in the mass media and articulated into acts of domination, repression, and policing. The racist architecture of the criminal justice system and the raced policies of schooling are just two obvious examples. The cues that are employed at the level of individual reception are difficult to determine without an ethnographic component (certainly a productive line of future research). Yet, the indexing of sign systems beyond the literal is very clear. Although audiences sometimes respond in laughter to strings of statements that are not jokes when embedded within the rhythm of comedic routines (a characteristic technique of many comedians), in African American stand-up comedy these statements often reference matters of political and sociohistoric significance. Its political function is all the more potent given its subterranean engagements, even while being transmitted through dominant channels (such as cable and other televisual mediums). Of course, the subversive elements of African American stand-up comedy aren't always anchored to masked discourses; very often the political tension produced is quite overt. At the center of the African American stand-up comedy narrative is the examination of raced, classed lives and the politics of whiteness. Concurrently, there is a social legitimation of sensibilities that must also be unpacked and subjected to a pedagogical center for purposes of transformation. These are the most ritualized topics within the narration of routines.

The techniques of delivery differ. There are African American comics who distance themselves from these types of analysis. The work of Bill Cosby serves as an influential example given his stature in the field. Yet, even his work is not free of occasional satire. Cosby cannot avoid controversial topics such as race. His comedy is heavily influenced by racial narratives, perhaps not in routine, but in his very reasoning regarding why he positions himself in the way that he does. And, of course, even as he lashes out at the most vulnerable by aligning himself with deficit model discourses, he too has benefited from the cultural capital of AAVE. Again, our argument is not centered on any politics of black authenticity. We don't believe that such a location can be framed. What we claim is that the very constitution of the medium privileges certain discourses, claims to knowledge, and ways of viewing the world.

Stand-up and Moving into Deeper Spaces of Transgression

To construct a deeper subversive agenda and form politically responsible networks of resistance through this medium and beyond, it is necessary that a critical pedagogical project be built alongside stand-up. The production, delivery, and beyond of the stand-up text needs to be built from a political pedagogy. The commitment to read the world from the perspective of those who are routinely pushed off the social map must be centralized. This would mean a cultural reidentification of the comic as pedagogue. Schools of education would have to widen the boundaries of what constitutes pedagogy/teacher identity and cross spheres in an effort to deinstitutionalize what counts as teaching and learning. One of the central moves of critical pedagogy has been the interrogation of what qualifies as "official knowledge" (Apple, 2000) and a call to engage the lived experience of students. What is often abstracted from this call is the question: How are teachers to engage the lived experience of students of color, working-class and poor youth, and bilingual youth, when the majority of teachers don't come from that location and may lack the political clarity to get there given the limitations of their institutional formation? African American stand-up comedy and the stand-up comedies from other cultural locations serve as a public transcript of alternative knowledge and are also an important source of engaging "lived experience" given its resonance/reflexivity and location as self-determined activity often grounded in ethnographic and auto-ethnographic exposures. Much of African American stand-up comedy does not rely on jokes as ordinarily defined, but rather on the representation of everyday events characterizing African American working-class life. The most wide-ranging interpretations of this life were enacted through the dramatizations of Richard Pryor, truly a first-rate comedic ethnographer and discourse analyst, as he spoke through different characters. The causes of cultural anxiety and visions of hope can be examined by analyzing what a group of people laughs at. Importantly, there is constant shifting between the personal and social/political, which opens up spaces for pedagogical projects that move beyond the field of decontextualized story-telling so common in classrooms. Granted, there are limitations to its force given that it, too, exists within capitalist modes of production and circulation. It is, however, one of the most profound vehicles given the license that the genre is afforded in crossing "normative" boundaries.

Bingham and Hernandez (2009) have shared powerful examples of how comedy may be integrated at the college level to assist students in paralleling the work of comedians and the specificities of sociological research methodology and the sociological imagination. What is important about their approach is that they integrate "popular culture" not as an add-on to the curriculum, but rather as a medium equally important to knowledge production in the academy. In their words, we must "face the realization that academic sociology [the discipline they teach] is not the final word on society" (p. 338). In addition to encouraging students to explore complex social problems through this medium and make connections to social theory, it is important to note that there also exists an element of self-reflexivity in the opening of a territory to examine why the very response of laughter is emitted.

These efforts in consciousness raising must be applauded. They do not, however, move beyond the consumption and analysis of these texts to exploring possibilities of production in the classroom and beyond. The tools and techniques of comedians must also be decentered and transferred to the masses to further the critical pedagogical project. Spectators must be moved out of the rigid role and produce satire themselves, thereby contributing to a broader politics of democratic participation.

Beyond analysis and production, spaces must be created for concrete action to transform the world. Without collective engagement in the transformation of the material realities that sustain subordination, stand-up comedy will remain only a vehicle for consciousness raising. This standpoint can be incited only if structures are built to sustain it. I conceive of nonprofit and community-based organizations utilizing stand-up comedy to address deep social, political, and economic issues in ways that involve not only the medium's exposure but also the transfer of the techniques for its production. These structures would also develop conferences, journals, critical ethnographies, university courses, engagement with stand-up in K-12 lesson planning and activities, open-microphone community-based stand-up political engagements, websites built on democratic structures allowing public input, political and social movements that utilize protest stand-up as a tactic, and so on. More importantly, all of these forms of contestation need to enter into dialogue, and we need to nurture and sustain those forms that are less tied to institutions. When progressive projects enter institutional politics and bureaucratic structures they are likely to be co-opted through reductionistic mechanisms of evaluation connected to funding (just one site of likely dominant control).

Several years ago, while serving as program coordinator for the Boston office of the National Conference for Community and Justice (NCCJ), one of the authors of this chapter facilitated a stand-up comedy event in Dorchester's Strand Theatre, built in 1918 and a center of vaudeville well into the 1930s. The site was also chosen because of historical, cultural, and racial tension in the area, as well as myriad institutional structures that preyed on youth by withdrawing material resources and life-sustaining services. By the late 1990s, at the time of this intervention, the area had one of the highest homicide rates in the country. The project was specifically designed and implemented to open up dialogues on controversial social issues as they touched down contextually. Advertisements for the event were posted in the police department, local schools, churches, and community-based organizations, and disseminated through the local government's calendar of events and well-known businesses catering to the community. The featured comic/activist was Jimmy Tingle, who at the time was already very well known; he was joined by several other comics of diverse backgrounds whose routines satirized controversial events and the history of discrimination in the U.S. The routines were unique in that they all pushed the political boundaries. Following the show, the comics formed a panel and opened up a dialogue with the audience about the content of the shows and their craft.

The dialogue that followed was extremely intense. Predictably, the questions and comments centered on whether or not the routines functioned to unmask institutionalized structural inequalities or to perpetuate them. Could entertainment simultaneously educate? These questions and comments were raised initially by audience members who were already knowledgeable about the intent of the project. They were members of various community-based organizations and antiracist initiatives in the Boston area. The initial spirit of critical dialogue enveloped the theater as community members from various ideological orientations entered the debate.

The event awakened a sense of possibility in several concrete ways. First, both the audience and the lineup of comics were comprised of diverse groups that historically have been subordinated differently, but at times along shared markers. The racial composition of the audience and comics, for example, was diverse, and yet common ground was sometimes found when topics converged on class and gender. This provided opportunities for the imagination of a politics and praxis of solidarity. These terrains must be nurtured for the further development of critical stand-up comedy. Muslim American comics have produced some serious critiques of American society and politics, particularly after September 11, 2001. Ahmed Ahmed, Tissa Hami, Dean Obeidallah, Azhar Usman, and Maysoon Zayid are just some comics deconstructing stereotypes of Muslims. George Lopez and Carlos Mencia routinely examine race relations and cultural conflict from the Chicano perspective. In doing so, they also integrate their own forms of border linguistic capital into their routines. A number of comics have built their careers on the "blue collar movement" in comedy—that is, on analyzing working-class life and class conflict. A number of queer comics are gaining ground in the stand-up scene. Also significant are the possibilities embedded in crossing national boundaries in the effort to connect with critical comedy being produced globally. Venues such as the annual Just for Laughs comedy festival in Montreal, the Edinburgh Festival Fringe, the Melbourne International Comedy Festival, various underground festivals throughout the world, and video-sharing sites such as YouTube, provide spaces for the nurturing of critical stand-up that crosses borders and produces grounded resistance.

The critical educational theorist Michael Apple (2000) has eloquently described such a possibility in his notion of a "de-centered unity." This means that our primary focus when building and rebuilding any political project would have to center on the analysis of power and how it is manifested in multiple sites. Such a realization will allow for relational types of projects that cut across markers of difference, contexts, memories, and so on. Such a project has the capacity to be sustained longer than projects that limit alliances. Henry Giroux (1992) insightfully observed that

> ...forms of identity politics that forgo the potential for creating alliances among different subordinate groups run the risk of reproducing a series of hierarchies of identities and experiences which serve to privilege their own form of oppression and struggle. All too often this position results in totalizing narratives that fail to recognize the limits of their own discourse in explaining the complexity of social life and the power such a discourse wields in silencing those who are not considered part of the insider group. (p. 208)

To build a pedagogical project alongside stand-up would mean thorough grounding in the community of praxis while not avoiding the integration of injustices done cross-contextually so that a broader subversive agenda may be built. African American stand-up comedy, and indeed stand-up generally, must avoid the common forms of demonization and infantilization of gay, lesbian, bisexual, and transgendered people. Rather, routines should be built through a penetrating analysis of how power functions to marginalize through the fracturing of communities and the fixing of discursive boundaries to limit the crossing of ideas that may potentially rupture it. This does not mean that a medium such as African American stand-up comedy must lose the very specificities that make it so powerful. Rather, it means realizing that its power is already limited and constrained by its reluctance to cross certain borders that normalize those very structures that it attempts to confront. What needs to be centered in the production of comedy, indeed in popular culture in general, is the furthering of deep democratic arrangements; this necessarily means forming powerful networks such as the possibilities mentioned above.

Second, the expectation on the part of the comics that their comedy served an educational function was subjected to the scrutiny of the knowledge of the community and the historical anxieties of people living in the immediate context. The comics were confronted with the realization that perhaps their framing of the public's problems was either too generalized or ambiguous to effectively address the set of exclusionary policies and practices at the level of the local. At one point, one of the comics questioned the very structure of the project and whether or not she should be seen as an activist or merely an entertainer who also lived/lives through the same set of oppressive conditions as the audience. Comedy, in essence, provided her with an economic avenue out of poverty, and her connection to it, in her own assertion, was merely utilitarian. She was challenged at several points by the audience regarding the responsibility to contribute to the community in more engaged ways, given that her routine referenced social and economic problems. In short, both audience members and comics were propelled into an engaged dialogue without the insulation of those normative boundaries that confines audiences to a certain set of cultural and spatial constraints and performers to others. The community was challenged to see the potential of the medium and their own limitations in envisioning what qualifies as political activism and the identity of an activist. Indeed, the historical record has produced many figures who deeply contributed to the shaping of a more humane world but never saw their role as one of activism. The comics were enticed to further deepen their craft, ideological contradictions, and perceptions of their role as activists by connecting their routines to the contextual realities before them. At issue was what constitutes political intervention and whether or not cultural contestation needs to move beyond awareness raising (not to mention the paternalistic location of some comics who assumed that the audience was not already aware), which is the location where satirical stand-up comedy has been. What was launched here was a profound community dialogue moving through and not around conflict, which is a precondition for any efforts at progressive social change.

Third, to further sustain an oppositional space, several community-based and national organizations at the forefront of political change in the community and beyond were invited to set up informational tables in an effort to connect people to concrete action. The organizers sought to create a space that was less an incidental "event" and more of an entryway into committed organizing. Also important was that all those participating in the event had an avenue to connect emotions raised to positive political projects. Had this element not been integrated, the project would have instantiated an irresponsible politics of further fracturing relations in the community. This aspect of the project was poorly integrated. On several feedback surveys, participants stated that the action-oriented dimension seemed an "add on" rather than the ultimate goal.

Yet, the continued convergence between the medium and social movements cannot be overstated. Critical stand-up comedy needs to be understood as cultural resistance and a symbolic movement in itself. The difficulty that we seem to have in seeing it as such stems from our own cultural definition of what qualifies as a movement. Because it lacks a "leader, a constitution, a legislative program" (Piven & Cloward, 1978), are we to dismiss it?

Comics and communities have histories. A critical comic's ability to engage audiences over time already signals an intellectual and material need on the part of both. The question is: How do we to expand the terrain of contestation? Part of the answer lies in the dialogue we referred to in the above example. That's insufficient, however. The tools of critical comedy need to be transferred to audiences so that a cultural terrain may be (re)produced where people are finding ways to come to voice through the medium. Here, we envision the spoken-word revolution (Youth Speaks, poetry slams, and so on) and imagine a critical stand-up comedy for radical social change. We envision the street-corner production of this comedy and its articulation in a number of other spheres. We envision a solidarity movement with critical strains of stand-up across multiple markers of difference and around the globe. More importantly, we envision the conversion of stand-up comedy and movements that are more concrete in demanding that the material realities of the oppressed be changed.

Stand-up comedy can and should be used in acts of civil disobedience and demonstrations; in acts of culture jamming corporate advertisement and the manufacturing of hedonistic consumer culture; in the occupation of private space that should be public, or public space that needs protection, as in the various acts of Reclaim the Streets; in labor union mobilization; and in protests against trade organizations. Such connections would certainly engender efforts at co-option. We've seen these efforts in the case of corporate advertisement and its recontextualization of the types of "subvertisements" found in the pages of activist magazines such as *Adbusters*. Yet, we cannot avoid producing progressive politics from "extra-ordinary" locations because of their likelihood of co-option. The fact that they become targets signals their importance. Just as the center will remain moving so as to perpetually counter cultural resistance, movements must also be creative in the manner in which they continually resist co-option. Perhaps these connections will engender a new generation of comics who, unlike Dick Gregory early in his career, will not have to question the limitations of comedy for social change, but rather will move in the direction he pioneered in the mid-1960s. Gregory's routines were more politically charged than other comic's, leading Howard Zinn to reflect, "never in the history of this area [Selma, Alabama] had a black man stood like this on a public platform, ridiculing and denouncing white officials to their faces. . . . [I]t was something of a miracle that Gregory was able to leave town alive" (1964, pp. 150–151). In recounting his own role, Gregory stated, "I kept pushing my material further . . . more topical, more racial, more digging into a system I was beginning to understand better and attack more intelligently" (in Kercher, 2006, p. 297). Gregory helped fuel the fire of the civil rights movement through his comedy while his craft was dialectically moved by the spirit of the movement.

One of the authors of this chapter is reminded of a class discussion on the diverse protest ideologies arising out of the various African American civil rights movements throughout U.S. history, particularly the contribution of a politically engaged middle-school student. After making a profound contribution to the dialogue, the student added, "I get most of my information from the barbershop." As schools uncritically disengage from a commitment to deepening and extending democracy and increasingly normalize standardized testing, scripted curricula, and neoliberalism and conservativism as educational salvation, and function as stratifying mechanisms and respond to the disturbances they cause by further policing youth, one must examine the institution of schooling closely for spaces of resistance (as they always exist) and simultaneously not lose sight of the various manifestations of critical pedagogy outside of schooling. These emerging (and perhaps not so emergent) spaces need to be exposed to deeper theoretical language so that their political nature may be utilized for the building of a more substantial transformative praxis. The reality is that a great deal of learning/ideological exposures goes on in these sites. As Peter McLaren has eloquently put it, "to ignore the ideological dimensions of student experience is to deny the ground upon which students learn, speak, and imagine" (2003, p. 242).

Schools are increasingly transmitting conservative and corporate values and abdicating their responsibility for the creation of democratic spaces capable of perpetually intervening in institutionalized structural inequalities. While we continue to struggle for more humane arrangements in the sphere of schooling, we simultaneously look outward and both border cross (Giroux, 2005) and blur the distinction of institutionally structured education and other sites of meaning making. African American stand-up comedy deals courageously with issues of race, language, poverty, and power while current dominant policies in schools sustain and/or realign these structural hierarchies. We must continue creating, cultivating, and deepening this form of cultural resistance. We must also traverse our respective fields of political engagement (given our respective social constraints) and find new ways to build organized solidarity, while always bearing in mind our organic responsibilities to change the material conditions under which people live and die.

References

Apple, M. (2000). *Official knowledge: Democratic education in a conservative age* (2nd ed.). New York. London: Routledge.

Bakhtin, M. (1981). *The dialogic imagination.* Austin: University of Texas Press.

Bingham, S. & Hernandez, A. (2009) Laughing matters: The stand-up comedian as social observer, teacher and conduit of the sociological imagination. *Teaching Sociology, 37*, 335–352.

Burke, L., Crowley, T., & Girvin, A. (Eds.). (2000). *The Routledge language and cultural theory reader.* London and New York: Routledge.

Cabral, A. (1970). National liberation and culture. Retrieved from http://www.history-isaweapon.com/defcon1/cabralnlac.html.

Charles, A. (2007, September 2007). Stand up black Britain. Retrieved from http://www.seeingblack.com/article_264.shtml.

Duncombe, S. (Ed.). (2002). *Cultural resistance reader.* London & New York: Verso.

Lepit, L. & Dowdy, J. (Eds.). (2002). *The skin that we speak: Thoughts on language and culture in the classroom.* New York: The New Press.

Du Bois, W. E. B. (1903). *The souls of black folk.* Chicago: A. C. McClurg.

Fanon, Frantz. (1952). *The Negro and Language.* In L. Burke,T. Crowley, & A. Girvin. (Eds.). (2000). *The Routledge language and cultural theory reader* (p. 419). London and New York: Routledge.

Fiske, J. (1989). Moments of television: Neither the text nor the audience. In E. Seiter, H. Borchers, G. Kreutzner, & E. Worth (Eds.), *Remote control: Television audiences and cultural power* (pp. 56–78). London: Routledge.

Folb, E. A. (1950). *Runnin' down some lines: The language and culture of black teenagers.* Cambridge, MA, and London: Harvard University Press.

Freud, S. (1960). *Jokes and their relation to the unconscious.* New York: W.W. Norton.

Giddens, A. (1984). *The constitution of society.* Berkeley: University of California Press.

Giroux, H. (1992). Resisting difference: Cultural studies and the discourse of critical pedagogy. In L. Grossberg, C. Nelson, & P. Treichler (Eds.), *Cultural studies* (pp. 199–212). New York: Routledge.

Giroux, H. (2005). *Border crossings: Cultural workers and the politics of education* (2nd ed.). New York and London: Routledge.

Giroux, H. (2009). *The mouse that roared: Disney and the end of innocence.* Lanham, MD: Rowman & Littlefield.

Hall, S. (1980). Encoding/decoding. In S. Hall, D. Hobson, A. Lowe, & P. Willis (Eds.), *Culture, media, language* (pp. 128–138). London: Unwin Hyman.

Hall, S. (1981). The whites of their eyes: Racist ideologies and the media. In G. Bridges & R. Brunt (Eds.), *Silver linings: Some strategies for the eighties* (pp. 28–52). London: Lawrence and Wishart.

Hall, S. (2002). Racist ideologies and the media. In P. Marris & S. Thornham (Eds.), *Media studies: A reader* (2nd ed., pp. 271–282). New York: New York University Press.

hooks, b. (1989). *Talking back*. Boston: South End Press.

hooks, b. (1994). *Teaching to Transgress: Education as the Practice of Freedom*. Florence, Kentucky:. U.S.A. Routledge.

hooks, b. (1998). Representations of whiteness in the black imagination. In D. Roediger (Ed.), *Black on white: Black writers on what it means to be white* (pp. 38–53). New York: Schocken Books.

Kercher, S. E. (2006). *Revel with a cause: Liberal satire in postwar America*. Chicago and London: University of Chicago Press.

Kernan, C. M. (1980). Foreword. In E. Folb, *Runnin' down some lines: The language and culture of black teenagers* (p. xviii). Cambridge, MA and London: Harvard University Press.

King, Jr. Martin Luther. (1967). Beyond Vietnam: A time to break the silence. Delivered 4 April 1967, at a meeting of Clergy and Laity Concerned at Riverside Church in New York City. http://www.americanrhetoric.com/speeches/mlkatimetobreaksilence.htm [accessed January 18, 2010]

Lears, J. (1994). *Fables of abundance: A cultural history of advertising in America*. New York: Basic Books.

Marris, P., & Thornham S.. (Eds.). (2002). *Media studies: A reader* (2nd ed.). New York: New York University Press.

McLaren, P. (2003). *Life in schools: An introduction to critical pedagogy in the foundations of education*. New York: Pearson Education.

Olson, A. (Ed.). (2007). *Word warriors: Thirty-five women leaders in the spoken word revolution*. Berkeley, CA: Seal Press.

Piven, F. & Cloward, R. (1978). Poor people's movements: Why they succeed, how They fail. New York, London: Vintage.

Pryor, R. (1976). *Bicentennial Nigger*. [audio recording]. Warner Bros. Records.

Pryor,R. (Producer). (1982). *Live on the Sunset Strip*. [film]. Los Angeles: Sony Pictures.

Pryor, R. (speaker). (1978). *Wanted: Richard Pryor live in concert*. [audio recording]. Warner Brothers.

Pryor, R. (2000). *Richard Pryor . . . and it's deep too! The complete Warner Bros. recordings (1968–1992)*. Los Angeles: Warner Bros.

Pryor, R. (speaker). (2000). *That "African-American" is still crazy: Good shit from the vaults*. [audio recording]. Warner Bros. Records & Rhino Entertainment Company.

Ricoeur, P. (1981). *Hermeneutics and the human sciences*. (J. B. Thompson, Ed. and Trans.). Cambridge, UK: Cambridge University Press.

Robbins, F., & Ragan, D. (1982). *Richard Pryor: This cat got 9 lives!* New York: Delilah Books.

Smitherman, G. (1977). *Talkin and testifyin: The language of black America*. Detroit, MI: Wayne State University Press.

Sommore. (producer) (2007). *Sommore: The Queen Stands Alone*. [film]. Code Black Entertainment.

Thiong'o, N. (1986). *Decolonizing the mind: The politics of language in African literature*.

London and Nairobi, Kenya: Heinemann.

Wallace, M. (1992). *Black popular culture*. (Gina Dent, Ed.). Seattle, WA: May Press.

Watkins, M. (1994). *On the real side: Laughing, lying, and signifying—the underground tradition of African American humor that transformed American culture, from slavery to Richard Pryor*. New York: Simon & Schuster.

X, Malcolm. (October 10, 1963). Message to the grassroots. Deliverd at King Solomon Baptist Church, Detroit, Michigan. http://teachingamericanhistory.org/library/index.asp?document=1145. [accessed January 18, 2010]

Zinn, H. (1964). *The new abolitionists*. Boston: Beacon Press.

Chapter Four

Symbolic Colonizations

Intersections of "Blackness" and Dis/ability as Negative Ontology in Film

If nations are narrated into being (Anderson, 1983) and if that narration is perpetual, it is imperative that we pay close attention to cultural production and industries. These productions have the capacity both to inform and to be informed by material social policy. Conceptions of the nation are inherently tied to cultural conceptions of the "norm." U.S. history may be narrated solely through the symbolic markers of dis/ability and the black body and the metaphors they've encoded sociohistorically. American literature, science, social sciences, and the peculiarities of its dominant historical reasoning are consistent and unrelenting in the regimentation of citizens toward particular readings of normativeness. Both markers are prominently figured in these texts because the U.S. was constructed from a unique form of racialized reasoning, politics of white supremacy, statehood (and all of the legal frameworks that support it) and imaginations of nation (Anderson, 1983). The pair surface as a result of capitalism's emergent social order and need to (re)produce a culture that sustains the hierarchical relations of power and institutionalized structural inequalities.

The formulation of an ideology of standardness and the "norm" is one of the ideological anchors of capital. Not only does it regiment bodies toward respective geographies of commodity production and manufacture respective consumer desires, it also builds institutions that function to discipline those that fall or resist out of the norm (and repositions the relationship as one a "compassionate capitalism"). The vertical structure of American capitalism is, of course, increasingly transported geopolitically through structural adjustment programs that break down traditional support networks for people with impairments (Talle, 1995). It also deepens the legitimacy of categories and the norm in locations where such structures may not have been as rigid. Contesting and fracturing dominant representation is essential in any space that claims democracy. To sustain a democratic sphere, it is not sufficient that the "ordinary" political structures are democratic (e.g., voting rights, a scripted yet vague list of personal liberties, and so on). Democracies must sustain and perpetually claim a democratic culture, which invariably means institutions that are democratic. Democracy should be a critical praxis that moves through us day to day. We cannot announce an arrival until we are able to imagine the relationships democracy brings into being. Therefore, an engaged, critical spectatorship of representation and contestation of the subordinate relations it (re)produces is vital to citizenship.

We must give props to the spaces of theory from which this chapter builds. Critical feminist theories have deeply examined the sociopolitical, economic, and representational engineering of gender and have pried loose significant space for the theorization of the body's historicity (DeLauretis, 1984, 1987; Shohat, 1994; hooks, 1996). Critical theorists of processes of racialization have also advanced significant theories regarding the subordination of blacks via mainstream media's power to produce meaning culturally (Smith, 1997; Guerrero, 1993; hooks, 1992, 1996). Dis/ability studies have followed with illuminating insights into the hegemony of able-bodiedism (Davis, 1995, 1997; Mitchell & Snyder, 2001; Garland-Thomson, 1997). These works have been analyzed through multiple epistemologies, from psychoanalysis to neo-Marxism to the various post positions. The Frankfurt School has blazed trails with deep and trenchant critique of mass media (Horkheimer & Adorno, 1972), placing it within an analytical frame of capitalism. Canadian scholars of media studies and critical film studies scholars have expanded the discussion of the media as medium and the ideologies it circulates as a grand technology as opposed to merely theorizing its contents (McLuhan, 1964; Innis, 1950). The Centre for Contemporary Cultural Studies has taken up the reflexive nature of production and spectatorship (Hall, 1980). We are also indebted to those theorists working extensively or partly in the field of critical pedagogy and critical education who theorize media as a form of pedagogy sutured to ideology and the assault on democracy (Kellner, 1990; Giroux, 1994, 2003; hooks, 1994). Lastly (and certainly omitting significant work due to lack of space) we credit border theories and critical race theory for analysis that centralizes subordinated (never total) identities and the workings of oppression as they intersect (Anzaldúa, 1987; Crenshaw, 1991).

In the spirit of this awakening of theoretical possibility, we take up the representational intersections of and the ongoing ontological assault on dis/ability and the black body and, by dialectical extension, the normalization of able-bodiedness and whiteness. Although the focus here is on representation and the architecture of language around the intersection of these markers, we must also contemplate and resist the real-lived material effects that these spectacles contribute in producing. Both corporeal markers have been culturally read as aberrations to be subjected to forms of social control. As studies that seek to "gender disability" have illuminated, ability and dis/ability have not been constructed uniformly. Studies that cross the social constructions of dis/ability and race remain at the frontier of theoretical development in dis/ability studies, critical race theory, neo-Marxism, and other paradigms. We cannot proceed without situating some of the terms that constitute the body of this chapter.

Definitions Employed and the Ideological Dimensions of Language

Relationships of power in any space cannot neglect the social and political function of language (Fairclough, 1989). We take up particular definitions of dis/ability and "blackness" so as to align ourselves with people and movements that seek resistance against both symbolic and real-lived violence against the dis/abled and racialized populations. We contend with the definition of any marker of difference that is vacuous in the sense that it does not presuppose a referent. It is possible to talk about difference without signifying what situates difference. We also resist definitions that restrict the natural movement of identities across boundaries. The common identification of "English language learner" in U.S. schools, for example, frames identities in the singular as if one's entire relationship to schooling is defined solely by the acquisition of a language. It also functions to manufacture a social order where any interrogation of the marker in relation to its dialectical relationship to the structural hierarchies of power is diffused. "Learning" signifies an active process in the space of "helping" technologies and institutions. In the space of the institutional discourses of schooling, therefore, an "English language learner" cannot be a "person subordinated linguistically," for example. The experience of subordination invariably calls into question who is doing the subordinating and how does the experience of subordination cut across various identities and hybrid formations. Such framings cannot be tolerated because they undermine power relations and potentially call for solidarities that may rupture it. It also marks the social actor as first and foremost a person. We wouldn't use "colored people" to refer to "people of color," and so should not utilize secondary or tertiary characteristics of people's identity to mark their presence in the social field. Somewhat similar lines of argumentation can be applied to dis/ability and "blackness."

The Merriam-Webster dictionary (2010) defines *disability* as "a.) the condition of being disabled" and "b.) inability to pursue an occupation because of a physical or mental impairment; *also,* a program providing financial support to one affected by disability." The *disabled* are encoded as "incapacitated by illness or injury; *also* physically or mentally impaired in a way that substantially limits activity especially in relation to employment and education." The *American Heritage Dictionary* (The New Second College Edition, 1983) defines *disability* as:

1. lack of adequate power, strength, or physical or mental ability; incapacity. 2. a physical or mental handicap, esp. one that prevents a person from living a full,

normal life or from holding a gainful job. 3. anything that disables or puts one at a disadvantage.

These definitions close off meaning by suffocating the full causation of dis/ability. They fix the boundaries of "disability" in the individual through a discursive lean on personal strategy and abnormality, sustaining the hegemony of normalcy through the attention they place on one's ability to contribute to the "normal" life of schooling and work. Certain questions are not raised: Who decides what normality is, and why are institutions (such schools and the workplace) constructed off of particular epistemologies of "normalcy"? Barnes and Mercer (2003) contend with individualized denotations such as these and claim that "in the individual model, 'disability' is attributed to individual pathology, whereas [a] social model interprets it as the outcome of social barriers and power relations, rather than an inescapable biological destiny" (p.12). The nearest approximation to a social definition in the entry above is the term *disadvantage*. Yet, that also functions to mystify the performance and effects of power, because the dialectical referent is screened out.

Definitions such as those referenced above mobilize certain orders of discourse and invite particular readings into dis/ability and the politics of disablement. They both construct the current institutional and cultural violence done to the dis/abled and are (re)constructed and (re)legitimized by those realities. Change happens largely through language. We must become conscious of definitions and conscientious in resisting those definitions that place populations in peril at the societal and institutional level. The stakes aren't merely semantic or symbolic— what we situate here is just one fraction of a social struggle over orders of discourse (Fairclough, 1989), which is essential in legitimizing dominant power. They mobilize certain public desires and disabling interactions that do not require force or coercion (Gramsci, 1971) as much as carefully constructed linguistic parameters. Rosemarie Thomson (1997) has lucidly defined *dis/ability* as

> a reading of bodily particularities in the context of social power relations. . . . [D]isability is a representation, a cultural interpretation of physical transformation or configuration, and a comparison of bodies that structures social relations and institutions. Disability, then, is the attribution of corporeal deviance—not

> so much a property of bodies as a product of cultural rules about what bodies should be or do. (p. 6)

We utilize the slash in *dis/ability* purposely to draw the reader into a reading that disturbs "ability" and culturally conceptualized bodily and mental normalcy. Impairment isn't dis/abling. Dis/ability, the translation of impairment into policies and cultural life largely defined by able-bodied people, is the conditions that (re)structure a dis/abling society. We simultaneously refract the able-bodied gaze of the dis/abled into language to signify the need for positive political projects that are centered on a reading of dis/ability as an ideological category that sustains harm not only for people who are disabled, but also for those who are able-bodied. For example, it is quite common for the able-bodied to dismiss equalizing the built environment to accommodate people who are impaired (if they do not dismiss it explicitly, then they certainly do through an insidious form of social constructed "not seeing"). The argument is that there are just certain spaces that the impaired cannot enter. Similarly, in a patriarchal society it might be said that there are just some forms of work not suitable for women—firefighting, for example. Rarely is it considered that the very technologies utilized in the built environment and the workplace were originally engineered on the basis of the imagination of the "normal" body (i.e., male and able-bodied). If these technologies had been subject to truly democratic imaginations initially, work and space would have been encoded in radically different way, making them safer and more productive for all. Furthermore, the social construction of able-bodiedness positions the dominant in zones of capitalist exploitation as people strive toward invidious consumption in order to attain an "ideal" and unrealistic image. This venture is doubly oppressive for women because the images are anchored to real lived social violence at the hands of men.

The orders of discourse (re)produced by definitions of dis/ability as solely a bodily condition allows for disabling concepts to enter everyday language and position people who are dis/abled as less than human. Take, for example, "lame ideas, blind justice, dumb luck, paralyzed wills, deaf ears, crippling traffic, and idiotic relatives" (Snyder, Brueggemann, & Garland-Thomson, 2002, p. 1). The circulation in schools of the term retarded to refer to anything negative is quite wide, and so is the lack of critical reflection behind such insults as "riding the short bus." Our very day-to-day metaphors serve to re-enforce the myth of bodily "norms" and "averages" and to cloud the institutional practices, policies, and cultures that subordinate the dis/abled. Even when attacks are rendered regarding an oppositional ideology, references to dis/abling terms are often employed. Glenn Beck, for example, has referred to progressive movements as "diseases and cancers," and said that their only role is to eat "our" Constitution. These metaphorical encodings are actually quite common in the language of multiple ideological positions. In the conservative imagination, however, the symbolic link between impairment and the coded subtext of whiteness as a norm is quite obvious.

Yet, beyond these articulations, what is most damaging is the integration of this language into legal frameworks that firmly establish a reading of dis/ability as bodies and minds out of control, in need of rehabilitation, and subject to market forces that abstract dis/ability movements and communities into the formulation of policy. The Individuals with Disability Education Act (IDEA), the premier legislation regarding dis/ability and education, presents many constraints in that it relies on definitions that are highly individualized. This effectively challenges our reading of the dis/abled as the largest minority group in the U.S. (Norden, 1994), for example: They exist as individuals and not a community. The self-advocacy language IDEA articulates presents problems for those whose cultural conception of family and advocacy differ. It also structures institutions in ways in which professionals revictimize families by coding them as dysfunctional.

The conventional definition of dis/ability creates other orders of discourses and realities. The ascendancy of the impairment-medical-industrial complex has been built from this rhetoric. In this terrain, dis/ability is a sickness or defect that must be cured through medical intervention. This definition of disability (a very common one in the west and increasingly circulated worldwide) invariably creates oppressive conditions through which those who fall under its label are subjected to control and containment under medical authority. Of course, there is also the "liberal" reconstruction definition, connected to the medical model, which constructs dis/ability as a deficiency to be fixed through rehabilitation. The definition that we privilege here is one that refuses to push structural hierarchies of power off the discursive map.

We write of the "black body" and "blackness" interchangeably. We resist the use of the term of reference in connection to the (re)structuring of essentialized identity categories. Within any space of identity formation, there exists divergence, particularly when taking into account the historicity and geographic context. The "black body" and "blackness" therefore signify a metaphor embedded in the respective sociohistorical context and cultural narrative (here the reference is to the U.S.) and expressed through the politics of racialized representations. It is a socially constructed reading of bodily characteristics within the context of power relations. Darnell Moore (2009) conceptualizes it, as we do, as "contested figures, signs, metaphors, as opposed to fixed typologies, unalterable essences or identities as determinative physiological distinctions" (p. 178). Its perpetuation serves the project of dialectically (re)constructing the hegemony of whiteness/white supremacy and restituting forms of identity formation, which may very well be essentialized, in the contestation of whiteness (as we've seen in the various anthropologies of black power movements in U.S. history). Our interest here is in the analysis of the use of these markers in the service of engineering and sustaining negative representations and relations of power.

The authors interrogate their intersection to make more transparent the predatory symbolic devices, sociohistorical scripts, and cultural narratives that the dominant utilize to sustain the "hegemony of normalcy" (Davis, 1995) by transacting the images against one another. The attempt here is not to fix yet another boundary in the study of "Othered" representations and realities. Rather, we seek the restitution (always an ongoing project) of the most critical of subversive agendas by analyzing elements that may be "pushed off the map" and theorizing the ways in which their analytical inclusion speaks to deeper forms of insurgency. In the end, we are less drawn to the politics of paradigmatic territorialisation, and realize that moving through the particularities of difference and its intersections means the expansion of democracy into cultural life; again, a necessary condition if we are to speak of democracy at all.

Hollywood's slant on dis/ability and "blackness" is pervasive

through all genres. The "Afro-Americanization" of U.S. and global popular culture (West, 1993) has invariably meant the widespread use of
black bodies as texts that contribute forcefully to the narrativization of
storylines as a whole. These representations are fully connected to corporate visions and dominant ideologies because their primary symbolic use is to sell and draw on sociohistoric racialized formations and
reasoning in the effort to license whiteness as normative state of being
(though not always consciously). As Michel Foucault (1972) would have
it, "the body is the inscribed surface of events" (p. 143). Granted, spaces
of resistance exist in transgressive independent productions and even
within certain spaces of the mainstream. The latter is overshadowed and
the former have considerably less power to circulate, though both open
up a challenge to the hegemony of normality as long as pedagogical projects are built alongside.

The use of people with physical and mental impairments in film and
literature is also pervasive. The survival of film, in its early stages,
meant taking up popular literature of the day and converting it into visual spectacles, particularly given the widespread protests of the treatment
of taboo social subjects (Norden, 1994). The exchanges between media
also meant mimicry of the representations of the dis/abled. With film,
however, the negative images were amplified given the visual effects.
Paul Darke (1998) cites notable examples in film:

> My Left Foot and Annie's Coming Out (cerebral palsy); Passion Fish, The
> Waterdance, The Raging Moon and Born on the Fourth of July (paraplegia);
> Breaking the Waves and Whose Life is it Anyway? (quadriplegia); Children of
> a Lesser God and Johnny Belinda (deafness); Pride of the Marines and Torch
> Song (blindness); The Best Years of Our Lives, Johnny Got His Gun (amputa-
> tion/war injury); The Elephant Man (bodily deformity); and Rain Man and The
> Eighth Day (mental impairment)...Moby Dick (amputee); Freaks
> (deformity/restricted growth); The Story of Alexander Graham Bell and The
> Tingler (deafness). (p. 132)

Darke's exploration of film led him to the conclusion that the recurring
representations warrant the identification of a new genre, namely, "the
normality genre." These genres do symbolic violence to the impaired as
well as to the able-bodied, although in different ways and degrees. We
see that through the setting of parameters and validation regarding the

constitution of "normality." He therefore resists the call for a politics of *tolerance* or positive representations of the disabled, because this would be ineffective in countering "normality," in favor of *respect* for difference on its own terms. We would cast the argument in a wider terrain of engagement and claim that *any* film is already a film that would qualify in the genre. The absence of an impaired character does not negate the existence of the embedded ideology of able-bodiedness and "normative" corporeality. David Mitchell and Sharon Snyder (2001) are insightful in stating that

> one cannot narrate the story of a healthy body...without the contrastive device of disability to bear out the symbolic potency of the message. The materiality of metaphor via disabled bodies gives all bodies a tangible essence, in that the healthy corporeal surface fails to achieve its symbolic effect without its disabled counterpart. (p. 28)

Although Darke's position is quite illuminating, we must also make more transparent the discursive and representational mechanisms at work through diverse film genres (and literary genres). There might be similarities of images across genres. Differences also exist and audiences are already predisposed to certain receptions given the genre of engagement. Capitalism remains the biggest producer of culture, and its launching of film genres isn't only about service at the altar of profit (although that is its strongest concern). It's also about manufacturing desire. Destabilizing dominant regimes is not in the interest of most "mainstream" filmmakers.

Abstracted from the majority of work on the representation of dis/ability is its relationship to racialization and particularly its framing of "blackness." Analysis of these alignments (and others) is critical because the (re)building of a sustainable dis/ability movement requires that borders be crossed and alliances formed (indeed, that is the life blood of any contemporary movement). Insulating respective movements means bringing less to bear on institutional life and losing significant populations along the way. There has been considerable effort made in the dis/abled people's movement to exclude other markers of liminality because dis/ability needed more visibility in the face of earlier movements that failed to engage it (Campbell & Oliver, 1996).

Scholarly work also has followed the same trajectory. Ayesha Vernon (1998) observes that "it is the fact that in all the numerous discussions and textbooks on disability, issues of 'race,' gender, class, sexuality and age have been either omitted as irrelevant to disabled people's lives or added on as an optional extra" (p. 206).

When Hollywood produces competition programming that seeks amusement in the very precipice of survival on some remote Pacific island (e.g., *Survivor* and the like), it simultaneously functions to manufacture desire for a certain able-bodiedness (despite the absence of the dis/abled) and erase the immiseration of billions of people struggling to survive in their respective geographies. Resistance to the "normative" representation therefore must not be built from atomistic analysis of one axis of difference, but rather multiple axes.

Because the location of this chapter is a work on education, we will begin with a brief sketch regarding the relationship between the wider need for analysis of film representation, its pedagogical power through the production of popular texts, and its centeredness in cultural imperialism. We make this last move for three reasons. First, to think through counter-representations would necessarily mean the need to decenter U.S. and Western cultural imperialism. Second, it is a myth to assume that scholarly work (particularly those tied to the hegemony of English) is implicated only in the space of the "nation." Third, theorizing film within the boundaries of imperialism and colonialism is no stretch at all. The beginning of film coincides with the growth of nationalism and the height of imperialism (Shohat, 1994; Stam, 2000). The medium therefore has a history tied to negative representation of the "Othered" and the imperialist impulse. Histories are important. We will follow with a definition of the various markers of engagement employed and analysis of several Hollywood texts and the complex ways they encode dis/ability and the black body. Lastly, we will look at ways in which pedagogical projects may be built alongside these productions in the effort to reframe the image and contemplate more democratic arrangements at the levels of representation and everyday material reality. To remain solely at the level of intellectual interrogation in the face of the symbolic violence(s) produced amounts to a standpoint that Joy James (1996) has called "the low threshold of political courage" (p. 3).

Cinema as Colonial Curriculum
for Classroom Contestation

The dismantling of dominant ideologies traveling through Hollywood cinematic productions continues to be of immense importance to education and anti-imperialism. Donaldo Macedo and Lilia Bartolomé (1999) insightfully observe that

> academia needs to understand that the popular press and the mass media educate more people about issues regarding ethnicity and race [and other markers of difference and their intersections] than all other sources of education available to U.S. citizens. By shunning the mass media, educators are missing the obvious: that is, that more public education is done by the media than by teachers, professors, and anyone else. (p. 223)

As state- and school district–sanctioned texts are critically examined for their complicity in corporatizing education (Kohn & Shannon, 2002; Molnar, 2005; Saltman, 2000; Leistyna, 2010) and transmitting dominant ideologies, we sometimes neglect the power of spectacles embedded in film at circulating those same interests. The most expansive incursion into the curriculum by corporations is mass media. They rationalize and justify virtually every aspect of dominant social relations despite the occasional cracks of agency. It would be a misstatement to claim that they operate outside of schooling, because their uncritical integration (particularly Disney films) circulates within schools. Sadly, the students who bear the greatest social cost for the media's unexamined integration are those already materially marginalized within the life of schooling (e.g., emergent bilinguals, those categorized as having a dis/ability, the "lower" tracks, etc.). Film and media are often utilized as forms of social control or, as one teacher recently put it, "a way to civilize them." Ironically, those who are often dismissed as unable to focus during classroom instruction (transmission pedagogies) are "civilized" when presented with film. Of course, the manufacturing of conservative and consumerist desire goes on well beyond the walls of schools.

In this current restoration of vicious U.S. conservativism, lethal U.S. nationalism, and the most arrogant of imperialisms, we must not limit our analysis of educational and curricular issues solely to what is so often imposed in schools. As the conservative alliance continues to produce and distribute in schools standardized texts and curricular materials that speak to neoliberal, conservative, authoritarian populism and new managerial middle-class sentiments (Apple, 2001), other public spheres are also plagued by conservative movements. The criminal justice establishment with its mandatory minimum sentencing also suggests standardization in the effort to police black, brown, and white working-class "bodies." It is vital that we also pursue an intersectional analysis of public spheres (e.g., schooling/criminal justice, curriculum/film). Substantial and important work has been done on representational politics in film by educational theorists (Giroux, 1989, 1994, 2003; hooks, 1992, 1996). The analysis of film and other popular cultural forms needs to continue not only in light of a politics of deconstruction and resistant and subversive reading, but also as a springboard whereby we create concrete action to counter those representations that perpetuate asymmetrical relations of power. We need to further theorize the fact that education is not limited to schooling.

A great deal of education happens outside of schools. James Lowen's insightful contribution *Lies My Teacher Told Me* (1995) eloquently points out the omissions and classic American fairy tales embedded within history textbooks. However, missing from the analysis is a more in-depth definition of "text" as anything that encodes meaning. While critiquing the "text," we need to remember Hollywood's textual power on the public's imagination and how it has already largely paved the way for conservative readings of historical, political, economic, and social conditions. It is not only youths entering classrooms with dominant theories of U.S. and world history gleamed from films; policy makers also are both captivated and capitalize on the pushing of racialized, classed, and ableist policy that reads youth as out of control—an image fully exploited by Hollywood and media in general through encodings of the hegemony of normalcy.

The "mainstream" U.S. film community wields great power in (re)circulating negative images and discourses of those who bear the social cost (both inside and outside the U.S.), and thereby assisting in the formation of rules, norms, and conventions by which social life is ordered and governed. Given the overwhelming control the U.S. media exercises over the manufacturing of "Othered" representations on a global scale, a critique of and resistance to the dominant discourses and practices of Hollywood necessarily speaks to an active anti-imperialist engagement. Hollywood and U.S. controlled media in general are major players in U.S.-led corporate globalization and imperialism. As Robert McChesney (1999) has pointed out, "the global media market has come to be dominated by the same eight transnational corporations, or TNCs, that rule U.S. media: General Electric, AT&T/Liberty Media, Disney, Time Warner, Sony, News Corporation, Viacom and Seagram, plus Bertelsmann, the Germany-based conglomerate" (p. 5).The overwhelming majority of Hollywood studios are owned by one of these conglomerates.

Despite the global connections and the power of the U.S. "mainstream" film industry, I would agree with critics who have attested that film criticism tends to be very U.S.- and Hollywood-centered and who have called for transnationalizing the media studies curriculum (Shohat & Stam, 2003). Given that the majority of films produced in the world are produced in Asia, Africa, and Latin America, it is of great importance to theorize the ways in which the politics of representation embedded in these films (especially if they are "non-mainstream") speak to different dominant ideologies or/and perhaps challenge Hollywood/U.S.-centric representations. This sort of analysis would more likely lead us into what Edward Said (1993) has called a "contrapuntal" reading of media representations. It would allow us a better lens to view not only dominant discursive formations in Hollywood, but also how these codings are contested by marginalized directors, writers, and actors. Although this type of reading is critically needed, our concern in this paper focuses on a major omission in critical film critiques of Hollywood—the representational alignments of black bodies and dis/ability, and by dialectical engagement, "whiteness" and able-bodiedness. Furthermore, we are also concerned with the production and (re)production of ableist/racist discourses and institutional policies that materialize to some extent on the shoulders of Hollywood codes (a major pedagogical machine). Barnes and Mercer (2003) cite Busfield (1996) in stating that "particular groups, including black people and women, disproportionally attract specific psychiatric labels such as 'schizophrenia' and 'depression' respectively" (p. 4). The manner through which Hollywood encodes intersections of "blackness" and dis/ability invariably speaks to the racialization of special needs and to the "normative" status so often assigned to schools within schools that function to incarcerate black and brown bodies.

Institutional and Symbolic Scars
in Dangerous Times

A double subordination exists both at the level of dominant cultural representation and institutionally lived realities when these markers are intersected. Similarly, double invisibilities exist when images of people who are gay and lesbian are transacted with spectacles of impairment (Corbett, 1994). Scholars who have taken up studies of the life histories and ethnographies of people who are dis/abled and black and case studies of their care have pointed out that reading their identities as separate is problematic given that their realities are shaped by structures of normative whiteness and abled-bodiedness simultaneously (Vernon, 1998) even though one of these realities may be more situated in a respective oppressive interaction than another. At times, both embodied imaginations may be at work—as in the case of a person who is black and dis/abled in the presence of a majority white able-bodied group or institution structured around that particular way of being in the world— and at other times only one—the same person in the presence of dis/abled populations who are in the racial majority, or in the presence of blacks who are in the abled-bodied majority. Although the media images consistently cross the identities in the effort to position spectators in a dominant reading of both embodied realities, rarely does the media engage the implicated social effects and institutional dehumanization.

Comparatively, Native Americans have the highest rate of dis/ability in the U.S., followed by African Americans and Latinas and Latinos (U.S. Census, 2000). African Americans have the highest rate of severe impairments (Bradsher, 1996). Not surprisingly, dis/ability is also associated with poverty, according to the census. It is important to note that the techniques employed in media and film regarding people who are black and dis/abled also affect other racialized populations, given the sociohistoric trajectory of the U.S. as a non-color–gradient society and the totalizing ideology that positions those outside of whiteness as invariably "black." Furthermore, the representations of "blackness" serve to uphold the normalcy of whiteness against which all other markers transact. African American women have a higher rate of dis/ability than men because their life expectancy is higher, and they experience the greatest difficulty in securing employment of any group. African Americans are doubly discriminated against, on the basis of race and because of employer's fears of high insurance premiums due to dis/ability status. The structured suffering of the dis/abled, particularly people of color, requires engaged responses at multiple locations. The politics of imagery and framing of language becomes just one site of contestation and one that should never be abstracted from others. The counter-discourses to the power of film encoding are just one path toward the deconstruction of the social effects of living in a nondisabled majority society.

Particular cultural products and images are shaped by the sociohistoric context (Norden, 1994). Norden succinctly traces out the historic counters of the edification and commodification of the dis/abled image in Hollywood film, or what he calls the "Cinema of Isolation," and ends (also by way of initiation) by pointing out that some positive moves have been made:

[T]he Cinema of Isolation has demonstrated a general sense of progress, a sense that will perhaps be more detectable if we divide the movie depictions into three general historical eras: the medium's origins to the late 1930's, the World War II years into the 1970's, and the 1970's through today. Films from the first period gravitated toward the highly exploitative, with their characters not much more than comic stick-figures, freakish beasts, or pitiable objects. Films from the second frequently had an exploratory quality, in which the characters' disabilities and struggles to overcome them take center stage. The third tended to feature movies that dealt with disability in more of an incidental way, in which rehabilitation issues often take a back seat to other concerns such as fighting for social justice, sexually expressing one's self, and simply getting on with day-to-day life. Though this history has been marked by frequent slippage back to the older forms of expression, the general movement from

exploitative treatments to exploratory to incidental does suggest a slowly
developing enlightenment on issues of physical disability. (1994, p. 314)

Underdeveloped in Norden's work, however, is the representational
interaction of race and dis/ability. He does take up an intersectional
analysis, but privileges gender and dis/ability by way of psychoanalyt-
ic engagement. He makes significant points regarding how the merging
of the two in one bodily reality signals the maintenance of a phallocen-
tric society, yet has little to say regarding the (re)architecture of white
supremacy and ableism based on the black impaired image.

In the case of the intersectionality of "blackness" and dis/ability, the
most important point of analytical entry is the era of the pseudoscience
of *eugenics* (early 20th century), a term meaning "good birth" coined by
the English scientist Frances Galton in 1883. Clearly, the ascent of this
practice and the theories that informed it (pioneered in the U.S. and
England) unleashed lethal forms of structured suffering and human
rights violations from cultural marginalization, immigration restrictions
(and the encoding of certain groups of immigrants as inferior), segregation, institutionalization, sterilization of "unfit" groups, euthanasia, and
mass exterminations such as those carried out by the Nazis. Sadly, the
remnants of these visions haven't disappeared, particularly if we examine its materialization in film representation. Their symbolic presence is
felt in institutional policies and practices (e.g., schools' standardization
practices that focus only on measureable and observable aspects of
behavior, and embryo selection procedures,) that seductively utilize
code words to refer to the inferiority of respective groups of people
(e.g., the dis/abled, immigrants, gays, lesbians, blacks, and the poor) and
large-scale violence based on the reading of certain bodies as less than
human. The horror of this pseudoscience and the atrocities it spurred
and continue to spur have been documented, and brilliant work continues to uncover their current manifestations and impacts. We will dispense with further framing of context and just say that this movement
also had profound impact regarding the cultural representation of the
black body and the dis/abled. Both culture and the deadly realities
inflicted informed and sustained each other's conception of the norm.

The landmark film *The Birth of a Nation* (released in 1915), based on
Thomas Dixon's *The Clansman*, introduced innovative techniques in the

technology of film and (re)ushered in vehement forms of racism and terrorism applauded by the likes of Woodrow Wilson and resisted by the
NAACP, W.E.B. Du Bois, the film director Oscar Micheaux, and rioting
protestors. The centralizing theme of the film was white anxiety over
contamination of white purity and its monumental significance to the
maintenance of the connection between whiteness, American identity,
and nation. *The Birth of a Nation* didn't invent these orders of discourses: They were let loose with the founding of the new liberal nation-
state and the discourses of the leaders behind its establishment (with
Thomas Jefferson as its key spokesperson). The highest grossing film of
the silent era, it also set the stage for the authorship of the visual
voyeurism of the black body (at least with regards to the technologies
of film—the black body as a spectacle was already on full display on the
slave block, systematic political terrorism of lynching, and lynch parties).

The Black Stork, released in 1917, was produced by Dr. Harry
Haiselden, who also had a feature part in the film. Haiselden was a
eugenicist surgeon who refused to treat babies born with severe birth
defects. The film served as propaganda for eugenics and euthanasia
and was re-released in 1927 under the title *Are You Fit to Marry?* The filmmaker Laura Kissel (2009) claims that the film had a "'better dead than
disabled' attitude, which remains a popular response to disability" (p.
33). Kissel also analyzes the techniques employed in the film: "The iris
motif, a black background with the disabled body encircled in the center of a field of blackness, guides the viewer to look toward the disfig-
urement, and objectifies the body" (p. 33). She goes on to analyze the
written textual production in the intertitles (today this convention is
rarely present in film; the soundtrack is used in lieu in the mobilization
of emotions that function in the Othering of the "abnormal"). One inter-
title reads: "You can blame the Black Stork for much of crime, poverty
and misery. The White stork brings us the babies that should make for
a nation of power" (1916, paper print; in Kissel, 2009, p. 33).

The signifying power of "blackness" in the *The Black Stork* is tremen-
dous, so much so that the film is the first powerful connection to be made
in the intersectional analysis of dis/ability, blackness, the reading of
the social scene, and the narration of the nation, at least in motion pictures. The interesting point here is that "blackness" is presented even

when the black body is absent. Borrowing from the term "persistence of vision" (meaning the technical process of viewing the movement of frames), what we have here is the persistence of ideological imagery. The producer of *The Black Stork* is capitalizing on the social anxieties already in play after the production of *The Birth of a Nation*. "Blackness" is not embodied physically, but it is present in the form of a semiotic technique. Since the production of *The Black Stork,* these techniques continue to be employed in the form of camera angle and lighting, and are used primarily to signal deviance and criminality. Hence, blackness is present even when it is corporeally absent. Paul Longmore (2003) documents this in analyzing the popular 1980s British miniseries *The Jewel in the Crown* (also broadcast in the U.S.). He states,

> like Dr. No, Doctor Strangelove, and a number of other maimed or amputee bad guys, he acquires a black leather-covered prosthetic limb. This dramatic device recurs frequently enough that one begins to wonder about the psychosexual significance of the connection between blackness, badness, amputation, and artificial arms. (p. 134)

D.W. Griffith's symbolic inscription of impairment within the representation of the black body is also noteworthy. The monumental technical achievements of *The Birth of a Nation* came largely as a result of disfiguring the black body (of course, all the major roles were taken on by white actors in black face) and refiguring the white able-bodied as the norm—a pervasive technique because what we are considering is a silent film that must necessarily highlight the image. The symbolic play is also evident when we consider the history of the producer. D.W. Griffith's ideological disposition was toward a rewriting of the nation as one that is rigidly white, able-bodied, and patriarchal. His conservative attitudes toward the dis/abled were on full display before *The Birth of a Nation*. In 1906 he produced the play *A Fool and a Girl*, which vehemently marginalized people who are blind through the play of metaphor. According to Norden (1994), "Griffith directed at least fourteen films . . . that dealt with physical disability...They ranged from primitive references...to relatively sustained levels of stereotyping" (p. 41). His ideological position on dis/ability is certainly in play in his representation of blacks, particularly when considering his history.

Of course, the cultural construction of blacks as dis/abled has a longer history in the discourses of scientific racism (genetic inferiority) and cultural dysfunction. These discourses are firmly entrenched in post-Renaissance literatures of Europe. The U.S. physician Samuel Cartwright attempted to codify a dis/ability he termed "drapetomania" in the early 1850s. Cartwright believed that it was a mental disorder that caused blacks to want to run away from slavery. One of its symptoms was the slave's resistance to "service," and one of its causes was the willingness of the master to make slaves too comfortable. An effective treatment of the impairment involved prompt and harsh beatings. These forms of scientific racisms have a deep history in Western discourse. Sadly, they are not behind us. Contemporary research continues to traffic in endeavors such as examination of supposed cultural and genetic inferiorities of people of color. Schools continue to advocate that students of color and poor students (disproportionately represented in special needs programs) be medicated. Such treatment is largely an act of silencing counter-discourses and resistance to racialized and classed institutional spaces.

The space of this chapter will not allow us a full historical treatment of the subject. Although we will reference historicity in what follows, our preference is analysis of film just prior to and following the landmark Americans with Disabilities Act (ADA) of 1990. We contemplate the representations in light of progressive (albeit very late) advances in the sphere of public accessibility and prohibitions against workplace discrimination. Yet, we read the times as dangerous, given the regressive oppression of vertical structures of capitalism, its erasure of public space, its propensity to unwinnable and unending wars, and the current financial crisis it has shaped. Of course, for blacks and the dis/abled, financial crisis is no stranger, given their historical existence on the economic cliffs and lifelines of the United States.

The similarities in the ways that both the black body and dis/ability are taken up in films are quite striking. Given the dominant coding of black and dis/abled people, what is particularly striking is the way that "mainstream" filmmakers play the images off each other to amplify dominant representational forms. These representations are by no means stagnant, however. It is necessary that the media constantly be repositioned so as to avoid and evade counter-discourses and reassert its power at hegemonizing a public that must necessarily be indoctrinated and averted from understanding power relations (in which the media is obviously implicated). The fact that the media must constantly reshift its discourse points to public engagement and critique rather than passive viewing and acquiescence. When analyzing these sociohistorical discursive shifts of the image, one begins to realize how incredibly destructive and organized is the shaping of oppression in the United States, particularly in its power to produce meaning, culture, and identity. (This process is always a precursor to the physical containment and deathly realities of colonialism—genocide, lynchings, the militarization of society, the enslavement of people, economic exploitation, environmental degradation, the building of the prison industrial complex, the systematic policing and attempts at erasure of counter-hegemonic narratives, and so on.) When such production is anchored to an immense technological superiority, the U.S. media establishment can instantly (re)legitimize and (re)encode certain ways of speaking, ways of seeing, and ways of being, not only nationally but globally.

Also, the representations of subordinated Others are never neat, never without tension, and never lacking the process of a certain negotiation with the periphery. We struggle with our own imaginations of "mainstream," as the center is constantly being moved through its very mediation with fluid peripheral discursive constructions and reconstructions. Through an analysis of this centric movement, it is quite clear that representations of the Other are increasingly more complex. One of the angles of complexity is rooted in the narrative slant on the simultaneous comparison and contrast of multiple "Othered" bodies and associated sensibilities in the effort to construct and reconstruct ontological normativeness. Although a full examination of this is beyond the scope of this work, we would venture to establish a link between such explicit plays on representation and the anxieties engendered in the dominant as multiple "Othered" counter-narratives emerged particularly in the civil rights movements of the 1960s and early 1970s (e.g., the African American civil rights movement, women's movement, American Indian movement, and disability rights movement, to name few). In the face of such multiple pushing of the center, it becomes necessary to reorganize dominant discourse for the counter-offensive. Such reorganization becomes evident both in the public sphere and in symbolic cultural productions.

Analysis of media texts must always be embedded in analysis of context. The films we analyze don't speak for themselves, but rather speak to familiar wider relations of power. In reading the texts, there is an unconscious play working to both activate and disturb history, culture, and memory, leaving us with the sense that what is there, despite its instability, has been "already written down elsewhere" (Lacan, 1968, p. 21). Our social movement is always mediated through social scripts or background narratives.

Our effort here is to focus in on the very architecture of films depicting dis/ability and "blackness" by analyzing the intentions of the filmmakers. To zoom in, we also have to inevitably zoom out and interrogate the sociohistoric and cultural context(s) of their productions. All art responds to and reflects the cultural context of its production. The meaning of a specific text does not live only in that text, but comes from somewhere. Filmmakers (like all producers of aesthetics) always initiate their aesthetics with the imagination of a certain audience type, a certain social context. Despite efforts to resist such a move, total escape is not possible. In this imaginary, there is always an effort to position audiences in certain ways (otherwise, the art would not encode any meaning). Lacan (1968) illuminates the play on certain notions of the "unconscious" in the effort to position the audiences:

> The unconscious is that...which is marked by a blank or occupied by a falsehood: it is the censored chapter. But the Truth can be found again; it is most often already written down elsewhere. That is to say: in monuments...in archival documents...in semantic evolution...in traditions...and in the linking of the chapters surrounding it. (p. 21)

Lacan correctly situates the reading of any cultural text as a negotiation between the intention of the author (i.e., filmmaker) and the respective ideological dispositions and experiences of spectators. Yet, the suggestion here isn't that all readings are trivial given individualized meaning-making psychological processes; rather, we situate a reading of the text as it indexes and also works on the context.

Much of what directors/producers say concerning the creation of films is not left at the level of unproblematized statements. They too live in the current cultural context, and reproduce (perhaps at times unconsciously) the same ideological manipulation via discourses and signifying systems. As Rosemarie Thomson states,

> not only is the relationship between text and the world not exact, but Representation also relies upon cultural assumptions to fill in the missing details. All people construct interpretive schemata that make their worlds seem knowable and predictable, thus producing perceptual categories that may harden into stereotypes or caricatures when communally shared and culturally inculcated. (Thomson, 1997, p. 32)

Such productions are never innocent. These texts are always produced and reproduced within asymmetrical power relations, and in the final analysis we must ask in whose service and benefit are the texts working. What regime(s) of truth does the narrative lean against and support? Normal Fairclough (1995) is very much correct when he asserts that "the invisibility of...power relations which underlie the practices...helps to sustain those power relations" (p. 309).

Very few Hollywood films take up the intersection of race and dis/ability explicitly, yet the two are always operative because they exist in dialectical relationship to encodings of the "norm." The reality is that all films produced within the U.S. are essentially about constructions of "blackness" and "whiteness," given that the very formation of the "nation" (another construct operative in all films) relates to the sociohistoric tensions with and oppression of the raced Other, and anxieties over abnormal bodies in the imaginations of the able-bodied. All mainstream films, despite the existence of black or dis/abled characters, are about the mobilization of a desire for "whiteness" and "able-bodiness" and other states of normalcy. When the two do appear, the characters are not normally centered as main characters in the narrative, but rather as peripheral "props" who function to uphold normative ways of being by mobilizing able-bodied desires. The explicit play on this intersection is recent and speaks to the changing nature of the dis/abled and black image on film.

The motivation behind representations of difference is always dialectical. In interrogating the dis/abled and black body, one is always simultaneously engaging the process by which the dominant encode a certain oppressor image, which never materializes on the surface but is embedded and reflected off the image and discursive formation of the Other. This production of meaning, culture, and identity is captured forcibly in Edward Said's (1978) *Orientalism*. It was necessary for westerners to construct an image of the Near and Far East, or, as Said puts it, "[deal] with it by making statements about it, authorizing views on it, describing it, by teaching it, settling it, ruling over it" (p. 43). The process is quite similar to the identity markers investigated in this paper. The representations function to re-inscribe domination not only from the top down, but also through the very manufacturing of consent of those it dehumanizes. The effort therefore is not only to simply dominate, but also to mobilize the desire for an ontological normativeness.

In any analysis of representation, it is important to analyze not only the image but also the language surrounding the image. Stuart Hall (1997) captures this connection in *Representation: Cultural Representations and Signifying Practices* when he says

> representation is the production of meaning through language. This is how you give meaning to things through language. This is how you "make sense of" the world of people, objects, and events, and how you are able to express a complex thought about those things to other people, or communicate about them through language in ways which other people are able to understand. (pp. 16–17)

It is not language per se that oppresses, therefore, but the meanings that are socially constructed, then fixed/encoded via signifying practices. What oppresses/colonizes are the socially constructed codes that we come to internalize. Lacan (1968) also moves in this direction. We will make reference repeatedly not only to the image but also to the language surrounding the image in two films, *The Bone Collector* (1999) and *Unbreakable* (2000).

The Bone Collector and the Biopolitics of Black and Dis/abled Sexuality

The Bone Collector presents an exceptional rupture in representation because here we have a dis/abled and black lead character embodied by Denzel Washington, a hyper-sexualized leading man of U.S. film. The title of this section suggests a dominant theme in the film, yet, several moves are made in intersectional representation in the film. Given the power of circulation, a plot summary follows.

The film opens up in 1990s New York City, and we are immediately introduced to Lincoln Rhyme (Denzel Washington), who is struggling to squeeze his body into a small crevice in order to investigate the homicide of a police officer. When he finds the corpse, he turns its over and sees that the corpse is himself. As he comes to this realization, he looks up and notices a massive beam coming down on him. The beam nearly cuts him in half. Four years pass, and we shift to an apartment in the west side of Manhattan where Rhyme is confined to a bed and cared for primarily by an African American nurse named Thelma (Queen Latifah). In this scene several characters are introduced. We meet Richard, a medical technology specialist who inspects Rhyme's medical equipment. We also meet Barry, Rhyme's doctor friend, whom Rhyme convinces to assist him in his final transition (suicide) by the end of the week. Rhyme has come to this decision after four years of disreflexia seizures (a result of a buildup of fluid in the spine that leads to a degenerative condition), which are becoming more intense and could at any time turn him into a "vegetable," as he states.

In the next scene we meet Amelia Donaghy (Angelina Jolie), who is introduced through a sexual encounter with a white male. Amelia does not want to commit to the relationship whereas the male character does; after this scene we are not certain if this relationship continues or not. We then note that Amelia is a police officer, and she rushes to a call made by a child. She uncovers a corpse and proceeds to take photographs of the crime scene. As a result of her natural talent for forensics (as Rhyme sees it) she is relieved of her duties in the youth unit and made to work a case of a serial killer against her will and at the recommendation of

Lincoln Rhyme. Rhyme is considered to be one of the top forensics experts in the country.

An incredible amount of technology is placed at the fingertips of Rhyme, who proceeds to work the murder mystery. However, he cannot work it solely with his brilliance—he needs an abled-bodied person through whom he works the homicide scenes. This person becomes Amelia, as he constantly encourages her as she investigates gruesome murders by stating, "I'm with you every step of the way." Throughout the movie we sense sexual tension between Rhyme and Amelia, and at one point it involves a physical encounter (touching).

At the very end of the movie we learn that the killer is the medical technician, who was really a police officer whose career was ruined due to an expert forensic testimony by Rhyme years earlier. Amelia rushes in just as Rhyme is about to be murdered, and she kills the villain. The film closes with a Christmas scene where we see Rhyme in a wheelchair next to Amelia. It appears that the two are a couple, though that is left ambiguous.

The Bone Collector is complex in many ways. First, it is based on a series of novels by Jeffery Deaver, who has a history of using dis/ability in his work. At the conceptual level we must understand the film as a derivative work (it utilizes the original literary text and subjects it to changes). As both the novel and the film are texts whose technologies of production differ (as they must, due to differences in the media), interesting questions of authorship, elision (sacrificing details from the literary text due to limits on the film's running time), interpolation (the mixing of literary material from a series of works), and adaptation surface. The level of reception produces interesting analysis given the sharing of an existing commercial audience. This provides for analysis regarding spaces of nonengagement or textual misrepresentations that shed light on the cross-textual treatment of dis/ability and the framing of "blackness." Second, like any film, it exists within the discursive frame of a genre. In this case, the genre is a detective mystery. This affords us possibilities of analysis regarding "Othered" representations and the conventions constructed primarily for commodity consumption.

Detective fictions, whether literary or filmic, offer us a certain socially and culturally situated identity (Gee, 1996) of the detective. One of the first fictional American detectives is Edgar Allan Poe's C. Auguste Dupin. The detective identity produced by Poe continues to be (re)produced in literature and film. Several recognizable character traits are utilized in the mystery genre: superior intellect, creativity in imagination (usually framed in the ability to enter the mind of the criminal), typically humble social backgrounds (because entering into the world of the deviant "Othered" representations requires an identity that is able to cross borders), maleness and hyper-masculinity, literacy, semi-professional status in the field of detective work, or eccentricity. The storyline often circulates in the play on a "super-crip" triumphing over tragedy. The detective is also utilized to mark the social identities of others. Often, the narrative is centered on an incompetent police force and the entry of the hero detective who offers clarity. What is interesting in Deaver's work, as Jakubowicz and Meekosha (2004) point out, is how dis/ability is used as a symbolic device to distinguish Rhyme from the mass of other detectives. They left race off the map, however. Also significant is the manner in which these identity markers encode other characters and play on and off the social narratives of dis/ability, race, and their intersection in the wider world.

The character of Rhyme speaks to a magnified projection of detective identity. Not only is he characterized as eccentric (he collects odd materials in the city to fuel his passion for and knowledge of forensics), but he also has the striking characteristic of quadriplegia with possibility of violent convulsions that may destroy him at any moment. Murphy (1987) characterizes this effort at representation well:

> The long-term physically impaired are neither sick nor well, neither dead or alive, neither out of society or wholly in it. They are human beings but their bodies are warped or malfunctioning, leaving their full humanity in doubt.... they are neither fish nor fowl; they exist in partial isolation from society as undefined, ambiguous people. (p. 112)

Here, the dis/ability functions to generate further suspense, as the mystery of the killer functions in parallel with the mystery of the dis/ability. Although dis/abled detectives are not new in this genre, the play on imminent death due to impairment is. Viewing this film is not a pleasant experience, as a number of critics have attested. The film critic William Arnold (1999) calls it "gruesome." It's terrifying not because it disturbs cultural conceptions of how bodies should work; rather, it disrupts what Mitchell and Snyder (2001) have called the "controlling narrative of medical and rehabilitative science" (p. 16). Dis/ability acts as "a metaphor and fleshly example of the body's unruly resistance to what Lennard Davis has theorized as the cultural desire to 'enforce normalcy'" (Mitchell & Snyder, 2001, p. 17). Some movement is restored in Rhyme's hand as a result of rehabilitation, but the likelihood of being fully rehabilitated is slim. Despite the catching of the "bad guy," the lack of resolution of his impairment leaves the audience uneasy. The casting of Washington as the dis/abled character is symbolic because his casting history reflects strong identifications with the audience given the role as protagonist.

Ironically, Rhyme is distanced from the audience by his hot-temperedness and arrogance. This serves to build not only the detective character, but also a dis/abling discourse: It functions to uphold the narrative of the bitter dis/abled in the space of an able-bodied majority. There is no possibility of a shared social identity as a person who is dis/abled (i.e., there no dis/abled community to belong to), only the anger of being positioned outside the "norm." Yet, when the narrative continues unfolding and the audience is presented with his brilliance and maverick style, positive identifications are established (especially considering the actor's public persona).

The fact that Rhyme is black is also deeply meaningful to the narration and spectacle. The novel presents him as white, and the film casts an African American. The sociohistoric anxiety over the black body's movement is utilized primarily through the relationship between Rhyme and Donaghy. Here we have the mobilization of suspense paralleling the capture of the criminal, the overcoming or self-effacing of dis/ability, and anxieties over black sexuality. This film works deeply at the emotional level because the images of "blackness" amplify dis/ability in the imaginations of the able-bodied, and the images of dis/ability enlarge "blackness" in a white supremacist culture. The dis/abled body and the black body are both utilized in the film to serve the ends of continued domination through the negative recirculation of the vilified "Other."

Sexual tension between Lincoln Rhyme and Amelia Donaghy pervades *The Bone Collector*. This is quite common in films depicting dis/abled characters. Paul Longmore (2003) has observed that "there is always an undertone of sexual tension, of sexual danger. We are never quite sure what he might do to her" (p. 11). The very casting of Denzel Washington and Angelina Jolie in the film is indicative of the intent behind the images. Both actors are celebrated in Hollywood for their ability to engender sexual fantasies in their audiences. Sexual tension between these two characters is heightened by representations of "blackness" and the quadriplegic body. As bell hooks (1992) elucidates:

> The commodification of Otherness has been so successful because it is offered as a new delight, more intense, more satisfying than normal ways of doing and feeling. Within commodity culture, ethnicity becomes spice, seasoning that can liven up the dull dish that is mainstream white culture. Cultural taboos around sexuality and desire are transgressed and made explicit as the media bombards folks with a message of difference no longer based on the white supremacist assumption that "blondes have more fun." The "real fun" is to be had by bringing to the surface all those "nasty" unconscious fantasies and longings about contact with the Other embedded in the secret (not so secret) deep structure of white supremacy. (pp. 21–22)

In the case of this relationship, the "nasty" unconscious fantasies are made more intense via the interracial dimension, as well as the possibility of sexual encounter with a quadriplegic.

The mystery concerns not only the discovery of the identity of the serial killer, but also and perhaps more importantly the uncovering of the pleasure and pain to be encountered in the sexual relationship with a black dis/abled body. This in essence would complete the mentoring process as Amelia moves from the world of inexperience (both in forensic work and in sexual terms, having never engaged in sexual activity with a black dis/abled man) to one of experience. Again this movement plays in deep cultural narratives where the dominant in this society have been "confident that non-white people had more life experience, were more worldly, sensual, and sexual because they were different" (hooks, 1992, p. 23). Throughout the film we are kept in suspense, anxiously and voyeuristically awaiting this encounter. Just as the possibility of an encounter presents itself, it is withdrawn and rearticulated later in the classic suspense style of Hollywood mystery film making. Of course, such representations work due to their deep sociohistoric trajectories.

White anxiety over black sexuality has been well documented not only in slave narratives but also in the very acts of violence and terror directed at black men believed to be in sexual relationships with white women or to have instigated sexual encounters with whites. The brutal murder of Emmett Till for whistling at a white woman is a case in point. The lynching of black men was most often caused by white anxieties over black sexuality and fears that they might invade the white race by raping white women and proving white men to be impotent or sexually inferior. Along with the brutal act of a lynching, whereby the central objective was to visually record the immobility of the black body collectively, the victim often was castrated (West, 1993). The castration was symbolic of fears of aggressive black male takeover of vulnerable white female bodies. Such fears engender cultural stereotypes and myths of black sexuality. As Cornel West (1993) put it, "the dominant myths draw black women and men either as threatening creatures who have the potential for sexual power over whites, or as harmless, de-sexed underlings of a white culture" (p. 83).

Clearly, the Lincoln Rhyme character is not an underling but rather one whose potential sexual power over Amelia is exploited. This power is represented directly in his desirous sexual gaze at Amelia despite the fact that he is in the presence of white men (there is no other white woman in the cast except for Jolie), and indirectly in his request that Amelia be made to work the case against her wishes. However, the only reason why such representation functions well in this particular film is that the dis/ability serves first to create a suspense effect as the audience wonders about the possibility of intercourse between the two, and then at the end to neutralize white anxiety over black sexuality as the possibility of such an encounter is proven to be impossible. Yet, it isn't only in this relationship that we find negative representations. Indeed, Rhyme isn't capable of having any constructive/positive relationship with able-bodied characters. His only value in the world is directly related to his ability to contribute to his line of work.

In *The Bone Collector*, Rhyme seems to have resolved his wish to completely self-efface through assisted suicide only as a result of now being able to live and work through an emblematic able-bodied character. The able-bodied character, Amelia Donaghy, who at first refuses to work with Rhyme due to her sense that Rhyme is too abrupt, ends up being forced to work with him as a result of the demands Rhyme puts on Amelia's supervisor. Her sensing of Rhyme's abruptness (after less than a minute in his presence for the first time) is connected to wider social/emotional solicitation of a demanding and parasitic dis/abled individual. Immediately the audience conjures up images of a dis/abled person using the dis/ability to make demands on normative ways of being. The demand is confirmed when she realizes that Rhyme has in effect ordered her to be in his service against her will. Such a fear of the demand on normativeness is further signified in the fact of blackness. The director plays on the social anxiety of whites when demands are made of them by marginalized Others. Sociohistoric examples that trigger this anxiety are numerous. In the end, we are forced to ask for the real hero to stand up. Is the hero the brainiac Rhyme, who has found the will to live through his detective work and, by extension, his able-bodied accomplice, or is it Amelia, who saves him from complete destruction through charitable service?

Of course, the capacity of Rhyme to fall back on the wish for a final transition is never fully retracted, even at the end of the film. At the very end we see a smiling Rhyme in a wheelchair surrounded by family, friends, and Amelia Donaghy (the body through which he has seemingly found the will to live). The implication is that without Amelia by his side, he may slip into a suicidal state. Incompleteness is built into the story's final structure. As audience members we are left with lingering questions. Does he ultimately go through with the suicide? Does he establish a romantic relationship with Amelia? Does he continue his investigative work with her? Such questions are left dangling in the end because the narrative cannot support a dis/abled body as positive ontology. The suspense narrative makes use of the representations of an incomplete body to signal an incomplete story. We are left with the feeling that dis/ability is malady. There is no possibility for that state of being to be positive in itself. It is possible to experience positive moments when the dis/abled body lives through the able–bodied, but only to the extent that the dis/ability serves to teach the able body a lesson. When

Amelia comes to the realization that she is capable of quality forensic work and gains confidence as a result of Rhyme's coaching (of course, Rhyme saw the quality in her work even before his mentoring), the narrative structure turns from a mentoring relationship to one based on a system of charity signified in romantic encounters and in Amelia's act of flying Rhyme's family in to celebrate his birthday at the closing of the film—the charitable and heroic thing to do.

Dis/abling and Racializing Deviance in *Unbreakable*

The first scene of the film *Unbreakable* opens in 1961 with the birth of Elijah Price (Samuel Jackson), a black child, in a department store. The doctor, who arrives after delivery, is horrified to find that the baby sustained many bone fractions while in the uterus. Later, in the character's adolescent years, we revisit him in a small run-down apartment sadly watching television with a broken arm in a sling. We learn that Elijah suffers from some type of bone disorder (not yet named) as his mother struggles to get him to go out and play in a park across the street (Bronx) and the child refuses so that he doesn't sustain a fracture.

Immediately after the scene of Elijah's birth there's a shift to the 1990s and the introduction of a white middle-aged male character (David Dunn) on a commuter train just outside Philadelphia. The train speeds out of control and derails. All passengers die except for David Dunn, who doesn't break a bone or sustain even a scratch. In the film's first act Elijah, now an adult (seen with a broken leg and a glass cane) and the owner of a comic book art gallery, meets David, and through their dialogue we learn that Elijah suffers from a genetic condition known as osteogenesis imperfecta. He states that he doesn't make a particular protein very well, which makes his bones very low in density and easy to break. He's had 54 breaks in his life, though he has the tamest version of the disorder, type I. He then attempts to convince David Dunn that the fact that he was not hurt in the trainwreck signifies that he has a special heroic gift symbolized by his choice of profession as a security guard. David is unconvinced initially, but later comes to the realization that he does have special powers. All of this is done through the metaphors typical of U.S. comic book hero/villain discourse.

In Act 2, David plays with his powers of fighting evil. In Act 3, Elijah, who has by now become David's guide of sorts, indirectly asks David if he believes in his power. David affirms. Elijah's response is "well, this is where we shake hands." In shaking Elijah's hand, David nearly faints as he comes to the realization that Elijah was responsible for the some of the worst atrocities in the world—including the train-wreck—all in the effort to find David, his opposite. As Elijah states in the end, "I knew if there was me there had to be you." In the closing message we learn that David led the authorities to Elijah's shop, where evidence of three acts of terrorism was found, and that Elijah was sentenced to an institution for the criminally insane.

Both *Unbreakable* and *The Bone Collector* position the disabled body as a parasite—an organism that lives in or on other organisms. Lincoln Rhyme's and Elijah Price's only significance throughout the respective films is that they support a narrative structure that encodes able-bodied-ness as the positive way to be in the world, and dis/ability as a narrative tool that serves to pedagogically open up spaces where the able-bodied character comes to the realization of his/her own taken-for-granted body. As Rosemarie Thomson (1997) has stated, their "social role is to symbolically free the privileged, idealized figure of the American self from the vagaries and vulnerabilities of embodiment" (p. 7). The more closely we inspect the characters' symbolic function, the more apparent it becomes that the dis/abled character really isn't the main character at all. The main character's disability serves as a "metaphorical device" (Mitchell & Snyder, 2001) to further construct a normative, able-body ontology. Mitchell and Snyder (2000) refer to this as a "perpetual discursive dependency upon disability [as] narrative prosthesis (p. 47). Lennard Davis (1997) and others have also argued, "if disability appears in a novel [in this case in film], it is rarely centrally represented" (p. 21). In the case of these two films, we sense (as an audience) that disabled characters are in fact the central characters. Upon closer inspection however, they are only walls sustaining the structure (never fixed) of normativeness.

The entire membrane of the film *Unbreakable* consists of the student/teacher relationship in David/Elijah. Elijah's very existence in the world is to demonstrate, at all costs, that David's body is extraordinarily normative. The foregrounded representation of disability is chiefly what serves to bring David to this realization. However, embedded throughout the narrative is the technique of invoking "blackness." We constantly see contrasts between David's able-bodied white world and Elijah's dis/abled black world. This technique is achieved in a multiplicity of ways:

- the invoking of common perceptions whereby class is racialized,
- the play on Elijah's fragmented body and fragmented family structure (we never see a father and we note that as an adult he doesn't have children),
- the linguistic distinctions between Standard English and African American English Vernacular (which shifts in and out),
- the camera/lighting effects of David's light world and Elijah's dark world,
- the distinction of Elijah's being born in the 1960s (the director is certainly invoking anxiety over perceptions of pro-blackness and the Black Power movement—all vilified through the symbol of Elijah, who in the end is incarcerated),
- the use of the name of a 1960s civil rights leader, Elijah Muhammad (who more than any other figure of the 1960s constructed the most radical narratives in challenging white normativeness),
- the physical reconstruction of a Frederick Douglass likeness, and
- the racist play on black biological propensity to crime.

The narrative structure leans on "blackness" in like manner. Lacan (1968) describes the distortions created when a "chapter [is linked] to the chapters surrounding it" (p. 21). In essence, the meaning lies not only in the immediate representation but in the representations intertextual relationship with other texts and cues from the cultural context. I would agree with Mitchell and Snyder (2000) that

> the dis/ability is central in that . . . the inherent vulnerability and variability
> of bodies serves literary narratives as a metonym for that which refuses to con-
> form to the mind's desire for order and rationality. Within this schema, disabil-
> ity acts as a metaphor and fleshly example of the body's unruly resistance to
> the cultural desire to "enforce normalcy." (p. 48)

Whereas Mitchell and Snyder claim the privileged position of disability in constructing normalcy in narrative by serving as a "crutch upon
which [they] lean for their representational power, disruptive potential-
ity, and analytical insight" (p. 49), I would also stress the importance of
interrogating multiple sites of difference as they intersect. Such an analysis is important because it allows us the angle from which to see the similarities and differences between the representations of the dis/abled
cross-racially and important distinctions and markers in intra-group
formations. If such differences are obvious, then the response to a more
responsible representation of dis/ability (or "blackness") must speak to
multiple constituencies comprising that identity marker.

Slowly, David comes to the realization that he has extraordinary
power over his body. He is able to bench press 575 pounds with relative
ease, he has never been sick in his life, he miraculously survives accidents where everyone else perishes, and he senses danger in people
through touching them or being in close proximity to them. While David
continues to struggle throughout the second act with whether or not he
is special, Elijah's character serves as a backdrop to further capitalize on
the audience's emotional response to David's obliviousness of his extraordinary body. As Elijah scurries, cane in support, to investigate whether
or not David has these powers, we follow him right into a tragic fall
where his fickle and awkward body gives in and we hear the bones
crackle, we see his body in desperate convulsion, and we hear the sting-
ing agony in his scream. This play on the delineations between the two
bodies serves to position us as an audience in a double suspense: We
voyeuristically await Elijah's ultimate fall and we anxiously await
David's discovery of his special powers as we are positioned to identify with his heroic qualities. Although we await Elijah's fall, we hope that
David can come to his realization quickly in order to end Elijah's mis-

ery of having to prove David's powers. In the final scene, we note that David is finally convinced of his unique power. His life is resolved through his choice to live normally—though he utilizes his powers covertly for heroic purposes in the end. This heroism is unknown to anyone except his son—again we see the play of a normative iconic heroic father figure in the backdrop of Elijah who, despite being introduced at birth, has no father and produces no children in life.

Elijah's life is insignificant. He does nothing and produces nothing that is not in accordance with the ultimate goal of his character's sketch—to convince an able-bodied man of the power of his taken-for-granted body. As soon as he does so, he is of no further use to the narrative structure. We learn that he is the epitome of evil. Paul Longmore (2003) has stated that the "most persistent [stereotype of people with disabilities] is the association of disability with malevolence. Deformity of body symbolizes deformity of soul. Physical handicaps are made the emblems of evil" (p. 78). This persistent stereotype is doubly amplified in *Unbreakable* as it functions to produce a subtext of fear of the super-deviant embodied in the intersection of "blackness" and dis/ability. Elijah's dis/ability is linked to an unredeemable evil. Of course, David cannot kill him as he killed a serial murderer earlier because it would reduce his positive qualities. Instead, the state takes over and institutionalizes Elijah in a facility for the criminally insane. Another discourse linked to late 19th- and early 20th-century figuring of disability is also at play here: The film categorizes disability along with another "undesirable" trait—criminality. This symbiotic relationship works in the film as it plays on the notion that both conditions are to be feared and controlled. Furthermore, this film exemplifies how disability is used in most films/novels; that is, the disability or physical "abnormality" is what makes the character of the villain work (Gartner & Joe, 1987; Fine & Asch, 1988; Davis, 1997). Throughout the movie we are not sure if Elijah is someone for whom we should show empathy or fear. During his very birth, even the doctor who was summoned after his delivery betrayed fear at the sight of the baby. Throughout the film, the character of Elijah is represented as someone we should empathize with and simultaneously fear. The character of David, however, symbolizes our aspirations. His body is not divine or so out of reach that we cannot attain it. He merely symbolizes normalcy at its height—a male, white, heterosexual, middle-class, father hero. He is the character to consume in the audience's reconstruction and re-identification with normalcy.

In *Unbreakable*, the anxiety over the black movement is central. Despite the fact that Elijah has a degenerative bone disease that causes him to stumble even when traveling very short distances, at the end of the movie we note that he has no problem moving rather quickly after having just created catastrophes such as the trainwreck, the plane bombing, and so on. The point reiterated throughout is that black movement should be regarded as suspicious and dangerous—and policed, institutionalized, and contained.

Both films also play on the desire of the dis/abled body to become able-bodied and the desire of the black body to become white. The most important utterance in *Unbreakable* is made by Elijah when he says, "if there is someone like me, there had to be you." In this statement he betrays his fascinated longing to find the perfect Other. Although it is made to seem that the longing is really about the eradication of the dis/ability, the careful casting of a black character serves to intensify this urgency of disability effacement while also calling forth deep-seated cultural feelings of black self-hatred and normative whiteness. In *The Bone Collector*, the deliberate casting of a white woman works in that it presents the audience with a rebirth of sorts—a rebirth of Rhyme into an able-bodied white woman. This rebirth is symbolized through the constant play on language in the film. Of course, a rebirth into an able-bodied white man would not have been possible given that it would suspend the sexual interracial anxiety and neutralize the bossy and demanding platform from which Lincoln Rhyme speaks to Amelia initially (which served the stereotype of the dis/abled using the dis/ability to exploit able-bodied weakness). Toward the end of the movie we see a half-upright Rhyme (in a wheelchair) next to a white woman who now seems to be his caretaker (earlier he was assisted by a black woman, who was killed). She becomes his counterpart—his body in action. Both films rely on self-erasure on two levels—dis/ability and blackness.

Both films abstract the possibility that the dis/abled body and the black body can be loved and embraced as positive ontology. Blackness is positioned as negative ontology through the symbolic use of a monkey being lynched (*The Bone Collector*) and in the cultural recirculation of blackness as evil (*Unbreakable*). These works therefore reproduce domination in their positioning of whiteness and able-bodiedness as a positive way of being.

Doing the Right Thingand the Spectacle of Smiley

Do the Right Thing (1989) is a positive film given that it was produced by a filmmaker who intervened in a terrain of representing "blackness," which had been almost an exclusive domain of whites and the imagination of whiteness (hooks, 1997). Granted, this space could have been filled by a black producer whose ideology speaks to dominant interests; Spike Lee is clearly not such a producer, considering the vehement treatment of his work (particularly his earlier films) by "mainstream" white film critics. There is much to be applauded in the film, though we must bear in mind that Lee wasn't originally intent on casting a dis/abled character in the film (he notes this in the *Do the Right Thing* audio commentary).

In the almost unbearable heat of Bedford-Stuyvesant, Brooklyn, we encounter street corners that exhibit a range of identities. *Do the Right Thing* presents us with a constructive image of community. Various tensions exist, including those that ultimately lead to violence. Within the conflicting space, community exists and questions regarding possibilities for the creation of deeper forms of community are constantly raised, but not answered. Spike Lee is masterful in allowing the audience to enter the minds of characters. Despite the negative traits of some characters, we somehow sympathize with them. The case of Smiley presents us with more difficulties however. He is both ordinary and extraordinary, simultaneously.

There is no struggle to amplify the character of Smiley like those of the others; the tendency throughout the film is to discipline and close down the audience's full reading of the character. This is achieved even while representing the dis/abled character as one who is integrated into the community and has a functional purpose. Smiley is not a burden to the community. He meanders through the neighborhood, often serving as a mere background for the unfolding of events (if the character is not present, we might overhear him selling his photographs in the background). Yet, his purpose is to sell the images of Martin Luther King Jr. and Malcolm X. He symbolically serves to amplify the main theme of the film, which is the importance of resisting oppression. Yet, there is no resistance to the stigma of dis/ability, no presented histories of the struggle for equality for people who are dis/abled, no presence of a dis/abled community, and no critique of the normative body (aside from that of whiteness). Snyder, Brueggemann, and Garland-Thomson (2002) are instructive:

> The fact that many of us will become disabled if we live long enough is perhaps the fundamental aspect of human embodiment. Yet, in our present collective cultural consciousness, the disabled body is imagined not as the universal consequence of living an embodied life but rather as an alien condition. This disability tends to be figured in cultural representations as an absolute state of otherness that is opposed to a standard, normative body, unmarked either by individual form and function or by the particularities of its history. (p. 2)

Smiley offers moments of socially constructing normalcy in the film, but he also is an object of pity.

He is a nuisance both to the characters around him and to the viewer of the film. His introduction in the background is at times disturbing to the spectator because one doesn't quite know how he fits into the narrative. Yet, Mookie stops to buy photographs from him, despite being in a rush. Sal gives him some money because of his son's mistreatment of him. The community verbally castigates Pino for his treatment of Smiley. All acts of pity, but situated in the effort to construct the character of the Other. There is nothing new in terms of dis/abled imagery here. What is different about the intersections of the black body and dis/ability in Smiley is that he is no victim. Even though there is no detailed construction of his character, we know that he embodies the most terrifying act of violence. The ultimate act of redressing Sal's noninclusion of celebrity blacks on his restaurant's wall is left in the hands of Smiley: He burns the restaurant. He is both pitied and vilified simultaneously. A similar representation can be found in the character of James "Radio" Kennedy in the film *Radio* (2003). The audience's identification with the character is subverted by the locker room scene where the spectator is teased with vilification for his sexualized transgressions against young white women. Throughout the film, Radio is a curious freak show whose symbolic entry into the historical representations of blacks in Hollywood serves to amplify the cliché of a white savior of a lost racialized soul or souls. The tired storyline is deepened due to the presence of the dis/ability. Both Radio and Smiley have no purpose but to fit into the world of bodily norms; Smiley in the late 1980s black community of Brooklyn and Radio in a segregated yet "pleasant" small South Carolina community in the late 1970s. Both are present to create an existential angst in spectators.

Smiley is initially presented as a character "in control" and integrated in the environment, and eventually becomes the "out of control" character. The loss of control is a frequent trope in *Radio*, too. The dis/abled often are coded as people who present social endangerment (Longmore, 2003). The threat to society actually is coded as a threat to whiteness through the historical slant on white anxieties over black male sexuality and the invasion of white women. Here again, each identity marker is used to deepen the already existent stereotypical representation of the Other.

Different media genres encode dis/ability differently, not only because they (sometimes) appropriate discourses unique to the genres, but also because of the manner in which spectators come into the reading. However, regardless of the genre, the encodings are mostly negative and relate the body and mind to a controlled climate in order to assuage the fears and anxieties of the able-bodied.

Spaces of Possibility

Pedagogy

Subjecting images of people of color (particularly as those images intersect with dis/ability) to classroom dialogue and critical reflection is essential. Schools are complicit in the formulation of policies and practices that read these two bodily realities in connection. But schools are not alone in this. Over the years an industry has been produced in connection with discourses of compassionate capitalism and the ideology of color-blind racism (Bonilla-Silva, 2003). Kalyanpur and Harry (2004) correctly describe "how the legal, medical, and educational systems have combined to bestow almost godlike powers on professionals to perceive or impute academic failure in certain students and create a disability where no real etiological discrepancies may exist" (p. 530). If institutions are readily entering into these readings, it is essential that critical education move against the grain. It gives critical educators not only a place to dialogue but also a concrete space to map out actions to subvert policies and cultures.

Critical teachers must not allow normative conceptions of the body/mind to orient their praxis within the space of schooling and outside. This would suggest that a re-examination of the "official" and unofficial curricula be brought to bear in the act of teaching. By unofficial curriculum we are envisioning the various alternative texts situated in the act of teaching; the relationships formed or not formed with students; a re-examination of the disabling and racialized language that enters our lexicon as a result of the abled-bodied and white upper-middle-class way of being in the world; a decolonization of the spatial politics of schooling (also a form of curriculum) so that space and the visual are factored as part and parcel of the ecology of a socially just world; resistance against destructive individualism and reward systems that privilege socially constructed normalcy; and active resistance of forms of exclusion through inclusion as practiced through any form of "tracking." And of course, as the subject of this chapter suggests, dialogue regarding representation in film and other media cultures must be opened, especially as identities intersect. Yet, dialogue alone and action within the school is insufficient. The boundaries of school need to be blurred with the social context so that both teachers and students contribute to and from ongoing social movements and cross-institutional resistances that seek the full humanity of those who bear the most social cost.

Here, we envision boycotts and staged protests in relation to films that do not hire dis/abled actors. We would not tolerate the representation of people of color in blackface or whites playing the roles of Native American characters, and should actively resist discrimination of the dis/abled in the workforce. Yet, we should also bear in mind that those who are black, brown, female, and dis/abled experience harsher consequences. We envision the production of alternative texts that attempt to "talk back" and the creation of a "de-centered" unity (Apple, 2001) able to maintain creative contestations with conservative ideologies. While forming solidarities with diverse interests, however, we must not seek compromise to the point that the political becomes inert and we contribute to the same forms of domination we mean to resist.

Digital media has powerful potential to instantiate positive political projects. Through social network sites students might actively call for boycotts of films that are disrespectful and disabling, and suggest that others do the same. Digital communities may be built to critique film both for positives and negatives and to suggest independent and "foreign" films that take up these intersections in respectful ways. (We don't wish to romanticize counter-perspectives from abroad; film production worldwide is dominated by individual models of dis/ability.)

Digital art and video sites may be utilized to produce counter-art and counter-videos that problem-pose mainstream images. Annie Leonard's short YouTube video *The Story of Stuff* presents an example of a project that is both possible to create with limited resources and potentially powerful in capturing attention.

Independent Filmmaking

Subversive agendas and floods of popular outrage promise hope. Independent films that challenge the dominant iconography of dis/ability are being produced, but they exist on economic cliff lines because funding for progressive productions is never acquired with ease. The most hopeful projects are those with diverse sources of funding that allow filmmakers a full range of aesthetic and political articulation. The disability arts movement, inseparable from the disability movement, continues to produce short but powerful films and other aesthetic texts that challenge "mainstream" representations. Also promising are those films produced outside the U.S. that resist ableism and fracture the dominant lens of Hollywood. Furthermore, they strive to be grounded in real lived insurgency from below in all paths of their production.

Laura Kissel (2009) is creating a more nuanced and engaged form of spectatorship in resistance to mainstream voyeurism of the impaired. She does not avoid historicizing eugenics, euthanasia, and institutional exploitation, but rather navigates a fine line between injustices done and oppositional narratives and representations for transformation. She destabilizes the spectator in a rearticulated Brechtian fashion (my analysis). She opens up space for the dis/abled to voice their own institutional oppressions and resistances, and displays more progressive interactions between the dis/abled and those who are able-bodied through unique interview techniques, experiments with technology, voiceovers, and camera angles that are more likely to summon critical engagement. Theoretical work on the various alignments formed between conservative sensibilities is critical not only at the level of the formation of internal institutional policy and "foreign" policy, but also at the level of the cultural. The shaping of cultural messages commands attention in the types of solidarities to be built in the ongoing struggles against conservative hegemonies. The interlocking architecture of normalcy requires a response that is both sensitive to the particularities of respective identity markers and yet sophisticated enough to move through the transactions. Such grounding is always complex, but necessary if we are not to fall victim to a politics of divide and conquer and erase and extinguish.

Aside from independent filmmaking in the U.S., other contexts must be considered. The film studies scholar Robert Stam (2000) insightfully observes that "even the branch of cinema studies that is critical of Hollywood often re-centers Hollywood as a kind of *Langue* in relation to which all other forms are but dialectical variants" (p. 22). We certainly are guilty of producing a chapter that examined Hollywood films exclusively; we did so given the relative omission of the topic in studies of the "Othered" image and due to the particularities of racialized formations in the U.S. Engaging cinema coming out of the economic south would certainly present nuances that would call into question the dis/abling Hollywood image. Despite Hollywood's power at circulating the image worldwide, we must remember that these representations are always mediated at the level of production and reception differently in other geopolitical terrains.

Documentary films are another important site of engagement, particularly given the success of current critical works. An example connected to our chapter in this text that discusses the power of comedy would be comedian Greg Walloch's *F**K the Disabled*. Tom Shakespeare (1994) notes that "just as humor is widely used to demean disabled people, so too it is employed by disabled people to generate 'insider' recognition and solidarity, by identifying common enemies and interests, and providing a bond of 'crip humor' to disabled people's culture" (p. 123). Walloch brilliantly alternates between stand-up acts and material realities of his life. He deconstructs the normative social scripts by critically examining the intersections of homosexuality and dis/ability. *Murderball* is another film that exposes important lines of inquiry regarding dis/ability, even though it traffics in discourses and imagery of the supercrip at times.

A World without Bodies by Sharon Snyder and David Mitchell examines the genocide of hundreds of thousands dis/abled people by the Nazi regime. *Whole: A Trinity of Being* is the story of a South African artist dis/abled by a bullet. It re-examines mainstream images of the dis/abled and sexuality. Deep and critical documentary explorations of race and dis/ability in American society are needed.

Moments of nonalignment with dominant representations also exist in mainstream film. *The Waterdance* (1992), written and codirected by Neal Jiminez, who became paralyzed following an accident, subverts common stereotypes of the dis/abled. Paraplegia is not positioned as a condition to be pitied, and the characters including Wesley Snipes's are humanized throughout. Honest representations of sex lives are presented. The film also dialectically treats able-bodied perceptions of the dis/abled and how the dis/abled navigate these perceptions. Importantly, we have in *The Waterdance* representations of a dis/abled community.

In the late 1970s a paraplegic named Reggie Green was cast in the television sitcom *The Facts of Life* and later in the film *Boyz 'n the Hood* (1991). Despite the limitations in the representations, the move to hire people who are dis/abled must be applauded. This might open up the possibility for stronger forms of political organization of dis/abled actors and their allies.

The Social Context and the Shaping
of Representation

Spaces of possibility also exist when taking into account the social context. People who are physically dis/abled and dis/ability rights organizations are actively contesting negative images of the dis/abled and their discrimination in hiring and casting. A productive and creative tension exists in the sense that the challenge is situated both outside the industry and inside (Norden, 1994). Those on the outside are less affected by the disciplinary silencing of the industry, and those on the inside have intimate knowledge of its inner workings and are capable of challenging the industry in their own interest and of contributing knowledge to activists on the outside. Without consistent and well thoughtout movements on the ground, the power politics of the image will remain in play. Without a dis/abled workforce in the industry, change is not likely. History also has instructed us on the social awareness of both dis/abled persons and other marginalized groups, particularly during times of war. Although the ideological reasoning behind war already does violence, both real lived and symbolic (consider the historical failure to fully integrate subordinated populations following their participation in war), it has also opened up a space for the visibility of oppressive forms. The U.S. Iraq war and the U.S. Afghanistan war (not really a war because the implication is that both sides are fighting) have opened up a space of public visibility of dis/ability and the institutional terror that dis/abled soldiers must endure at the hands of the U.S. government. In the current healthcare debate, the politics of dis/ability is also important. As Williams (1991) has put it,

> disablement makes an important contribution to the ideological crisis surrounding health and welfare in capitalist societies. This is because disabled people, being both deserving and expensive, pose a crisis of legitimacy for the State in those capitalist societies which seek to be both profitable and civilized at the same time. (p. 517)

When taking into account the effect of dis/ablement in the lives of people of color, it subjects conservative (Tea Party type) imaginations to deeper forms of dissonance given the racialized nature of their discourse. Reading these realities into current social controversies, therefore, is a powerful challenge.

This challenge must originate from diverse locations. The power of boycotts remains significant. We need to consider films as not just uncontestable cultural knowledge(s) situated for a passive citizenry, but rather as capitalist commodities to be challenged the way one would challenge the Nike Corporation—by boycotting. The marketing of such films could be subjected to forms of cultural jamming quite common in the subversion of Coca-Cola ads worldwide. Furthermore, the digital world that we now live in provides us a great opportunity to subvert oppressive representations by engaging in a politics of digital democratic counter-productions. We need to both interrogate and produce the images we want. Digital media may also be utilized to sustain deeper forms of critique through cross-border activism. The protesting of the image might therefore take place at various sites simultaneously, producing globalized resistance from below while fashioning contestation through grounded knowledge of the local. Ultimately, for these negative representations to change, it is essential that social movements that take up their intersections exist and be continuously strengthened. The interruption of the discourses and visual rhetoric of "normalcy" means the freedom of us all.

References

Anderson, B. (1983). Imagined communities: Reflections on the origins and spread of nationalism. London: Verso.

Anzaldúa, G. (1987). Borderlands/la frontera: The new mestiza. San Francisco, CA: Aunt Lute Books.

Apple, M. (2001). Educating the "right" way: Markets, standards, God, and inequality. New York: Routledge Falmer.

Arnold, W. (1999, November 5). Brutal "Bone Collector" wallows in gruesome absurdity. Seattle Post Intelligencer. Retrieved from http://www.seattlepi.com/movies/boneq.shtml.

Barnes, C. & Mercer, G. (2003). Disability. Oxford, UK and Malden, MA: Blackwell.

Bernardi, D. (2009). Filming difference: Actors, directors, producers, and writers on gender, race, and sexuality in film. Austin, TX: University of Texas Press.

Boggle, D. (1973). Toms, coons, mulattoes, mammies, and bucks: An interpretive history of blacks in film. New York: Viking.

Bonilla-Silva, E. (2003). Racism without racists: Color-blind racism and the persistence of racial inequality in the United States. Oxford, UK: Rowman & Littlefield.

Bourdieu, P. (1991). Language and symbolic power. Cambridge, MA: Harvard University Press.

Bradsher, J. (1996, January). Disability among racial and ethnic groups. Disability Statistics Abstract, 10, 1–4.

Busfield, J. (1996). Men, women and madness. London: Macmillan.

Campbell, J., & Oliver, M. (1996). Disability politics: Understanding our past, changing our future. London: Routledge.

Corbett, J. (1994). A proud label: Exploring the relationship between disability politics and gay pride. Disability and Society, 9(2), 343–358.

Crenshaw, K. (1991). Mapping the margins: Intersectionality, identity politics, and violence against women of color. Stanford Law Review, 43(6), 1241–1299.

Darke, P. (1998). Understanding cinematic representations of disability. In T. Shakespeare (Ed.), The disability reader: Social science perspectives (pp. 181–200). London and New York: Cassell.

Davis, L. (1995). Enforcing normalcy: Disability, deafness, and the body. London and New York: Verso.

Davis, L. (Ed.). (1997). The disability studies reader. New York and London: Routledge.

DeLauretis, T. (1984). Alice doesn't: Feminism, semiotics, cinema. Bloomington, IN: Indiana University Press.

DeLauretis, T. (1987). Technologies of gender. Bloomington, IN: Indiana University Press.

Enns, A., & Smit, C. (Eds.). (2001). Screening disability: Essays on cinema and disability. Lanham, MD and New York: University Press of America.

Fairclough, Norman. (1989). Language and power. London: Longman.

Fairclough, Norman. (1995). Critical discourse analysis. Boston: Addison Wesley.

Fairclough, N. (2000). Critical Analysis of Media Discourse. In P. Marris& S. Thornham (Eds.), Media studies: A reader (2nd ed.,pp. 308–325). New York: New York University Press.

Fine, M., & Asch A. (Eds.). (1988). Women with disabilities: Essays in psychology, culture, and politics. Philadelphia: Temple University Press.

Foucault, M. (1972). The archaeology of knowledge and the discourse on language. New York: Pantheon.

Foucault, M. (1984). The order of discourse. In M. Shapiro (Ed.), Language and politics (pp. 108–138). Oxford, UK: Blackwell.

Garland-Thomson, R. (1997). Extraordinary bodies: Figuring physical disability in American culture and literature. New York: Columbia University Press.

Gartner, A., & Joe, T. (Eds.). (1987). Images of the disabled, disabling images. New York: Praeger.

Gee, J. (1996). Social linguistics and literacies: Ideology in discourses. Bristol, PA and London: Taylor and Francis.

Giroux, H. (1994). *Disturbing pleasures: Learning popular culture.* New York: Routledge.

Giroux, H. (1997). *Channel surfing: Race talk and the destruction of today's youth.* New York: St. Martin's.

Giroux, H. (2002). *Breaking in to the movies: Film and the culture of politics.* Malden, MA and Oxford, UK: Blackwell.

Giroux, H. (2003). *The abandoned generation: Democracy beyond the culture of fear.* New York: Palgrave Macmillan.

Giroux, H., & Simon, R. (1989). *Popular culture, schooling, and everyday life.* Granby, MA: Bergin & Garvey.

Gramsci, A. (1971). *Selections from the prison notebooks of Antonio Gramsci.* (D. Forgacs & G. Nowell-Smith, Trans. and Ed.). London: Lawrence and Wishart.

Guerrero, E. (1993). *Framing blackness: The African American image in film.* Philadelphia: Temple University Press.

Hall, S. (1997). "The work of representation. In *Representation: Cultural representations and signifying practices* (pp. 13–73). London: Sage.

Hall, S., Hobson, D., Lowe, A., & Willis, P. (Eds.). (1980). *Culture, media, language.* London: Hutchinson.

hooks, b. (1992). *Black looks: Race and representation.* Boston: South End Press.

hooks, b. (1994). *Outlaw culture: Resisting representations.* New York: Routledge.

hooks, b. (1996). *Reel to real: Race, sex, and class at the movies.* New York: Routledge.

hooks, b. (1997). *Cultural criticism and transformation* [DVD]. Northampton, MA: Media Education Foundation.

Horkheimer, M., & Adorno, T. W. (1972). *Dialectic of enlightenment.* New York: Herder and Herder.

Innis, H. A. (1950). *Empire and communication.* Oxford: Clarendon Press.

Jakubowicz, A., & Meekosha, H. (2004). Detecting disability: Moving beyond metaphor in the crime fiction of Jeffrey Deaver. *Disability Studies Quarterly,* 24(2), http://www.dsq-sds.org/article/view/482/659 [accessed January 18, 2010]

James, J. (1996). *Resisting state violence: Radicalism, gender, and race in U.S. culture.* Minneapolis, MN and London: University of Minnesota Press.

Kalyanpur, M., & Harry, B. (2004). Impact of the social construction of LD on culturally diverse families: A response to Reid and Valle. *Journal of Learning Disabilities, 37*(6), 530–533.

Kellner, D. (1990). *Television and the crisis of democracy.* Boulder, CO: Westview.

Kissel, L. . (2009). Disability is us: Remembering, recovering, and remaking the image of disability. In D. Bernardi (Ed.), *Filming difference: Actors, directors, producers, and writers on gender, race, and sexuality in film* (pp. 17–40). Austin, TX: University of Texas Press.

Kohn, A., & Shannon, P. (2002). *Education, inc.* Portsmouth, NH: Heinemann.

Lacan, J. (1968). *The language of the self: The function of language in psychoanalysis.* Baltimore, MD: Johns Hopkins University Press.

Leistyna, P. (2010). Taking on the corporatization of public schooling: What teacher education can do. In S. Macrine, P. McLaren, & D. Hill (Eds.), *Revolutionizing pedagogy: Education for social justice within and beyond global neo-liberalism* (pp. 65–86). New York: Palgrave Macmillan.

Longmore, P. K. (2003). *Why I burned my book and other essays on disability*. Philadelphia: Temple University Press.

Lowen, J. W. (1995). *Lies my teacher told me: Everything your American history textbook got wrong*. New York: Simon & Schuster.

Macedo, D., & Bartolomé, L. I. (1999). *Dancing with bigotry: Beyond the politics of tolerance*. New York: St. Martin's.

Macrine, S., McLaren, P., & Hill, D. (Eds.). (2010). *Revolutionizing pedagogy: Education for social justice within and beyond global neo-liberalism*. New York: Palgrave Macmillan.

Males, M. (1999) *Framing youth: Ten myths about the next generation*. Monroe, ME: Common Courage Press.

Mitchell, D. T., & Snyder, S. L. (2001). *Narrative prosthesis: Disability and the dependencies of discourse*. Ann Arbor, MI: University of Michigan Press.

McChesney, R. W. (1999, November 29). The new global media: It's a small world of big conglomerates. *The Nation*, 11–15, 1999.

McLuhan, M. (1964). *Understanding media: The extension of man*. New York: McGraw-Hill.

Memmi, A. (1965). *The colonizer and the colonized*. Boston: Beacon Press.

Molnar, A. (2005). *School commercialism*. New York: Routledge.

Moore, D. (2009). Theorizing the "black body" as a site of trauma: Implications for theologies of embodiment. *Theology and Sexuality, 15*(2), 175–188.

Morris, J. (1993). *Independent lives? Community care and disabled people*. Basingstoke, UK: Macmillan.

Murphy, R. (1987). *The body silent*. London: Phoenix House.

Norden, M. F. (1994). *The cinema of isolation: A history of physical disabilities in the movies*. New Brunswick, NJ: Rutgers University Press.

Said, E. (1978). *Orientalism*. New York: Routledge and Keegan Paul.

Said, E. W. (1993). *Culture and imperialism*. New York: Vintage.

Saltman, K. (2000). *Collateral damage: Corporatizing public schools—a threat to democracy*. Lanham, MD: Rowman & Littlefield.

Scott, J. W. (1999). *Gender and the politics of history*. New York: Columbia University Press.

Shakespeare, T. (1994). Cultural representations of disabled people: Dustbins for disavowal? *Disability and Society, 9*(3), 283–299.

Shakespeare, T. (Ed.) (1998). *The disability reader: Social science perspectives*. London and New York: Cassell.

Shohat, E. (1994). *Unthinking Eurocentrism: Multiculturalism and the media*. New York: Routledge.

Shohat, E., & Stam, R. (2003). *Multiculturalism, postcoloniality, and transnational media*. New

Brunswick, NJ: Rutgers University Press.

Smith, V. (Ed.). (1997). *Representing blackness: Issues in film and video*. New Brunswick, NJ: Rutgers University Press.

Snyder, S. L., Brueggemann, B., & Garland-Thomson, R. (Eds.)., (2002). *Disability studies: Enabling the humanities*. New York: The Modern Language Association of America.

Stam, R. (2000). *Film theory: An introduction*. Malden, MA: Blackwell.

Talle, A. (1995). A child is a child: Disability and equality among the Kenya Masai. In B. Ingstad & S. R. Whyte (Eds.), *Disability and culture* (pp. 56–72). Berkeley: University of California Press.

The American Heritage Dictionary. (The New Second College Edition). (1983). New York: Dell Publishing.

Thomson, R. (1997). *Extraordinary bodies: Figuring physical disability in American culture and literature*. New York: Columbia University Press.

U.S. Census Bureau. (2000). *Population profile of the United States*. Washington, DC: U.S. Census Bureau.

Vernon, A. (1998). Multiple oppression and the disabled people's movement. In T. Shakespeare (Ed.), *The disability reader: Social science perspectives* (pp. 201–210). London and New York: Cassell.

West, Cornel. (1993). *Race matters*. Boston: Beacon Press.

Williams, G. (1991). Disablement and the ideological crisis in health care. *Social Science and Medicine, 32*(4), 517–524.

Chapter Five

Planned Disruptions

Rethinking Knowledge and Power

We are political militants because we are teachers. Our job is not exhausted in the teaching of math, geography, syntax, history. Our job implies that we teach these subjects with sobriety and competence, but it also requires our involvement in and dedication to overcoming social injustice. (Freire, 2005, pp. 103–104)

Section One: On Curriculum and Teacher Dispositions

In reflecting on the national influences in the field of curriculum development during the last century, Herbert Kliebard (1995) observed:

The twentieth century became the arena where these four versions of what knowledge is of most worth and of the central functions of schooling were presented and argued. No single interest group ever gained absolute supremacy, although general economic trends, periodic and fragile alliances between groups, national mood, and local conditions and personalities affected the ability of these groups to influence school practice as the twentieth century progressed. In the end, what became the American curriculum was not the result of any decisive victory by any of the contending parties, but a loose, largely unarticulated, and not very tidy compromise. (p. 25)

We would add that today, capitalism, as a producer of culture and in particular the neoliberal economy, with its increasing stranglehold on schools, where there is an increased reliance on prepackaged curricula (Kohn, 1992; Apple, 1999) as mediators of a structured drive towards a test-centric society (McNeil, 2000; Kohn, 2000; Valenzuela, 1999), must be confronted strategically, yet unabashedly, if we are to remain faithful to the most important pieces of the puzzle, the children. The critical theorist Peter McLaren (2005) echoes this need to confront the leviathan that has become our institutions of (mis)education when he articulately and boldly announces:

> If we wonder how it is that here in the twenty-first century we are witnessing the steady erosion of human rights and civil liberties, of the trammeling of the freedom to make history, the abandonment of the poor to the ravages of capital, as well as the devastation of our ecosystems, we only have to examine the extent of our political denial and its implication for miseducation our citizenry. (p. xxviii)

In our view, the development of transformative curricula and lesson plans is of utmost importance in reclaiming possibilities and contesting apathy, because to assume that institutions (including schools) in a neoliberal economy have a vested interest in developing a critical citizenry is tantamount to complicity in the very act of perpetuating hegemonic interests by succumbing to willful ignorance. Donaldo Macedo ruptures any consideration of unintentionality when he notes that "ignorance is never innocent inasmuch as it predicated on the privilege of not needing to know" (personal communication, April 5, 2010). As Freire (2005) points out, "teachers' political, ethical, and professional responsibility puts them under an obligation to prepare and enable themselves before engaging in their teaching practice" (p. 32).

If Freire is right, and we think he is, both the curriculum and the act of teaching cannot be divorced from the daily reality that students face, much as it cannot be divorced from the inhumanity of society at large. In other words, we believe there is a pressing need to fragment the boundaries between lived reality and academic disciplines, and the reluctance on the part of educators and institutions to engage in this endeavor is, in our view, part of a structural complicity with capital commodification and accumulation that becomes realized in one of two ways. First, such curricula and teaching practices (embodied in educational institutions) may ultimately produce students who, despite being legitimated by an accreditation process in the form of a "diploma," are unable to make use of their natural critical faculties in connecting the "theoretical" or academic to the real. Under such circumstances, the miseducation that McLaren speaks of may be due to a range of factors: genuinely "not seeing" the nexus between the academic and the real (again, a constructed phenomenon); unwillingness to engage in the tedious work of critically examining the implications of what is taught; fear of engaging with "controversial" material (which itself comes from a fear of losing control); or blind abidance to the restrictive educational environment that is partly governed by testing directives. Second, the reluctance may exacerbate the all-too-common condition of students holding on to their cultural penetrations (Willis, 1982) and then realizing that the entire process, both curriculum and teaching practice, are entirely disconnected from their realities, naturally causing them to ask "why do we need to know this stuff?" This of course exacerbates the "forced-out" phenomenon (we call them "dropouts"). Freire (2005) is illuminating in both respects. As he reflects on fear in teaching, he insightfully notes that

> when faced with fear of any kind, one must first objectively ascertain whether there are real reasons for that fear. Second, if those reasons do exist, one must match them against the available possibilities for overcoming them successfully. Third, if an obstacle cannot be overcome right away, one must determine what steps to take toward becoming better capable of overcoming it tomorrow. (p. 50)

Freire's admonition contains within it an underlying connection between fear and degree of difficulty, a subject that we take up in the next section of this chapter. His analysis of the degree of difficulty has been supported by other critical educational theorists (Fine, 1991; McNeil, 2000; Valenzuela, 1999). He observes:

> The use of linguistic manipulations to hide a particular ideology does not necessarily mean that the dominant class schemed to develop discourses disguising concrete situations that in reality push students out of school or prevent

them from going to school. In reality, we do not have children who drop out of school for no reason at all, as if they just decide not to stay. What we do have are conditions in schools that either prevent them from coming to school or prevent them from staying in school. (Freire, 2005, p. 10)

In both scenarios—that is to say, in the fear of rigorously confronting the task of developing meaningful lessons and curricula, and in the fury of remaining faithful to testing directives—there is a complicity on the part of educational agents and institutions that, besides leading to students being "forced out," stagnates the creative potential of both teacher and student and in so doing, limits growth. In making this claim, we realize that the current environment requires that teachers take testing seriously, for to do otherwise is to neglect a political responsibility that teachers have to equip students with the necessary tools to move forward; however, we believe that the work of critical teachers requires the capacity to mediate these external constraints as much as possible so that students are able to develop not only their critical sensibilities but also a sense of democratic citizenship that will allow them to both effectively read the world and remake it in the interests of humanity. When confronted with meaningful curricula and teachers bold enough to be reflective practitioners, such students may in fact be able to connect their positionalities to those of their brothers and sisters anywhere in the world; hence, the civil war in the Ivory Coast would be connected to the price of cocoa here in the U.S. and Hershey's capacity exploit consumers, or the deluge of commercials and infomercials by pharmaceutical companies would be connected both to the plight of indigenous populations that are being decimated as a result of ecocide and to the never-ending rows of pain medication in local drugstores. In both cases, the lesson(s) would then be connected to progressive political movements that would seal the connection between the academic and the real. This is the inevitable result of a praxis that fuses theory and practice and that refuses to cower in the face of intellectual work, or to segment commonsense knowledge from academic-based knowledge. Freire's (2005) observation in this respect is clear and succinct:

In truth, discussion of these two types of knowing implies a debate over practice and theory that can only be understood if they are perceived and captured in their contradictory relationship. They are never isolated, each one in itself; there is never only theory, never only practice. Thus the sectarian political-ideological positions—positions that, instead of understanding their contradictory relationship exclude one another—are wrong. The anti-intellectualism denies validity to the theory; the theoretical elitism denies validity to the practice. The rigor with which I approach objects prohibits me from leaning toward either of these positions: neither anti-intellectualism nor elitism but practice and theory enlightening each other mutually. (p.168)

These observations are mediated by our understanding that the disposition of teachers toward this way of being and becoming vary among current teachers as well as teachers-in-training. Not all teachers seek to create a space where, as bell hooks points out, agents can enter the dominant culture and make it speak beyond the boundaries of conquest and domination.

A Conversation with Teachers

In *Bushido: The Soul of Japan* (2010), Inazo Nitobe notes that "rectitude is the power to take a certain course of action based upon reason. Without wavering—to strike when to strike is right, to die when to die is right" (p. x). As we have engaged in this project, we have continuously deliberated on who we are writing for. Nitobe's insight into rectitude captures in a certain sense our belief that this text is written with a sense of urgency and with particular educators in mind. Our conversation, though broad and inclusive as a means of growth in the profession, is particularly meant for those educators who grow weary of an education driven by benchmark testing, standardized tests, flawed accountability systems, and the general malaise that has more and more affected both the psyche and practice of educators; those who with a sense of rectitude put the interests of their students ahead of the labyrinth of schemes that is the nexus between education and the neoliberal order. In defense of such teachers and indicting these conditions, the critical theorist Henry Giroux writes:

The rhetoric of accountability, privatization and standardization that now dominates both major political parties does more than deskill teachers, weak-

en teacher unions, dumb down the curriculum and punish students; it also
offers up a model for education that undermines it as a public good. Under such
circumstances, teacher work and autonomy are not only devalued; learning how
to govern and be a critical citizen in a fragile democracy are hijacked. (2010, p. x)

We realize that even within such environments there are those who are
able to create innovative curricula and lessons that capture the reality
and imagination of youth while pushing the boundaries of the limited
autonomy provided by educational institutions in spaces under the current assault of the neoliberal order. These teachers, who are able to bor-
der-cross into the realm of possibility in a work environment dominated
by the returning model of social efficiency, are found within all institutions of learning. Though they are not the majority, and in most circumstances, given the nature of the profession, they work in isolated
environments, they do exist. In most cases, they are the ones who rarely
have problems with classroom "management" and rarely send students
to be disciplined by administration. They are usually also the ones who
go to great lengths to deepen their understanding of their craft and discipline, invest in local relationships of affinity, make strong connections
with students, and know the parents of their students outside of the
"speed-dating" context of parent-teacher conferences. They know the
environment that students come from, and appreciate and respect the
differences that their students bring to the classroom, while seeking
meaningful ways of relating curricular material. They don't work under
a deficit model of education. Such teachers don't "psychologize" the academic or social issues of students to a "dysfunctional home" or absen-
tee parent. They see all students as capable of succeeding, and most
importantly, they embody an ethic of caring that reverberates in an
embodiment of an internal professional struggle to continuously reex-
amine their own sociopolitical and pedagogical positions relative to the
student reality facing them in relationship to the wider social context. As
Freire (2005) articulately points out:

Citizenship is not obtained by chance: it is a construction that, never finished,
demands we fight for it. It demands commitment, political clarity, coherence,
decision. For this reason a democratic education cannot be realized apart from
an education of and for citizenship. (p. 161)

For these professionals, this constant self-reflection and struggle becomes a source of pride and professional satisfaction even though it also takes a toll on the body and spirit. In our experience, such teachers are often hampered more by the inefficiencies of administration than by the arduous work of developing meaningful ways of engaging students.

Lest we fall into the trap of heroifying these teachers, we must also point out that these professionals are real and struggle like everyone else. Lessons don't always go according to plan, time is always an issue, and their commitment to students often puts them in a space where there is occasional tension with administration. Even with such normative experiences in the profession, these teachers refuse to engage in a pedagogy of complacency. They don't see their professional role as that of a surrogate parent to students who come from difficult situations in a paternalistic scenario that abdicates the responsibility to teach, but rather as a caring professional who respects the craft sufficiently and loves the students abundantly so as to inspire and demand engagement.

The end result of these characteristics is a corporeal embodiment of those whom Giroux (1988) has described as "organic intellectuals": a type of teacher/activist who, being fully grounded in the sociohistoric context, both theoretically and practically traverses the confinements of institutions through a living pedagogical praxis. Hence the work of the activist informs and is informed by the experiences of the classroom. Speaking of such a pedagogy, Peter McLaren (2007) notes that "critical pedagogy is a way of thinking about, negotiating and transforming the relationship among classroom teaching, the production of knowledge, the institutional structures of the school, and the social and material relations of the wider community, society and nation-state" (p. 24).

The current threat (and dialectically the power) of such a pedagogy is evidenced in the reaction of Arizona Superintendent of Public Instruction Tom Horne, who was interviewed by CNN reporter Anderson Cooper about the proposed ban on ethnic studies programs in Arizona:

> **AC:** But what's wrong with that...if African American kids want a class that has a focus on African American studies?

TH: What's wrong with it is that it divides students up by race and I believe that one of the principal ideas of the American school system is that we bring kids together and we teach them to treat each other as individuals....What matters about a person is what does he know...what can he do...what's his character or hers...not what race he was born into....One of our important functions is to teach kids...kids from different backgrounds to treat each other as individuals...and not to infuse them with ethnic chauvinism about a particular race and teach them narrowly just about the background and culture that they happen to be born into...but to teach them about different cultures and different races...and different traditions and not divide them by race....I think that that is really backwards. (Tom Horne, 2010)

The visceral reactionary politics embedded in this response in terms reflecting the educational establishment's complicity in the wider social movement toward a kind of erasure of particular segments of the population (Apple, 1999) is both enlightening and daunting. On the one hand, it brings to light discourses that often are concealed in the condescending smiles of those who are in a position to oppress and marginalize, and as such, renders plain their draconian intentions. On the other hand, Machiavellian schemes highlight the need for teachers with a resolute tenacity of spirit, sociopolitical clarity, and the methodological expertise to bring to bear the power of education in a liberatory pedagogy. The development of ethnic studies programs during the 1970s was itself a contestation to the erasure of the histories of marginalized populations from a largely Eurocentric and male-centered curriculum in a nation where the very fabric of society was built on the commodification of the black body and the dialectical formation of the dominant white identity as inherently superior. Beyond the historicity of curriculum, any critical examination of the economic and sociopolitical conditions of ethnic "minorities" in U.S. society—whether it be with respect to employment, unemployment, discrimination, racism, adequate health care, education, probability of being incarcerated, and so on—indicates that the systematic nature of "disenfranchisement" of these populations is structural in nature, and as such, that their experiences in society are qualitatively different. One wonders if this articulation of the need to treat others as "individuals" is not part and parcel of the larger project to disarticulate collective struggles through a discourse of meritocracy; the resulting rationale is that if Native Americans have the highest rate of suicide, the highest unemployment rate, the highest poverty rate, and the highest alcoholism rate in the U.S., it must be a result of personal failures and not the end result of centuries of discrimination and structured social warfare that deserves concentrated study for the betterment of the group.

Democratic citizenship in an era when "democracy" has become a sliding signifier to mean "free-market economy" (never truly "free" because it normally induces heavy exploitation of the most vulnerable) requires that educators become particularly adept at highlighting the contradictions embedded in such discourse (Macedo, 1994), and also capable of structuring spaces of contestation leading to transformative engagement (Lesityna, Woodrum, & Sherblom, 1996). Such educators need to be organic and transformative intellectuals capable of fusing the roles of teacher and activist. A countering discourse often heard (particularly in teacher education programs) posits a fear of indoctrinating students, but that misses the point entirely. First, the normative experiences that students are exposed to in schools is not "indoctrination" in the normative system of power relations that favors some while marginalizing most. Second, the task is one of structuring a possibility of engagement where both the teacher and student grow through the possibility of a critical analysis of the lived. Hence, the reliance on the countering discourse is integrally part of the structure of complicity in a system that prevents students from linking the lived to the theoretical in the service of a more critical reading of the world. Such discourse then is supportive of the very structure of domination that reduces education to the uncritical mode sought by a socioeconomic and political system that thrives on students remaining captive to the ravages of unfettered consumption through a claim of the pseudoscientific objectivity of knowledge (Macedo, 1994), all the while removing the most fundamental pillar of democratic citizenship, the capacity for critique. No current educator can engage in such transformative praxis without careful consideration of the limitations present in the social context; it is to this critical area that we now turn to reflect on systemic constraints.

Structural Impediments

Donaldo Macedo (2007:xxx) captures both the power and the urgency of the need for a liberatory praxis based on a critical media literacy when he observes that

> given the sophistication of the propaganda apparatus in the wholesale domes-
> tication of American minds, it is most imperative that educators embrace forms
> of literacy that encourage critical thinking and the ability to make linkages
> among historical events as a process to read reality more comprehensively
> and critically. (pp. xxi–xxx)

Critical media literacy, as a transformative praxis capable of rupturing the dominant neoliberal ethos that engulfs the educational structure, is bound to encounter numerous obstacles because by its very nature such a praxis undermines the ideological and practical base that sustains the current asymmetrical power relations. Given that such an engagement problem-poses the very institution of schooling, it should be no surprise that we believe that movements toward such radical pedagogical inter-ventions engender both individual as well as collective resistance. On the one hand, one's tendencies toward individualized actions, born out of a constant barrage of messages geared to individual consumption and the conceptualization of individual well-being as being sacrosanct (even at the expense of collective good), must be boldly confronted; on the other, the social dynamics outside of the individual also need also be rig-orously deconstructed and reshaped so as to map out new terrains and socioideological scripts. One's capacity to clearly analyze the nature of these obstacles is fundamental in equipping educators with the neces-sary foresight to fracture impediments.

One of the fundamental obstacles to the development of such ped-agogical interventions rests in the types of administrative support that educators are able to mobilize. While we perceive the dynamics between administrators and educators to be significantly more complex than simply a reductionist model of good/bad, critical educators who are buffered and supported by effective administrative staff (as measured by putting the needs of the students first) are more likely to develop comprehensive pedagogical interventions that in the long-run are more meaningful and allow for better performance in state standardized tests. Such administrators possess a more critical reading of the world, which ultimately is evidenced in a teaching force more willing to take on critical interventions. Those who are faced with administrators more concerned with the performance on state standardized tests than with a collective critical praxis are arguably more likely to be inclined toward a pedagogy driven by the tenets of social efficiency and banking education, even while realizing the futility of such endeavors. Because in the current test-centric environment no one is entirely "untouched" by Adequate Yearly Progress (AYP) and systems of "accountability," and most administrators do in fact have to contend to some extent with standardized testing, critical educators need to be able to explore whatever cracks of agency are available for the development and introduction of more meaningful and applicable curricula. In pedagogical environments where standardized testing is a reality, progressive teachers need to be particularly careful that the curriculum utilized reflects the reality of the students. Such teachers would, for example, utilize readings on racial profiling as a means of exploring search and seizure as conceived in the Constitution, followed by engaging possible ways of contesting the violation of civil rights for urban youth.

Another critical obstacle that progressive teachers must contend with is the tendency toward the development of an insular practice. The isolated nature of teaching is such that educators often operate as if in a world unto themselves, an island in the middle of the ocean. Admittedly, the current movement toward a social efficiency model is gradually eradicating this possibility as teachers are increasingly forced into models of accountability that forcefully and regressively restrain such tendencies; yet, all too often we still see teachers who are professionally disconnected from their colleagues in the same institutions and, at times, even in the same departments. This isolation prevents teachers from forming productive alliances with other professionals, and often reduces the act of teaching to a "one-actor play" in a multiaudience theater. It is through these various possible alliances that critical educators are able to collaborate for the development of the craft and the continued critical engagement of students. Beyond collaboration for the sake of pedagogical intervention, this professional interdependence can lead to a type of mutual mentoring that can counteract the pressures of what is routinely an isolated practice. As many studies on teacher turnover rates have demonstrated, lack of mentorship contributes significantly to educators leaving the field. Again, one can conceive of a practice where an English teacher and a history teacher may collaborate by exploring Langston Hughes's " A Dream Deferred" as a background for an analysis of Jim Crow laws or healthcare. Insularity of practice must give way to more interconnected and meaningful projects for the sake of a more critical reading of the world.

Progressive teachers need to be critically aware of these interconnections and movements away from insularity of practice in order to avoid the lack of a critical socioenvironmental reading of the wider teaching context. A reading of Freire (2005) is particularly instrumental in this respect; no teaching should occur independently of the context of teaching. The often-heard cry from students that teachers "just don't get it" is usually attributed to the "disconnect" between the teacher's reality or reading of the world and the everyday lives of students, particularly in urban areas where the teaching force normally resides outside the context where the teaching occurs. A pedagogy based on an effective reading of the sociocontext relies on a professional engagement with the community to the extent that teachers develop meaningful personal ties in the community, and have a vested interest in the local even if they themselves live outside the community (Ladson-Billings, 2009). Misreadings of the social context often lead to strategic blunders such as pedagogical contestation of war in a context where there is an abundance of families with members serving in the military. In such an environment, the pedagogical approach would need to take into account the lived reality of the families and their connection to the military.

One other structural impediment that we want to mention is the financial strain that is often the reality of teachers as professionals. It's not unusual in the media to hear of the luxuries of teaching (with respect to time off), yet in our experience, and as many studies in the field have shown, educators often work well beyond the school day and routinely (particularly during the summer months) take on multiple jobs in order to keep up with the cost of living. These financial stressors are all too real, and given the extent to which such educators are consumed with finding effective ways to engage students, it is easy to feel that one puts in much more than one receives (in terms of financial compensation); this is not surprising if one analyzes the institution of education from a macro-perspective. The huge disparities among school districts in terms of funding, and the appalling lack of resources, particularly in urban schools compared to wealthy suburban schools (Kozol, 1992), is indicative of the value that we place on education generally. Ironically, while we spend $7,000 to $8,000 to (mis)educate students and gripe about having to pay a few thousand more, we have few problems spending $50,000 to $60,000 incarcerating these same youths later on in life. Perhaps our inclinations stem from the fact that jails are increasingly becoming the fastest-growing private industries in the United States, fueled essentially by the very students whom we opt to spend so little to educate (James, 2000). When we have English departments rationing paper to their students, students being asked to bring toilet paper to school, and an archaic system of school funding devised during colonial times which is based on property taxes, it is not surprising that critical educators feel as though their efforts at educating the young are being minimized. Even under these circumstances, critical educators can default on their car payments or mortgages and yet refuse to allow the disciplinary structures that are transacted between capitalism and institutional power to have the last word. In the area of financial stability, as in many other areas, critical educators need to form alliances for better social conditions among all colleagues generally through a much more active citizenry model. The current financial crisis affecting education often pits programs against each other, and veteran teachers against new teachers, and in the process eliminates decades of improvements in the profession. Contestation of those models that advocate a solitary and reactive practice in the face of budget constraints must be relinquished in favor of more communal formations in which the interests of the whole supersede the interests of the individual. Regular participation in school committee meetings, PTAs and PTOs, and city council and local nonprofit organization meetings must take priority if teachers are to embody the traits of critical citizenship that they seek to develop in students, and in the process ameliorate their working conditions.

Section Two: Critical Pedagogical Interventions in Process

Warning: Stay away from buying into an uncritical ideological model that subscribes to the magic bullet fetish—these plans are not rigid models to be followed, but rather examples of what can be possible through a critical transformative pedagogy utilizing the very modality that we propose to deconstruct: media.

Our aim here, as in the previous four chapters, is to interrogate the epistemological validity of the traditionally rigid, compartmentalized curriculum. The increasingly test-centric environment under which teachers labor (Apple, 1999) has in our opinion served to solidify barriers between traditionally conceived domains of study and the living world outside the terrain of schooling. As you will note in the accompanying lesson plans, we provided state standards based on the national movement to create a unified and cohesive curriculum of study. We believe that such efforts, particularly while operating under the subtext of "accountability," serve to stifle creative teaching and the propensity of teachers to engage in a critical praxis. Nevertheless, given the terrain that we traverse and our ethical responsibilities as teachers, we feel that we must heed and indeed deal with the limitations that teachers encounter in the field daily. The lesson plans, in various disciplines and with their respective standards, serve to attest to critical possibilities even under the duress of neoliberal strains. The plans are just that—plans! It's our hope that classroom teachers can in some way make connections to critical engagements in and through their own spaces and realities.

GRADE LEVEL: 8th
SUBJECT: History
THEME: Imperialism
DURATION: Two days

Day 1

MA State Curriculum Frameworks Standards:

WHII.11 Describe the causes of 19th-century European imperialism. (H, E)

A. the desire for economic gain and resources
B. the missionary impulse and the search for strategic advantage and national pride.

Objectives:

- SWBAT identify areas of the world that have been subject to colonization.
- SWBAT define key terms related to imperialism.
- SWBAT link past imperialism and physical control to newer forms of control such as cultural imperialism.

Strategies and Procedures:

As students enter the classroom they will note a word splash on the board containing the following words: *imperialism, natural resources, mercantilism, cultural imperialism, Berlin Conference,* and *demarcation line*. The instructor will then ask the students to pick and define three of the listed terms in their own words. Once the students have done this, the instructor will ask them to hold on to the definitions as they will become useful as the lesson progresses.

Students will then be shown a historical map highlighting all the countries in the world in which English is spoken. Students will be asked to try to name some of the highlighted countries and what they think the highlighted areas represent. After allowing students to venture some responses and comment on each other's responses, the teacher will explain that the highlighted areas represent English-speaking areas of the world. The teacher will particularly point out that English is spoken in every continent at some level. The teacher will then give the students a few minutes to write down some responses to the following questions (responses should be brief but reflective):

1. Why do you think English is spoken in so many areas of the world?
2. What were some of these countries' original languages and why did they change to English?

3. Would you voluntarily change the language that you speak for another language?

4. Is the way that a person speaks important for how they see themselves?

The teacher will then ask students to share some of their responses. Once students have had a chance to provide their opinions, the teacher will explain that in fact some of these countries speak English because at some point in their history they were conquered by an English-speaking country. The teacher will then pull out another map displaying the various Western powers' territorial conquests across the world. Students will be asked to visually estimate which Western power conquered the most territories or people.

Students will then be asked what their reactions would be if suddenly they were told that they could no longer speak English. After sharing their thoughts, the teacher would then point out that imperialism caused many social changes that affected people across the world differentially, and that language changes were just one way among many. The teacher will then define *imperialism* on the board as:

> The process whereby countries seek to enrich themselves by expanding their influence through the territorial, physical, or cultural conquest of other peoples.

The teacher will then explain that in the past much of this was done with the justification of "civilizing and Christianizing" other peoples and regions of the world, and it implied that one nation or people was viewed as superior and the other inferior. The teacher will then put up the following quote and ask the students if they can guess who the author is:

> It would be a strange thing if Six Nations of ignorant savages should be capable of forming a scheme for such a union, and be able to execute it in a such a manner as that it has substituted for ages and appears indissoluble; and yet that a like union should be impracticable for ten or a dozen English colonies, to whom it is more necessary and must be more advantageous, and who cannot be supposed to want an equal understanding of their interests.

After eliciting some responses from the students, the teacher will explain that the quote came from Benjamin Franklin in 1754, when he pleaded for a political union of the colonies. Students will be then be asked to write one paragraph commenting on whether or not they would consider the Native Americans to be civilized or savage/uncivilized at the time of their conquest.

Informal Assessment:

After five to ten minutes the teacher will open up the floor for student responses and acknowledge the various viewpoints. The teacher will then instruct the students that for homework they will have to make note of an ad (television or newspaper) that had imbedded in it the message that one person or group was superior to another in some way.

GRADE LEVEL: 8th
SUBJECT: History
THEME: Imperialism
DURATION: Two days

Day 2
MA State Curriculum Frameworks Standards:
WHII.11 Describe the causes of 19th-century European imperialism. (H, E)

A. the desire for economic gain and resources
B. the missionary impulse and the search for strategic advantage and national pride.

Strategies and Procedures:

The teacher will initiate the class by having students comment on what they were able to find on the previous night's homework. After hearing all the responses, the teacher will point out that in the case of imperialism, the implied message of superiority was central to justifying the conquest, killing, and plunder of other regions and peoples.

The teacher will then split up the class into groups of four or five. Each group will have a timekeeper, a note taker, and a reporter. Each student will be given an Uncle Scrooge Disney comic adventure story and asked to read the story. (The students will be given 20 minutes to read the short story.) As a group, students will be asked to respond to the following questions:

1. How are Disney characters represented? What are their traits?
2. How are natives represented? What are their traits?
3. What are the ultimate goals of each set of characters?
4. Are there any connections between the exercise and the ideas of imperialism?

After responding to the questions on paper, the teacher will ask each group's reporter to comment on his or her group's responses. Once all the responses have been given, the teacher will explain that rationalizing and dehumanizing natives as "savages" and "uncivilized" made it easy to justify slavery, segregation, genocide, and territorial conquest, and that even today many of these same messages are given in the media with respect to other peoples of the world.

The teacher will then put up the following two quotes on the whiteboard and ask the students to reflect on what the authors may have been thinking in relation to domination as they spoke these words:

> Speak softly and carry a big stick; you will go far.
>
> TEDDY ROOSEVELT

> The world is not looking for servants, there are plenty of these, but for masters, men who form their purposes and then carry them out, let the consequences be what they may.
>
> WOODROW WILSON

Students will be asked to view a 5-minute video clip of Glenn Beck on immigration. After viewing the clip, students will be asked as a group to compare the video clip with the posted quotes and reflect on the following questions:

1. Are there similarities and differences in the ways that people are viewed?
2. How do you think their views would be justified?

Once students share their responses, the teacher will provide the students with a similar Uncle Scrooge Disney story with the dialogue left blank. The students will be asked to "invent the dialogue" and recompose the story from the perspective of the native. Students will have 30 minutes for the exercise, after which they will share their differences from the original.

For homework, students will write two paragraphs on whether or not the U.S. is an imperial power today, justifying their answers.

GRADE LEVEL: 10th
SUBJECT: Mathematics
THEME: Data Analysis, Statistics, and Probability
DURATION: Two days

Day 1

MA State Curriculum Frameworks Standards:

Select, create, and interpret an appropriate graphical representation (e.g., scatterplot, table, stem-and-leaf plots, box-and-whisker plots, circle graph, line graph, and line plot) for a set of data and use appropriate statistics (e.g., mean, median, range, and mode) to communicate information about the data. Use these notions to compare different sets of data.

Objectives:

- SWBAT compare and contrast sets of numerical data.
- SWBAT define *mean, median, range,* and *mode*.
- SWBAT represent numerical data through graphical representation.

Required Materials:

- 5 posterboards
- markers
- set of magazines/Army video game covers
- computer with online access

Strategies and Procedures:

As the students walk into the room the instructor will point out that on top of a desk at the front of the class there are four piles of colored index cards with words written on the reverse side. Students will also be told that each one of them will have to pick three cards (each of a different color) to bring back to their desks to define, and that each colored card has a different monetary value. After allowing the students to come up and obtain the cards the instructor will give each student 10 minutes to define the three words. The instructor will then ask for volunteers who want to share their definitions with the class. After hearing the various responses, the instructor will provide the values for each of the colored cards and ask the students to calculate how many points they have. As the students begin the calculations the instructor will write out the definitions for the following words on the board: *mean, mode, median*, and *range*.

The instructor will then explain that these terms are important for an understanding of the relativity of figures. The instructor will then ask students to calculate the mean value of the three cards depending on the colors they chose. The instructor will then point out that the mean changes depending on the total value given.

The instructor will then point out that statistics are used to determine everything from state and federal taxes to the amount of gas a car consumes, the fuel necessary for a particular flight trip by a pilot, and even the trajectory of projectiles by crime scene investigators.

As an example, the instructor will point out that the average working person pays approximately 33 percent of their yearly income in taxes for any given year. The instructor will then ask the students to get in groups of four to calculate how much money citizens who earn $25,000, $40,000, and $65,000, respectively, would pay in taxes yearly. Once the students have determined this amount, the instructor will model the required calculations on the board and point out to the students that at 33 percent yearly, the citizens would be working from January to April to sustain the government. The instructor will then pose three questions on the board for the student groups:

1. Would it be fair if these people were taxed equally?
2. Who would have the greatest disadvantage among the three?
3. What percentage of one's income should be directed for taxes?

Students will be given approximately 10 minutes to discuss respond in one or two paragraphs, after which they will share their responses with the class. The instructor will then inform the students that they will be doing a timed exercise. The instructor will access the U.S. national debt clock online and inform the students that the class will be evaluating the changes in the national debt every 5 seconds.

At a given time the instructor will refresh the image and ask the students to record the monetary value. Twenty seconds later the instructor will freeze the image and re-record the value. The students will then be asked to calculate changes every 5 seconds. Once the students have had the opportunity to calculate the changes, the instructor will ask the students to get in groups of four prepare a posterboard that demonstrates through a bar graph how much the national debt changes per minute, per hour, and finally per day.

The groups will be given 20 minutes to develop the various graphs. For homework, the students will be asked to research what functions of government consume the greatest amount of taxes.

GRADE LEVEL: 10th
SUBJECT: Mathematics/Literacy
THEME: Data Analysis, Statistics, and Probability
DURATION: Two days

Day 2

MA State Curriculum Frameworks Standards:

Select, create, and interpret an appropriate graphical representation (e.g., scatterplot, table, stem-and-leaf plots, box-and-whisker plots, circle graph, line graph, and line plot) for a set of data and use appropriate statistics (e.g., mean, median, range, and mode) to communicate information about the data. Use these notions to compare different sets of data.

Objectives:
- SWBAT compare and contrast sets of numerical data.
- SWBAT represent numerical data through graphical representation.

Required Materials:
- 5 posterboards
- markers
- set of magazines/Army video game covers

Strategies and Procedures:

As the students walk into the room the instructor will have a pie graph representing the proportionate representation of government spending on the board, yet the respective government sectors will be left blank. Students will be asked to report on what they found from their homework research. The instructor will then ask the students proportionately which department or sector spends the most in government funds.

Once students have volunteered some responses, the instructor will point out that the military consumes proportionately a substantial amount of federal taxes. The instructor will list the percentages on the board. The instructor will then ask the students if they can venture a guess as to why the military consumes so much of the federal taxes. After the students volunteer their responses, the instructor will list the amount of money spent daily in Afghanistan and Iraq. The instructor will then list the amount spent daily on education.

Students will be asked to calculate, compare, and graphically demonstrate the resources spent on each of the wars in relation to education during a period of one week. After each student has had the opportunity to calculate, compare, and graph, the class will be once again broken down into four groups representing different interest groups: prowar senators, antiwar senators, businesses, and educators.

Each group will be asked to compose a mutually agreed-upon letter (supported by graphs developed on a posterboard, illustrated with pictures from the various magazines) arguing the pros and cons of continuing or ending the wars. Students will be evaluated on their ability to make their case utilizing both graphs as well as text.

GRADE LEVEL: 10th
SUBJECT: Mathematics/Literacy
THEME: Data Analysis, Statistics, and Probability
DURATION: Two days

Day 3/4

MA State Curriculum Frameworks Standards:

Select, create, and interpret an appropriate graphical representation (e.g., scatterplot, table, stem-and-leaf plots, box-and-whisker plots, circle graph, line graph, and line plot) for a set of data and use appropriate statistics (e.g., mean, median, range, and mode) to communicate information about the data. Use these notions to compare different sets of data.

Objectives:

- SWBAT compare and contrast sets of numerical data.
- SWBAT represent numerical data through graphical representation.

Required Materials:

- enlarged video game covers
- graph paper
- cutouts of newspaper headlines on troop deployment

As students walk into the room there will be newspaper cutouts and game covers prominently displayed at the front. The instructor will inform the students that today's lesson will continue our work on graphing and comparing sets of numerical data. The instructor will then inform the students that today we will be looking at video games as an entertainment mode and the perceptions associated with gamers and game playing. Students will be asked to reflect on paper (one paragraph) about what types of games they play and whether or not they feel that games can influence behavior. After 5 minutes or so, the instructor will assess the types of games that students play, paying special attention to shooter games.

The instructor will then point out that according to the NAE in 2007, one video game was sold for every second of the entire year. The instructor will ask the students to calculate how many games that would mean in one day. The instructor will assign an assumed value of $15 per game and ask the students to calculate the amount of money spent on video games in a day. Students will then be asked to demonstrate how they arrived at their responses.

The instructor will then hand out some graph paper and ask the students to graph the sales of video games for one week given the values stated. Once students have had an opportunity to do this, the instructor will point out that shooter games are particularly popular, and that even the U.S. Army utilizes shooter games to train soldiers for combat. The instructor will then distribute to the class a small newspaper article on the use of simulators to train soldiers. Students will be given 10 minutes to read and underline important information from the article.

Students will then have an opportunity to comment on what information they found relevant in the text. Once students have had an opportunity to comment and share their opinions, the instructor will have the class break into groups to discuss the following questions:

1. If shooter games accounted for 50 percent of the daily sales of games, given the values stated, how much money would be spent on shooter games on any given day?
2. What types of strategies do companies utilize in marketing shooter games?
3. Based on the games presented, who are shooter games marketed to?
4. Do games influence behavior?
5. What types of games are not created, and why?

Once the students have had the opportunity to discuss the questions and form opinions, the instructor will open up the floor for discussion. After the students share their responses, the instructor will present two articles on games/gaming (one for and one against the benefits of gaming).

The instructor will then ask the students as a group to pick a side on the debate and have students research pro and con debates online and in national newspapers and form a coherent argument. Students will be informed that during the next class session they will have to present their views in a panel format.

Day 4

As students walk into the room, the class will be arranged in a panel format. Students will be allowed to choose various roles in today's exercise (senators, pro-gaming advocates, anti-gaming advocates, doctors, and one reporter and one camera operator). Once they have chosen the various roles, the instructor will act as moderator and open up a senate hearing on gaming. Each side will have to present their case based on economics (through statistical data), social impact, and overall educational value of gaming.

This exercise will last the entire class period. For homework, students will be asked to reflect (two paragraphs) on how statistics helped to shape the opinions of class members during the debate.

GRADE LEVEL: 11th

SUBJECT: Social Studies and Language Arts

THEME: Elements of Satire and Addressing Social Injustice through
    Comedy

DURATION: Five Days

The standards and materials outlined below cover the expanse of the three days.

Florida Sunshine State Standards:

LA.1112.2.1.5

The student will analyze and discuss characteristics of subgenres (e.g., satire, parody, allegory) that overlap or cut across the lines of genre classifications such as poetry, novel, drama, short story, essay or editorial.

LA.1112.5.2.3

The student will use research and visual aids to deliver oral presentations that inform, persuade, or entertain, and evaluate one's own and others' oral presentations according to designed rubric criteria.

SS.912.A.1.4

Analyze how images, symbols, objects, cartoons, graphs, charts, maps, and artwork may be used to interpret the significance of time periods and events from the past.

SS.912.H.1.5

Examine artistic response to social issues and new ideas in various cultures.

It is important to note that several standards in addition to those outlined would also apply. The purpose is to allow ample space for students to cross disciplinary borders and not be constrained by discrete skills.

Required materials:

- several types of texts, including: political cartoons; *Adbusters* advertisement or other forms of "subvertisements"; short literary piece; song lyrics; and news satire piece (such as a piece from *The Onion*)
- graphic organizer for vocabulary
- graphic organizer for text analysis
- flip chart paper
- short video clips of stand-up comedy routines (from diverse ethnic groups)
- props for the creation of stand-up comedy club/café

Day One

Paired dialogue—students will discuss what constitutes humor from their perspective, why it is utilized, when, how, and where. The effort is to open up a space for the understanding that humor serves diverse purposes and that these social uses of humor directly bear on the lived experiences of students. Furthermore, the effort is to engage background knowledge as much as it is to generate theory from within.

Introduction to the essential question—students will be introduced to an essential question that will serve as an anchor throughout the lessons. The suggested question: Is comedy able to effectively challenge social injustice? This question will be projected for the duration of the lesson, and students will have to answer it at the conclusion of the lesson by assuming the role of a speaker at the World Social Forum. The speech will function as a creative assessment.

Interactive lecture—a vocabulary graphic organizer will be distributed to the class. Students will be exposed to key vocabulary: satire, irony, sarcasm, parody, exaggeration, juxtaposition, comparison, analogy, and double entendre. Students will be exposed to a definition as well visual images that capture the particular technique. (The author chose to highlight the terms using bumper stickers and protest signs advocating certain social causes from diverse ideological orientations, locations, and historical epochs.) Students will then define the term in their own words, create a sentence using the term, and illustrate the term in the space provided. (Note: the point is to begin a class dialogue on the use of the social use of these devices.)

Day Two

Collaborative group assignment—students will work in groups of four to analyze a respective text and relate it to the techniques of satire in the previous lesson. Each group will analyze a different type of text. Text suggestions:

- Political cartoon: Kelley, S. (1994). *San Diego Union Tribune.* The cartoon depicts a white man pointing to a family and stating, "It's time to reclaim America from illegal immigrants!" A Native American standing opposite him states, "I'll help you pack."
- Lyrics: Bruce Springsteen's "Born in the U.S.A."
- Counter advertisement: *Adbusters* ad for a product consumed by youth
- Counter news: A piece from *The Onion* or *Saturday Night Live*
- Literature An excerpt from Joseph Heller's *Catch-22* or George Orwell's *1984.*

Group discussion questions may include:
Which aspect of satire is utilized?
Why is this particular aspect being utilized?
What is the author's opinion on the social, political, and/or economic issue?
Who is the author speaking to?
Is the perspective communicated effectively? Why or why not?
Students will then present collaboratively, while the audience takes notes on the medium and the aspect of satire employed.

Day Three

Students will analyze diverse stand-up comedy routines. The instructor will utilize routines that centralize social injustice and expose it through diverse forms of satire. These routines will be accessed from sites such as YouTube and will be short excerpts. Examples will cross races, ethnicity, and gender and might include the works of Richard Pryor, Margaret Cho, Whoopi Goldberg, George Carlin, George Lopez, Russell Peters, and so on.

Groups of three—think—share: Students will answer several questions on flip chart. What are the topics/themes that the comic uses? What are some of the comics' nonverbal cues? What is it that makes us laugh or not laugh? What's the message? What is the implication of such a message? For which audience do you think this comedy is intended?

Class discussion—the class will debrief the various performances. The question of language will consistently be centralized in discussion as students problem-pose whether or not the comedy can be performed outside of the original vernacular. Through the analysis, students will also compare how the respective linguistic medium, although varied, is able to perform similar functions. This will extend into a discussion of language variants and socially constructed linguistic hierarchies.

Days Four and Five

Groups of three project—students will produce an original piece of satirical stand-up comedy utilizing the theme of "school life and policies." All students will serve as writers of the piece. One will have the added role of integrating visual/bodily techniques, another in researching elements of school life and policy that should be put under the gaze of satire (examples: standardized testing, zero-tolerance policies, etc.), and another will be the presenter/comic.

Publication/dissemination—students will perform their routines in a "Comic Justice Café" during class or after school for peers and staff. They might also have the option of publishing short parts on social networking sites and then follow by analyzing the jokes and the responses engendered.

Day Six

Students will write a speech addressing the question: Is comedy able to effectively challenge social injustice? Students will assume the role of a speaker at the World Social Forum. The speech will function as a creative assessment. The speech should integrate the various topics and themes covered the previous days and utilize the key vocabulary, texts, authors, and comics discussed. The speech should also make reference to language equality.

References

Apple, M. (1999). Official knowledge: Democratic education in a conservative age. New York: Routledge.

Fine, M. (1991). Framing dropouts: Notes on the politics of an urban high school. Albany, NY: State University of New York Press.

Freire, P. (2005). Teachers as cultural workers: Letters to those who dare teach. Boulder, CO: Westview.

Giroux, H. (1981). Ideology, culture and the process of schooling. Philadelphia: Temple University Press.

Giroux, H. (1988). Teachers as intellectuals: Toward a critical pedagogy of learning. Westport, CT: Bergin & Garvey.

Giroux, H. (2010, April 15). In defense of public school teachers in a time of crisis. Retrieved from http://www.truth-out.org/in-defense-public-school-teachers-a-time-crisis58567.

Horne, T. (2010) Anderson Cooper AC 360—CNN. http://www.cnn.com/video/data/2.0/video/bestoftv/2010/05/12/ac.ethics.study.ban.cnn.html. Retrieved on November 15, 2010.

James, J. (2000). States of confinement: Policing, detention, and prisons. New York: St. Martin's.

Kliebard, H. (1995). The struggle for the American curriculum: 1893–1958 (2nd ed.). New York: Routledge.

Kohn, A. (1992). No contest: The case against competition. Boston: Houghton Mifflin.

Kohn, A. (2000). The case against standardized testing: Raising test scores, ruining the schools. Boston: Heinemann.

Kozol, J. (1992). Savage inequalities. New York: Harper Perennial.

Ladson-Billings, G. (2009). The Dreamkeepers: Sucessful teachers of African American children. San Francisco,CA: Jossey-Bass. Lesityna, P., Woodrum, A., & Sherblom, S. (Eds.). (1996). Breaking free: The transformative power of critical pedagogy. Cambridge, MA: Harvard Educational Review.

Macedo, D. (1994). Literacies of power: What Americans are not allowed to know. Boulder, CO: Westview.

Macedo, D. P., & Steinberg, S. (Eds.) . (2007) . Media literacy: A reader. New York NY: Peter Lang Publishing.

McLaren, P. (2005). Preface: A pedagogy for life. In P. Freire, Teachers as cultural workers: Letters to those who dare teach (pp. xxvii–xxxix). Boulder, CO: Westview.

McLaren, P. (2007). A pedagogy of possibility. In A. Ornstein, E. Pajak, & S. Ornstein (Eds.), Contemporary issues in curriculum (4th ed., pp. 22–31). Boston: Pearson.

McNeil, L. (2000). Contradictions of school reform: Educational costs of standardized testing. New York: Routledge.

Nitobe, I. (2010). Bushido: The soul of Japan. Kojimachi, Japan: Teibi.

Valenzuela, A. (1999). Subtractive schooling: U.S. Mexican youth and the politics of caring. Albany, NY: State University of New York Press.

Willis, P. (1977). Learning to labor: How working class kids get working class jobs. New York: Columbia University Press.

Index

minding the media

CRITICAL ISSUES
FOR LEARNING AND TEACHING

Shirley R. Steinberg & Pepi Leistyna
General Editors

Minding the Media is a book series specifically designed to address the needs of students and teachers in watching, comprehending, and using media. Books in the series use a wide range of educational settings to raise consciousness about media relations and realities and promote critical, creative alternatives to contemporary mainstream practices. *Minding the Media* seeks theoretical, technical, and practitioner perspectives as they relate to critical pedagogy and public education. Authors are invited to contribute volumes of up to 85,000 words to this series. Possible areas of interest as they connect to learning and teaching include:

- critical media literacy
- popular culture
- video games
- animation
- music
- media activism
- democratizing information systems
- using alternative media
- using the Web/internet
- interactive technologies
- blogs
- multi-media in the classroom
- media representations of race, class, gender, sexuality, disability, etc.

- media/communications studies methodologies
- semiotics
- watchdog journalism/investigative journalism
- visual culture: theater, art, photography
- radio, TV, newspapers, zines, film, documentary film, comic books
- public relations
- globalization and the media
- consumption/consumer culture
- advertising
- censorship
- audience reception

For additional information about this series or for the submission of manuscripts, please contact:

Shirley R. Steinberg and Pepi Leistyna,
msgramsci@aol.com | Pepi.Leistyna@umb.edu

To order other books in this series, please contact our Customer Service Department:

(800) 770-LANG (within the U.S.)
(212) 647-7706 (outside the U.S.)
(212) 647-7707 FAX

Or browse online by series:
www.peterlang.com